Desirable Power

Take control of your life,

health and relationship

By Jacob Korthuis

ISBN: 0-9786598-1-3
Publisher: BCE Institute, Inc.
PO Box 470475
Celebration, FL 34747, USA
www.awayfrompain.com
www.pmacontrol.com (Corporate world)
www.mydatemylife.com (Relationship)

Table of content

Table of content **2**

Warning! **12**

About the writer **13**

Preface **15**

Are you living or just surviving? *16*

Chapter 1 – The desire for answers **18**

A passionate vacation *18*
Nobody will ever know *18*
The fear kicks in *19*
Did they know? *19*
Finally, relief! *20*
It was all real to her *21*
A million times more in the subconscious *21*
It can all be changed *22*
Theory versus practice *23*
Finding desirable power *24*
PMA, the power to control *25*
Don't underestimate yourself *26*
What can you expect? *26*
Don't sabotage yourself *27*

Chapter 2 - The human mind – The center of our behavior **29**

Two major areas of the brain *29*
The conscious and the subconscious *29*
Clearing things up *31*
The Life Force *32*
How does the human brain work? *32*
We all start out the same *33*
Understanding of the basic patterns of the brain's mechanisms *33*
Our brain is preprogrammed *34*
You don't need medical training to understand your own brain *35*

Questions that need an answer 36
The overall picture 36
Our genetically determined constitution 39
Our personality is not genetic 40
Our comparison material 40
The Database 41
Characteristics of PMA words 41
Clusters 42
Bad Clusters 43
Storage spread all over the Cortex 44
The comparison process 45
Level 1 - Fragments 46
Level 2 - Sub-clusters 46
Level 3 - Clusters 47
Factual data is always connected to physiological aspects 47
Your past determines your conscious awareness 49
Comparison material needs to be encoded 50
The absolute code 51
How do you know it's coffee? 52
How the subconscious works 54
Unknown objects 55
You connect it to what you do know 56
The relative code 57
The conscious part of the brain determines the relative code 59
How does this work in the subconscious? 59
We are all the same and yet so different 60
Physiological codes are not the same as emotional symptoms 60
Your Clusters determine what you perceive 61
Automatic selection of the material with the highest relative code 65
Find the answers in yourself 66
The most basic measuring system: Pain – Pleasure 67
Ingredients of a decision 68
Consider the ordinary things 70
Surfing the subconscious 71
Step-by-step comparison 73
Old codes become handy 78

Suddenly, I was thirsty 79
You fancy yourself in Spain 80
The miraculous sensitivity of our sensors 82

Chapter 3 – Physiology **83**
Physiology is not a coincidental process 83
Don't blame it on your genes 84
No response without stimuli 84
Without input, no physiology 85
Our most powerful drive 85
The two main operating systems of our physiology 86
Proto-physioclusters 87
Proto-physioclusters maintain balance 87
Physiology – starting at the beginning 88
Away from pain, our most basic drive 89
Cells are like people 89
Our communication and response system 90
Your genes do not control you 90
Genes can change 91
Without environmental signals there is no life 91
The nucleus, our Database of potentials 92
The gate guard of our cells 93
Proto-physioclusters can be misled 94
Physio-clusters 94
Physio-clusters are always connected 95
Physio-clusters never happen on their own 96
Nature vs. nurture 98
Taste is a matter of experience 99
The physiological data is packaged separately 100
The separation of factual data and physiology 101
The reversed process during the comparison 102
The subconscious makes it easy for itself 104
Compassion must be learned 104
Gathering comparison material 105
Physio-clusters determine our emotions 106
The development of your emotions 106

Individual perception 107

Chapter 4 – The language of our subconscious **109**

You really need this 109
The subconscious does not make mistakes 109
The capacity of the brain 110
Some facts about our brain 111
The smallest contribution to the transport of information 113
The bigger route of transporting information 114
Don't vegetate but live with passion 115
Ligands: the messengers between our cells 115
Instructions from cell to cell 116
Ligands, the fundament of our feelings and actions 118
Limbic System 119
Physio-clusters related to Bad Clusters 120
Activated comparison material activates physiology (ligands) 120
Physio-clusters never act by themselves 121
Emotions 124
Ligands determine the relative value of data 125

Chapter 5 – The activation of Clusters and Bad Clusters **128**

The subconscious sees no difference 128
Emotions are individual 129
Emotions are inborn 129
Intensity is learned 130
The neuro-physiology behind emotions 131
Your perception is your reality! 132
Feelings override thoughts 134
Why is that? 136
The dentist 137
Clusters and Bad Clusters 138
All the sensory data has the same relative code 138
Why we call it a "Bad" Cluster 138
Imagine a huge library with millions of books 139
Bad Clusters 139
How and when are Bad Clusters created? 140

A matter of perception 141
An extreme physiological state during rest 142
Obstinate physiological reactions 142
It cannot reject it 143
"Houston we have a problem" 144
Clusters with negative physiology 145
It is a matter of speed 147
No logic in a Bad Cluster 149
Why are Bad Clusters created? 151
The existing physiology is the real problem 152
Emotionally loaded data is remembered better 153
A Bad Cluster is not a suppressed memory! 156
A fundamental difference 156
You cannot or you do not want to remember 158
The cause of suppressed memories 160
The mechanism of suppressing 161
"I lost the memory of several years of my childhood" 162
It is all a matter of decisions and choices 164
You surround yourself with activating signals 165
Clusters, Sub-clusters and Fragments 166
Activating Bad Clusters on a low level 167
Likes and dislikes, a matter of physiology 169
Realize why you like things 169
Things we love become unhealthy triggers 171
More Sub-clusters become active 172
How to use the activating items to your benefit 174
A lifetime tool 175

Chapter 6 – The hidden Power Of Bad Clusters **176**
The effects of eliminating Bad Clusters 176
Pay attention to the activation of Bad Clusters 176
The activation of Bad Clusters 178
The story continues 182
Bad Clusters get stuck in the process 183
Re-activation 187

Chapter 7 – The secret of psychosomatic health problems **189**
Psychological or physical? *189*
Our conscious and the physiology *190*
Your mind directs your body *191*
The executed Physio-cluster *193*
Your conscious does not control the physiology *194*
Physiology and Bad Clusters *196*
The past controls our behavior *201*
Continue on medication *201*
What does psychosomatic mean? *202*
We are masters in deceiving ourselves! *204*
The development of psychosomatic symptoms *204*
No emotion without physiological information *205*
The chain breaks at the weakest link *206*
Change or die *207*
A long-lasting, undesirable physiological state *208*
It is much deeper *211*
Sick from long lasting memory moments *212*
A temporary problem *213*
It could be the wine *214*
It must be the wine *215*
I can't fall asleep *216*
The contents of a Bad Cluster are not logical *218*
The power to compensate *219*
The energy drainer *219*
With clenched fists *220*
Take a vacation every day *221*

Chapter 8 – The power of our Friend Mechanism **222**
Our protection mechanism *222*
The Friend Mechanism *222*
The Warning Friend Mechanism *223*
The loss of control is unacceptable *224*
Focusing *225*
What we do register *228*
The rituals of our Friend Mechanism *229*

It feels so right 230
Why it is so difficult to change people 231
We always search for ways to feel better 238
Recognize your Inhibiting Friend 243
Related to many Bad Clusters 244
Each Inhibiting Friend Mechanism is different 244
Our mediator between the conscious and the subconscious 246
Clusters before and after a Bad Cluster 247
Belief systems and the Inhibiting Friend Mechanism 248
Creating the Inhibiting Friend Mechanism 250
A belief system develops 251
We always look for confirmation of our belief systems 254
The Friend Mechanisms and the sessions 255
The purpose of our dreams 256
Decisions controlled by nightmares 257
Learn to trust your subconscious 259
Distinguishing characteristic of the Inhibiting Friend 260
Identifying the Friend Mechanism 262
Self-deceit to confirm your belief systems 263
Blind and deaf for reasonable arguments 264
They are not looking for the truth, but for their truth 265
The Friend Mechanism interacts with the conscious brain 266
The ultimate form of not feeling 275
Cooperate with your Friend 275
Do not lie to yourself 277
Go to the final room 279
Don't be misled 281
Just continue and everything will fall into place 282
Looking for the unknown 284

Chapter 9 – Our belief systems **288**
For everything there is a cause 288
The foundation of our behavior lies in our belief systems 291
The origin of our belief systems 292
Challenge your belief systems 292
Why find our belief systems? 294

A great tool to discover our personal belief systems 294
A tool to find and change belief systems 295
Let us consider our belief systems 298
What belief systems did you find? 310
Are all belief systems wrong? 311
Change your belief systems 313
How do you do that? 315
What will happen if you start doing that? 316
Making changes 317
Chronological module 319
Effects on your present and future life 320
Remember Janine 322

Chapter 10 – How to use Progressive Mental Alignment **324**
Go for it! 324
The tension disappears forever 325
The effects of the PMA technique 326
Grow to your full potentials 327
An enjoyable process with major benefits 327
Go the whole nine yards 328
Can I practice PMA all by myself? 330
Allow your subconscious to deliver 331
Become aware of your senses 333
Trust your brain 338
All the pictures are relevant 339
Points of origin 340
Do's and don'ts in your sessions 342
Experience the language of your subconscious 344
Do not combine PMA with other techniques 345
The tools that allow you to communicate with the subconscious 347
Signals to train your brain 349
The importance of language in your session 353
You will be surprised 356
The PMA session based on activation 356
The basis of the PMA method 357
Find the moment 360

The procedure 360

Chapter 11 - Build happy relationships with PMA **362**
You cannot understand a Bad Cluster 363
The result 364
He doesn't understand her violent reaction 365
A Bad Cluster is activated 366
Will you go to Atlantic City with me? 368
Both Bad Clusters are activated 368
It is not the other, it is your comparison material 370
The suitcase clicks shut 370
Did you learn anything from it? 373
The secret of successful relationships 375
PMA means freedom! 376

Chapter 12 – Take control of your life **378**
Learn to understand yourself and others 378
Pay attention to the solution 379
Don't ask why, but ask when 380
Good advice, no help 381
The origin of your goals 381
How to achieve your goals 382
You have to believe in your goals 384
Widen the circle of your possibilities 385
Courage is the only thing you need! 385
Do the pleasurable things you never did 387
Application in your daily life 388
The opportunity to grow 389
How far and how deep can you go with PMA? 390
Do something with what you've learned! 391
Fear versus freedom and pleasure 392
Freedom is the absence of inhibiting fear 394
Practical tools to apply your new knowledge 395
Changing your belief systems 397
No taboo during a PMA session 399
Get the leverage you need to become more successful 400

Tools that help you practice PMA to your benefit *400*
Continue on *401*

Acknowledgement **402**

References **403**
References and Literature Progressive Mental Alignment *403*

Notes **410**

Warning!

Anyone who reads this book and/or wishes to apply the PMA method as described herein, whether on his own or together with a PMA Coach, must understand that the contents of this book can drastically change his or her behavior and perception of life. The book describes in detail specific processes of the brain, such as the origin of psychological, psychosomatic and physical problems, as well as the hidden source behind our belief systems, habits and behavior. Reading this book and/or applying the information contained herein can bring about great changes in the behavior, emotions, and lifestyle for the reader, as well as the relationship with his/her partner, friends and family members. The application of PMA can evoke powerful reactions and physiological and physical reactions. Neither the author nor the publisher can be held in any way responsible for these changes. This book is mainly written for individuals that look for answers and wish to confront themselves with the root cause of their belief systems, behavior and health. If you accept this challenge, then perhaps you will soon belong to the great group of people that before you, have gone and experienced extreme improvement in every aspect of their lives. Many are of the opinion that it was only after applying the PMA method, that they discovered their deeply hidden sources of energy and potentials.

About the writer

Jacob Korthuis was born in 1950 in the Netherlands and has over 25 years of medical and personal coaching experience, including 10 years of teaching rhetoric. During his practice in natural health, combined with his holistic way of thinking, he developed the Progressive Mental Alignment® Training and Coaching Method (PMA).

He wrote his first book, *Oog in Oog* (transl.: Eye to Eye), in 1986. This book is still used today as one of the official textbooks of natural health in The Netherlands and Belgium. In 1991 he appeared on national television were he represented the professional holistic health community. In 1996, he developed a totally new approach to solve psychological and psychosomatic complaints and behavioral problems. The method is called Progressive Mental Alignment® (PMA). In 1996, he published the first book, titled *Free Yourself* (published in English, Dutch and Danish), which presents this powerful method as a self-help tool to free people from psychosomatic and/or psychological complaints and let them understand their behavioral patterns.

Jacob is the co-founder of the VBAG, one of the largest natural health practitioner organizations in The Netherlands. There, he is well known as a speaker and teacher in homeopathy, iridology, chiropractic and holistic health. He is the authority on the Progressive Mental Alignment® method and in teaching it to professionals in the health care, relationship and coaching industry.

In 1995 he founded the BCE Institute in The Netherlands, and in 2002 he also founded A-way from pain®, Inc. in the USA. He trained many professionals in The Netherlands, as well as in the USA, Denmark and Germany, on how to practice the PMA method. Since 2002 he has resided in the USA and developed a special program for trainers and coaches in the corporate world to teach the PMA Training and Coaching techniques to management and sales personnel.

Preface

Desirable Power presents an entirely new understanding of the subconscious processes of our brain. It shows how powerful and yet, how delicately sensitive our nerve cells are, and how easily they can go into overload, causing unhealthy and incorrect neuro-physiological connections. These incorrect connections, called *Bad Clusters*, become subconscious jamming stations that inhibit us from reaching our goals and are also responsible for all psychosomatic illnesses. To change these incorrect connections we first need to make subconscious data and processes 'visible' to the conscious part of our brain. By doing so we are able to create a pathway to a permanent positive change in our behavioral patterns and health. This process can be mastered by the method called *Progressive Mental Alignment®*, abbreviated to *PMA*. In a way that is easy to understand, you will be guided through the neuro-physiological processes of the brain and gain insight about our deeply hidden drives and belief systems. By practicing the PMA self-help method, as explained in this book, you will experience a positive change in your behavior and health. You will discover how hidden and wrongly stored data in your subconscious contains large amounts of positive energy, waiting to be unleashed. This book is written for those who are willing to embark on an adventure and who are not afraid to look at themselves squarely in the mirror. It is a straightforward approach; simply written. Above all, it is a book loaded with information on how you can free yourself from countless psychological and psychosomatic symptoms and how to change reactive behavioral patterns into a positive and proactive existence and create solid and happy relationships. An increasing amount of scientists agree on the same conclusion: the mind makes the body sick and subconscious processes inhibit us from reaching our true potentials. PMA will enable you to discover how the subconscious mind dictates negative behavior and how easily this can be changed. Rising health care costs and demanding jobs force us as individuals to seek a way to take the state of our health and the driving forces behind our performances back into our own hands. Our behavior determines how we interact with other people. These interactions establish the quality of our relationships. Today, more and more relationships are unhappy. There is a great demand for direction and support that reach beyond the conventional methods. This publication will surely provide you with that direction and support.

Are you living or just surviving?

Do you get up in the morning feeling that although the day has just begun, it's all too much? Are you tired all the time? Don't feel like doing anything? Burned out? Depressed? Scared about the future? Do you get the feeling that there is more to life than what you are now experiencing? Are you caught up in routines? Do you want to bring more meaning, joy and contentment to your life? How often do you hear people say: *"I am suffering from physical complaints but doctors cannot find the cause"?* Or: "*The doctors told me that it's all in my head"?* It may surprise you to discover that your brain actually does play a crucial role in psychological and physical complaints. These complaints are not imaginary, they are very real. What are the root causes? Events in the past experienced as traumas, that have been incorrectly or insufficiently processed by the brain. They are often the cause of negative feelings, fears and many physical complaints in the present. Furthermore, these traumas influence your daily functioning more than you may realize. They can even make you ill and determine the majority of your decisions and behavior. Therefore, it is worthwhile to take a look at the subconscious processes of the brain. Where do irrational fears (such as phobias, the fear of failure, fear of change or repetitive irrational habits and/or behavior) come from? Why is it so difficult to change negative behavioral patterns? What stops us from achieving our goals? Do you recognize that gut feeling that you are capable of much more than you have achieved up to now? How can you unleash your hidden potentials and energy to a maximum? What is the effect of the recently discovered, incorrectly processed neuro-physiological data, called "Bad Clusters", on our health and behavior in daily life? Just continue reading and enjoy the exciting discoveries of your own subconscious processes and how they control your emotions, belief systems, actions and health.

Jacob Korthuis

Chapter 1 – The desire for answers

A passionate vacation

Janine was a beautiful woman with a promising career. Her colleagues and friends loved her because of her cheerful character and magnetic personality. However, nobody recognized that Janine lived in constant horror. It all started when she was 22 years old and had a great vacation in Italy with some of her friends. One night they all ended up in a bar. There was an abundance of *Chianti*, sensual music and passionate Italian men. The next morning she woke up next to Gino, a handsome Italian guy. Although she never again saw him after that, she did hear something about him that completely changed her life. It was one year later, when one of her friends traveled back to Italy. Janine will never forget the day that this friend called her and said: *"Do you remember Gino, the guy we met in Italy? I met some of his friends today when I visited the same bar. They told me that Gino is not doing well at all. They found out that he is HIV-positive!"*

Nobody will ever know

Janine's heart rate was skyrocketing! It felt like all her energy was flowing away and she almost fainted. *"HIV-positive!"*, she frantically thought to herself, *"That means AIDS; and I slept with him! I will die!"* Instantly, all sorts of pictures that she had seen on television and stories she read in magazines about HIV flashed through her mind. Janine felt a fear inside that was ripping her apart. She was brought up in a very conservative and religious environment. Sex before marriage was unacceptable! Her family would find her disgusting if they ever found out what she did. She was so afraid of their rejection and so ashamed of what happened on her vacation that she decided not to speak to anyone about this. When she was in Italy, she never told her friends the truth about what happened that night! Now, she became afraid that Gino's friends also knew about her *one night stand* and may told her friend. She was a nervous wreck when her friend returned from Italy, but felt some relief after she realized her friend knew nothing about her brief affair with Gino.

The fear kicks in

Janine decided to continue her life as before, like nothing ever happened. Her relief only lasted a few days. After a week, she suddenly felt feverish and had a sore throat. Instantly, the fear kicked in! *"HIV-positive... oh my God, my immune system is already damaged!"* Going to the hospital for a blood test was out of the question. Nobody could ever know! She would live as healthy as possible from now on. But she lived in fear more and more every day. Whenever she felt even the slightest negative change in her health, she panicked. For five years Janine lived in this horror! Finally, on one particular evening she came home from work and felt sick. She wasn't very hungry so she just made herself a sandwich with some left over tuna from the refrigerator. A few hours later she felt even worse. She decided to call her parents, who lived just a few blocks away from her.

Did they know?

Janine's parents found her laying unconscious and immediately rushed her to the hospital. When she gained consciousness and realized that she was in the hospital, she panicked! The doctor came in and told her: *"Janine, Janine, don't worry, everything will be alright! We examined you thoroughly and found that you had some innocent virus in your blood which has led you very close to a burn-out; and it turned out that the tuna you ate was spoiled and caused food poisoning. This was too much for your body to handle and you fainted, but I promise everything will be fine."* At that moment, thousands of thoughts circled in her head: if they examined her blood, did they also test it for HIV? The uncertainty almost killed her!

Finally, relief!

After her family was gone, she asked the doctor: *"What did they actually find in my blood?"* The doctor politely responded: *"Oh, some innocent virus that is causing flu-like symptoms."* Unsatisfied with his answer, Janine asked again: *"Is it possible that there is another condition they may have overlooked?"* The doctor answered convincingly: *"That is always possible, but not likely. We performed a thorough examination. We examined the functions of the kidneys, liver, thyroid, and pancreas. We also checked for HIV, mononucleosis, as well as other infections, and all came up just fine... no problems."* It was like a huge bubble exploded inside of her, suddenly releasing all the pressure that was bottled up inside her for five years! She felt very dizzy and gasped for air. She felt a huge desire to jump out of bed and start to dance, but instead, she started to cry! The doctor grabbed her hand and with empathically said: *"Calm down Janine. Believe me, everything will be fine. You are a strong woman, and in a few days you will feel great again!"* How little did he know! She had lived five years of uncertainty, tortured by guilt, shame and fear. All those sleepless nights, worries and fear, especially during the moments she felt the slightest symptom that something was wrong with her body. He could not even understand a fraction of the relief she felt when she learned that she was not HIV-positive. The constant fear and uncertainty during the last five years shaped her whole behavior, decisions, belief systems and health. It robbed her of her energy and made her a lot less proactive. Yet, it all disappeared in a fraction of a second when she realized that she was not infected, not suffering from AIDS.

It was all real to her

Just imagine the emotional price she paid these five years. Was the fear she constantly experienced real? What about her sleepless nights and her health problems? Were they real? And the tremendous relief she experienced when she found out that she was not infected? Was that real? However, the changes in her belief systems, decisions and behavior the last five years were very real. But, was it all based on objective information? Was the actual reason of her fear based on medical facts? In *her* mind it was! Why? Because the neuro-physiological connections she made in her conscious brain, and especially in her subconscious, made her believe that! Of course, it all began with the message given to her that Gino had been diagnosed HIV-positive. However, it was her conscious and subconscious interpretations, her neuro-physiological connections, dictated by the emotional load of that message in combination with what she already knew about HIV, that caused her emotional and physical problems and reactions.

A million times more in the subconscious

Science shows us that our brain is not a computer, that it just stores and analyzes dry facts. Every piece of data that enters our brain through our senses is extensively processed and finally stored as factual data, but at all times unbreakably connected to the feelings that were felt at that moment. These feelings are caused by the physiological status of your body at that time. It is stored as a neuro-physiological code that is unbreakably connected to the factual data. The consequence of this will be discussed later. As a human being we have feelings and have that unique 'thing' we call: *awareness*. To explain awareness is still a complicated issue that trouble scientists. Complicated experiments demonstrated that in order to become 'aware' of what we see, smell, hear, taste and feel, our subconscious has to compare and analyze all incoming sensory data. It has to encode that data properly and process all the information before it can finally create 'awareness'. To manage that huge task, the subconscious will process more than a million times the quantity of data than the amount that will ever reach the conscious brain. By connecting the dots, PMA reveals that all of us carry a tiny amount of 'wrongly stored' data, called Bad Clusters, which has an enormous influence on every aspect of our lives. The subconscious possessing this type of incorrect encoded data is responsible for a lot of behavioral problems and all existing psychosomatic complaints. Just think about the ongoing fear Janine suffered. It was not based on physical failure or malfunctions, but purely caused by her emotions, originating from her belief systems, in connection to a simple phone call. Her problems were 100% psychosomatic! Some may conclude: *"Oh, I understand; so she was a little bit crazy?"* But this is not so!

It can all be changed

One may ask: *"But doesn't psychosomatic mean that your brain makes your body sick?* Absolutely! But that has nothing to do with being crazy! Instead, we should ask ourselves: *"Why would the brain do such a thing? Is the brain out of its mind? Does it do that on purpose?"* No, of course not! Our brain, especially our subconscious brain, would never purposely do something to hurt us. Actually, it is genetically programmed to always push us as far away from pain and damage as possible. But what, then, causes the brain to act like this? We could say it is due to a 'short-circuiting' during an overload. The process of psychosomatic illness was a mystery for a long time. By connecting the dots in biology, neuro-physiology and quantum-physics, it became clear how our brain goes into overload and makes wrong connections and how this is harming us and making us sick. It did not only shed light on the root-cause of psychosomatic problems, but also on what are the drives that dictate our behavior. Let's discover how we are able to create permanent positive changes and regain our health and energy.

Theory versus practice

The human brain is the most ingenious and complex mechanism on the planet. Although we all posses one of these gray masses in our head, there is no other organ studied so thoroughly as the brain, and yet, so little of its secrets have been discovered. If we learn to know its way of working, its natural rules, possibilities and limitations, we will be able to reach amazing goals an levels of performance! We will have the ability to achieve so much more in life than we do now! But we have to play the game by the genetic rules and programs of the subconscious brain. The subconscious brain uses his own language. If we want to communicate with our subconscious, then we first have to learn that language. One of the most basic rules of that language is called stimulus/response. Scientists worldwide are busy investigating this most fascinating matter. Through scientific research with humans and animals and utilizing the most modern techniques, scientists have already developed some unique insights into the complex construction and workings of the human brain. This sort of research is extremely important and meaningful. Their primary mission is to discover how the brain works: Which chemical, electrical and biological processes are taking place? What exactly happens during the thinking process? What reactions are taking place in the brain as it gathers experiences through the senses? How many neuropeptides (or ligands) and IMP's (Integral Membrane Protein) exist? What are they made up of? What do they react to and why? And how do the synapses work? Why does the brain, on one hand, continually make connections to different nerve cells while, on the other hand, degenerate many of these very same connections? How do the different components of the brain work together? How do we remember? How do we forget? How do we suppress? Science is industriously seeking the answers to these and hundreds of other questions. Next to these purely scientific approaches that are taking place in various laboratories and research centers, there is also a group of scientists who are engaged in a more philosophical approach as to how the brain works. Many theories have, in the meantime, seen the light. However, many of these theories unfortunately dispute each other in their opinions. Next to science and philosophy, there is yet another approach: *practice*. That is primarily what this book is about. It helps us to discover what we experience in ourselves, our emotions, our frustrations, our physical and psychosomatic complaints and repetitive unwanted behavioral patterns on a daily basis. Observations made from the medical practice have led to logical conclusions and have been described in an easy to understand language. How the brain works will be explained, and especially, what can go wrong in our minds and how this effects and controls our behavior, health and relationships.

Finding desirable power

Of course, the workings of our brain can be explained by chemical, electrical or biological means, but at present, we want to try another approach. We're discussing the daily practice of acquiring an understanding of the mechanisms of the brain. This approach will give us answers to questions such as: Why do you behave the way you do? What are the motivations behind your behavior? Why do you feel so bad sometimes? Why do you sometimes overreact or behave aggressively? How do depression, phobias, negative emotions, fears, perfectionism, eating disorders, fibromyalgia and a large variety of psychosomatic symptoms develop? Why is it so difficult to accomplish goals? Moreover, the big question is: How can you, once and for all, rid yourself of these problems? Is this really possible? Can we also really unleash the hidden powers and capacities inside of us? Let us find out how PMA will help us get answers to these and other questions. This book shows us the way to this *Desirable Power* we all carry inside of us.

PMA, the power to control

PMA is based on a very direct and fundamental approach of the subconscious human brain. Before you begin to work with this method, it is very important to know the fundamentals on how the brain functions and how this knowledge leads to understanding why this technique works. If you want to obtain the maximum benefit from this method, then you will have to correctly apply what you learn in this book and approach your subconscious in its own language, based on its own rules. If you do that, then you will discover its positive effects and you will be surprised by what you can learn about yourself, and others, and how much hidden desirable power you possess to control your health and behavior. To understand the hidden drive behind our belief systems, decisions and behavior, we must look inside ourselves and learn to understand *how* our mental and emotional systems are controlled. In other words, we must understand the 'operating system' of the body and mind. Regardless of what it is that we experience in our body, such as hunger, thirst, desire, illness, happiness, pain, love or any other change of feeling or emotion, it is all the result of one thing: *physiology*! So before we continue our discovery journey into the subconscious, we have to understand some basic principles about physiology and neurology.

Don't underestimate yourself

Understanding the basics of neuro-physiological processes is not as hard as it seems. Everyone can comprehend this. Some people assume they can't grasp things, so they condition themselves by creating a belief system that subjects like these do not interest them. By making that true for themselves, they actually say: *"I have no interest in understanding myself... how to become happy and successful in life and how to achieve the things I want! That's too difficult for me; I just go with the flow!"* Don't fall into that trap! We all have the ability to learn and to grow! Even more, we always grow as long as we take in new information, whether we like the information or not. We only stop growing when we're dead. Therefore, it's good to take control of your growth and direct it to your benefit. There is no one that is unable to practice the PMA method! But we do find people that only condition themselves with belief systems that they are unable to it!

What can you expect?

No other training, coaching or counseling method has yet acknowledged the existence and role of a powerful protection mechanism that determines at least 75% of our belief systems and behavioral patterns. Unfortunately, other methods often empower this protection mechanism, without even realizing it, and never go beyond that point. PMA calls this protection program: *the Friend Mechanism.* In fact, this mechanism conceals the real cause of our strongest negative drives and paradigms from our conscious brain. So far, PMA is the only existing method that will go to the original source of our beliefs and attitudes. During an exciting journey, PMA will show you how to remove hidden blockades in your subconscious. You may expect to achieve the following:

- More energy
- Greater effectiveness in handling everyday events
- Better and happier relationships
- Enhance the quality of your judgment
- Achieve your goals more easily and set new ambitious ones
- Make better decisions in business and personal affairs
- Experience inner peace, freedom and balance

Experience your own exciting and surprising adventure when you embark on your discovery journey into your subconscious brain! Feel the releasing power of the self-help sessions you will master while reading this book. A neurologist who practices PMA once said: *"To study PMA is enlightening, but to experience the effects of it during and after a session is an eye-opener first class!"*

Don't sabotage yourself

Before we look into the control center of neuro-physiological processes, I would like to share a real story with you: Are you familiar what a *"flea circus"* is? It is a circus performed by fleas on a little 2x2 foot table with a short wall surrounding it that measures 3 inches high. The fleas are trained to perform little circus acts, like pulling a silver carriage or playing with a little ball, etc. Naturally, fleas can easily jump 10 feet high, and more. So why, in the flea circus, do they not jump way over that little 3-inch wall? That's because the trainer conditioned them in two ways. First by feeding them with his own blood so they get attached to him! Secondly, he puts them in a little jar before he starts to train them. The jar is only <u>two</u> inches high. The fleas start to jump, hitting the lid on the jar, time and time again. Finally, they get a headache and give up! After that moment they stop using their genetic jumping capacity! Here is the lesson we can learn from this: Don't be a circus flea! You *can* use all your genetic capacities to the fullest! Too many people are conditioned by inhibiting belief systems that dictate them so they cannot "jump" high! With this in mind, please join me in discovering our *Desirable Power* and experience how high we can really jump!

Chapter 2 - The human mind – The center of our behavior

Two major areas of the brain

Most people might believe that the mind and body are separate entities. But science and common sense increasingly show that the mind and body are one! The mind is not disconnected from the rest of the body, instead, the *result* of all the functions of the body. Or if you prefer a more spiritual approach, it manifests itself through the functions of the body. The whole body, including the mind, is one biological unit that closely works as one entity. Purely for educational purposes, in order to understand the functions of the brain and the mind/body relationship, we have to make a distinction between the separate modules. Examples of what we mean with modules are: senses, body organs, special skills, language, movement, emotions, etc. Each of them has a specific task or function. After we understand the modules, we'll focus on their interactions with one another. First of all, let's divide the functions of the brain into two large segments:

The conscious and the subconscious

We divide our brain into two parts: the conscious and subconscious brain. The conscious cannot exist without the subconscious, and the subconscious would be of no use to us without the conscious. We will discuss them separately for educational reasons. Let's examine what are the distinct functions of both. To put it into a few words you can say:

- The definition of the conscious brain:

Everything that you are aware of.

- The definition of the subconscious brain:

  Operates like an advanced computer; it's a piece of exact equipment following strict genetically determined rules.

Consciousness MAKES MISTAKES	**Subconscious** DOES NOT THINK OR FEEL MAKES NO MISTAKES
1. Understanding	1. Observing/Perceiving
2. Reasoning	2. Comparing
3. Planning	3. Analyzing
4. Focusing	4. Physiology
5. Conclusions	5. Connecting
6. Decisions	6. Storing
7. Action	7. Retrieving
8. Feelings	

The subconscious is not some sinister name for a mystical mechanism. It is the technical part of the brain that processes and analyses all incoming perceptions and impressions. It has its own set of rules and logic, which is different from the way our conscious makes its connections. It is important to always keep the following in mind: The conscious is the only part that can feel! Feeling is a conscious sensation.

> ***Example*:**
> When you are under anesthesia during an operation, you do not feel the pain. How is this possible? Your consciousness is temporarily shut off.

The subconscious doesn't think or feel but only executes programs! It works like a highly advanced computer of a very high caliber with unparalleled capacity. Every mistake we make is made in the conscious part of our brain. Mistakes are usually the result of judgments and decisions. These are always conscious and always based on our feelings! The subconscious does not make a single mistake. It just carries out processes in a predefined way, based on a very simple rule: Stimulus/Response.

Clearing things up

It is now time to clear up some matters regarding the false reasoning of the French philosopher and mathematician, René Descartes (1596-1650), whose interpretations have long dominated in science. Descartes proposed that conscious (spirit or soul) is not physical and takes up no space in the physical body. He came to the conclusion that the soul and the body are two entirely different entities, distinct units. His words, *"I doubt, therefore, I think"* (dubito ergo cogito) and *"I think, therefore, I am"* (cogito ergo sum), are famous. Descartes came to the conclusion that no one could doubt that he/she has a spirit or soul because the very act of doubting one's self constituted in having a soul. Without a soul you cannot doubt, he stated, but we could doubt the fact that we have a body. From that, he concluded that the soul is an independent existence that only uses the body as a mechanism. He perceived the soul as an immaterial thing, an elusive occurrence. Without going into 'why' it is important to understand that, for centuries his ideas have directed science in the wrong path. Clinging to his interpretations will inhibit or even prevent us from unraveling the secrets of the human brain and our behavior!

The Life Force

Our brain is definitely a corporeal and therefore, tangible substance. This corporeal part would not be able to function without the *Life Force*, just as a computer would be unable to function without electricity. This universal Life Force, or *Chi*, can best be compared to electricity. Similar to electricity, it is impersonal. The human mind cannot exist without a body, any more than the body cannot live without the mind. They are in fact *one* biological unit! This conclusion gives us an entirely different understanding of the brain. Our mind has to be treated as a part of our body. From this viewpoint, psychosomatic illnesses (physical symptoms caused by the psyche) are a logical occurrence. If the mind and the body are viewed as two separate entities, then all sorts of complicated explanations for the mysterious psychosomatic influence they have on each other will be sought after. We will truly see that there is nothing mysterious about this. If we consider the body and mind as one, then a number of things become evident. Our genetic material and our individual experiences make us into what we are.

How does the human brain work?

What is awareness? This is perhaps one of the questions that most baffle scientists. Scientific researchers admit that they actually know very little about the processes in our brain, how we think, how emotions come to be, how we remember, how we judge and process our experiences, and how consciousness is created by our brain cells. Diligent research into these topics is regularly undertaken. The functioning of the human brain can be described in two ways:

1. The technical and organic functions with electrical and bio-chemical processes scientifically determining what, why, how and where things occur in the brain.

2. The practical functioning of the brain, without going too much into the organic processes. Not a technical or a difficult account, no chemistry or physiology, instead, feelings and reasoning are central.

We will discuss the ways and processes in which someone experiences his/her environment and reacts to it, the thought processes, including emotions and frustrations.

We all start out the same

Scientists in the fields of biology, neurology, physiology and quantum physics have discovered a lot about genetics and the functions of our body. The fact is, that every healthy baby is born with the same basic ingredients and behavioral patterns. They all move, cry, laugh, pee and poop exactly the same! They all use the same muscles (facial and body) for that type of behavior. From that point on, we start to learn. We usually don't think about this normal process of life and developing experience because we consider it "normal" that we can do those everyday things (such as thinking, talking, eating, sitting, walking, maintaining balance, etc.). However, performing this kind of "normal" behavior is far from easy, from a neuro-physiological point of view. Scientists who try to build robots find it very difficult, if not impossible, to build and program robots that can do these elementary, *normal* things!

Understanding of the basic patterns of the brain's mechanisms

It is essential to understand the basics of this learning process because the brain always follows a strict pattern in this operation. It is this same pattern that we use in PMA. As soon as we understand the operating system of the brain, we can start to use that knowledge to our full benefit. Just like a computer, if you don't understand how the programs work and what these programs are capable of, you will never use or enjoy the computer to its full extent. Don't get scared now, it won't get too technical! To understand how to drive a car and have full benefit from it, we don't necessarily have to go under the hood to find out every technical detail. We just need a good instructor who can tell us how to operate and drive that car. And this is exactly what we're going to do!

Our brain is preprogrammed

Why are these diverse mechanisms and their function more interesting to us than the clinical, technical, physiological and scientific sections? Because, everyday, each one of us is confronted with his or her own personality, fears, frustrations, guilt feelings, humor, psychosomatic sicknesses and so on. We need a method that enables us to better control our emotions, or perhaps, even control them completely. This will bring about marked improvement in the quality of our life. Also, this has everything to do with the understanding of the functioning of the brain. There is no computer on the face of this Earth that can hold a candle to the human brain. And yet, making the comparison with a computer can assist us in acquiring a better understanding of what we are discussing. We need to ask ourselves: *Is it mere chance that the computer has been developed to its present form or is this merely a subconscious replication of our own brain?* A computer is made up of a box filled with an incredible amount of technology. We can compare the box and its sophisticated content with our body. A computer can only do what it has been programmed to do. It has its own language that can be translated into ones and zeroes, which are then grouped into bytes of 8 bits. With only that, all the possible and necessary combinations can be made in order to do the wonderful things that computers can perform these days.

Likewise, our brain has its own language, its own processing mechanism based on its own rules. If we want to understand and approach our subconscious brain, we need to know and accept the genetically determined rules and language of the brain.

You don't need medical training to understand your own brain

However, in order for a computer to function, more is needed than just a box and its technological innards. It has to be programmed with some sort of basic operating program, the so-called "operating system". This operating program (for example Linux, OSX, Windows) can be compared to the genetically programmed aspects that we, as people, receive at birth. Our basic emotions are included at birth, such as fear, joy, surprise, sadness, disgust and anger, but also included is the inherent possibility to develop the primary attributes of love, power, wisdom and justice, which are the foundation of all our emotions. A computer operates on the basis of a fixed pattern: regularity. Our brain also operates on the basis of a similar sort of regularity. There are two ways to explain the workings of a computer to someone who has never before worked with them. You could begin to explain all the technical components inside and what each one does. Or, you could just sit down at the keyboard and begin to explain which keys or keystroke combinations need to be used in order to gain the most benefit from the computer. It is through the latter that you can quickly learn how to use the computer to your best advantage. In a similar manner, we will examine the functioning of the brain. It requires no great technical or medical knowledge to understand how your brain functions and how you can use your brain to increase your own personal health, energy and happiness.

Questions that need an answer

We are interested in how the brain processes information and how it creates emotions and behavioral patterns. Why are certain people the way they are? Why can one person laugh at something that actually frightens another? Why do some people experience intense revulsion at some things that others have no reaction to, or perhaps, even find it attractive? Why do our emotions change so quickly without any easily discernible reason? Why do we sometimes feel that there are certain things that we must do, no matter what? What is psychosomatic? Where does anger, fear, aggression, depression, guilt feelings, perfectionism or our countless belief systems come from? Why is it so difficult to control them? How can they continue to embitter our lives after so many years?

The overall picture

In order to understand and influence the way we act and feel, we have to acquire some basic knowledge about how our mental and emotional systems work. Progressive Mental Alignment® (PMA) is not a lecture in Neuro Sciences, but we will go into the subject just as much as we need to for our practical purpose. Like we mentioned earlier, PMA often compares the brain to a computer in order to visualize similarities in its structure. So let us look into the primary functions of the brain. Roughly we can say:

- The outside of the brain, called the Cortex, stores all the factual data. These are all the pieces of information that we perceive through our senses.

In PMA, the combined factual data that form together one mental picture, or memory, is called a Cluster. The front part of the Cortex is considered the basis of our awareness or consciousness.

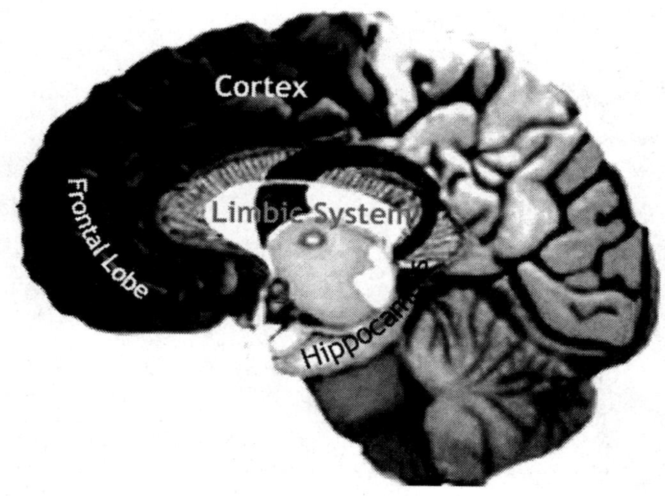

- The inner part of the brain, called the Limbic System, takes care of the physiology. It controls our physiological processes.

Neuroscience makes a distinction between the short-term memory and the long-term memory. Short-term memory is mainly located in the Hippocampus. Long-term memory is found in the Cortex (excluding the frontal lobe, the part behind your forehead). New incoming sensory data always has to be processed. To do this, the Cortex and other areas, called the Hippocampus and the Thalamus, work closely together. You can compare the Hippocampus to the RAM (Random-Access Memory) of your computer. The short-term memory (Hippocampus) prepares the new data for storage in the long-term memory (the Cortex). The frontal lobe is where all higher processes take place. This is the place were the end results of all the data are sent to, and where we make our decisions. Also, it is where all the analyzed information comes together and creates awareness. The different modules of the brain are strongly interwoven with each other, working closely together as one biological unit. The distinction between these modules is a functional one.

Important!

Although there are many wonderful, yet complicated, mechanisms in the brain, it is important to remember the two basic areas:

1. The Cortex – the upper layer of the brain where we store all our sensory, factual data, such as colors, shape, movement, smell, taste, sounds, words, etc.

2. The Limbic System – the inner part of the brain where we store all our physiological information.

The factual data (Cortex) is always connected to physiological components (Limbic System). The result of that physiology gives you your drives. It is that physiology that creates emotions. The symptoms of our emotions are the indicators we will use to communicate with the subconscious who controls our physiology. Once we can do that, we are able to change major aspects of our health and behavior. It is great fun to discover what really controls your drives and feelings. You will be amazed how many answers you will get by "looking in the mirror of life". Why is it that so many people – especially men – have a hard time confronting themselves with their own emotions? They are YOUR emotions, not someone else's! Obviously people are not keen to see the things that can benefit them in growing. Don't be too shy and reserved to look and find out what is your personal hidden strength in order to grow and become successful. You will discover that everything you do, say, decide, how you behave and feel, originates from the emotions (physiology) you experienced and stored throughout the course of your lifetime. Most of your emotions are stored just as they should; they will support your thoughts and actions as they are supposed to. In specific circumstances, however, they are stored in a way that can harm you. In that case, they have a disturbing and inhibiting influence on your total behavior and will block your potential drives.

Our genetically determined constitution

It is obvious that our experiences shape and color our emotions, but how does our genetically determined constitution relate to our emotions? Actually, genes do not control our emotions; they only determine the original constitution of our physical body! If genes do not control our emotions, then how do they control our life? Genes play only a minor role in that process. Our constitution is genetically determined by the combination of stronger and weaker organs or organ-systems. This means that the status of organs (like our nervous system, liver, kidneys, heart, thyroid, etc.) determine, to a certain degree, *how* we feel our emotions. As an example, we can compare our genetic constitution with the make of a car. There are many different types and models of cars. Each model has its unique shape and power, but also has its unique stronger and weaker parts. If we use a car in a wrong way, regardless of what brand it is, the weaker parts will break down first. The same applies to our genetic constitution. Each one of us has a unique constitution, but also its unique stronger and weaker parts. Use your body wisely and the weak parts will sustain and serve you for a long time. Use your body irresponsibly and abusively, and your weaker parts will be the first to break.

Our personality is not genetic

You can compare emotions to a piece of music. Each emotion has its own specific preprogrammed melody. Our nervous system and other organs act like the strings of a piano. Their strength, weakness and "tuning" are genetically determined. There are millions of pianos, each with their own unique tuning of the individual strings. They will not be tuned, but played as they come from the factory. You will probably agree that none of the pianos will sound the same because each one is tuned slightly different than the other. Now, play exactly the same melody on all of the pianos. Do you agree that the same melody will sound different on every one of the pianos? This works the same with our emotions. The basic program (melody) is the same, but we reflect them differently because of the genetic "tuning" of our organs and organ-systems. That is where the genetic part ends. All the rest of our emotional controlled responses and behaviors that shape our personality are determined by our choices based on our subconscious comparison material.

Our comparison material

What is exactly meant by the phrase: "subconscious comparison material"? It describes everything we ever learned and experienced in our life that was significant enough to store in our 'Database', our brain cells. Do we constantly remember all those stored events? *Thank God* we don't! We would go crazy! So, then, why do we need them? They create our reality. If we would not have this Database full of previously stored experiences, we would not know where we are and what we say or do. We would still experience life at the level of a newborn child. Everything that enters our brain through our senses (what we see, smell, taste, hear and feel) needs to be analyzed to give it meaning so that we can understand the sensory information. If you see an object you have never seen before, you would not know what this object is. How come? This is because you have nothing in your subconscious Database to compare it to. Even the understanding or carrying out of the most elementary moves, gestures, words, choices, etc. are based on previously stored data. Without all this stored data you would not even be able to walk, sit, talk or eat by yourself. Where do we store all this information?

The Database

The Database of all our factual sensory data is the Cortex and is where we store all our memories. All the data is neatly stored and categorized in the Cortex, such as all the new incoming sensory data in connection with previously stored data. The Database cannot think, act or feel. Its functioning is bound to the stimulus/response rule. It's similar to a 'super' hard disk, filled with data that becomes meaningful only when needed as comparison material to analyze new incoming information. We have two Databases: one for sensory factual data (Cortex) and one for the physiology (Limbic System). In PMA we call a stored memory, with all its sensory data, a "Cluster".

Characteristics of PMA words

Here we introduce a typical PMA word: *Cluster*. We will use this word in abundance, so it will be helpful to remember what we mean by it. The word "Cluster" is used in the computer world and in astronomy to describe *"single pieces that belong together as one unit"*. In PMA it refers to *an amount of neuro-physiological data that belongs together as one unit*. In PMA it refers to *factual data stored in the several areas of the brain that form together one memory*. This stored data can be of an event or something we have learned. A Cluster also refers to *an amount of physiological commands that form together a unit, which mostly defines the source of an emotion* (in this case we always place the word "Physio" in front of the word "Cluster"). In PMA we refer to five different types of Clusters:

1)	**Cluster**	*Correctly encoded and stored memories*
2)	**Bad Cluster**	*Incorrectly and improperly coded events*
3)	**Sub-cluster**	*A fraction of a Cluster or Bad Cluster (one sense)*
4)	**Proto-physiocluster**	*Genetic mechanism that controls basic physiology*
5)	**Physio-cluster**	*Physiological commands that are always connected to a Cluster or a Bad Cluster*

In the future, we will discuss each of them separately. But for now, because they are often used throughout this book, let us try to remember them starting at this point.

Clusters

Clusters are properly analyzed memory units; a collection of data that together forms a meaningful event or 'mental picture'. Everything that we experience, think about and conclude is stored in the form of Clusters. All the data in a Cluster is always analyzed and encoded. Clusters serve as subconscious comparison material for newly incoming sensory data in order to assign a code to this new data.

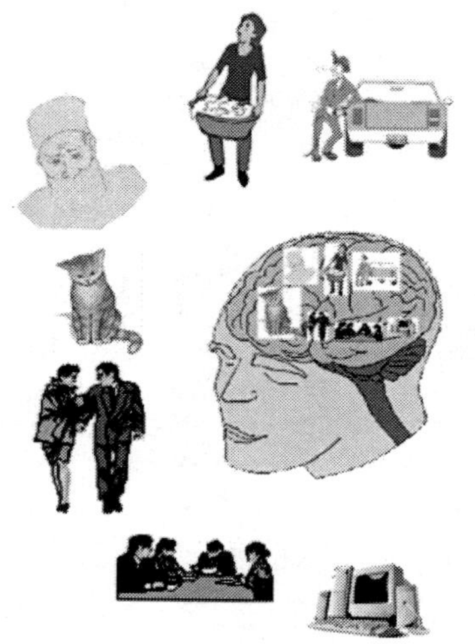

Cluster

Correctly stored memories of everything we experieced, observed or learned

Stored as sensory factual data

The codes are based on the already existing code, or value, in previous analyzed and stored Clusters. Clusters contain all kinds of information: All the things we ever studied, learned, and thought about, as well as all the experiences that where important enough to store, whether they were nice, or not so nice experiences.

Bad Clusters

We will discuss the origin, content and power of Bad Clusters later on. But for now, please pay close attention to this short explanation about Bad Clusters because its meaning is so very crucial to our whole existence: By means of protection, some experiences are stored "wrongly", they are not properly encoded and therefore, not available for later conscious retrieval. We call these wrongly stored Clusters: *Bad Clusters*. They are created only during an event that you experience as traumatic. However, there is a general rule that describes exactly when a Bad Cluster will be formed:

A Bad Cluster is the unavoidable result of a moment when we feel we lose total control.

What do we mean with the words "lose total control"? These are painful, scary or embarrassing moments that we have no control over a situation. It gives us a feeling of panic, for there is nothing to hold on to. It feels like if you were to fall into a deep hole without anything to hold on to. In a situation like this, your subconscious will be partly blocked for reasons we will discuss later. This causes, for that specific moment, a "short circuiting" in the processing of new incoming sensory data. This results in the fact that the incoming data will be stored in connection with the extreme emotions you experience at that very moment of storage. What kind of emotion (physiology)? A situation when you felt you lost control, a moment of panic! That's the moment you create a Bad Cluster! Unfortunately, Bad Clusters are stored in the same Database cells (Cortex) as similar, but normal, encoded Cluster data. This means that the subconscious will also use Bad Clusters as comparison material the same way it will use normal Clusters. However, the physiological loads of both types of clusters differ tremendously!

Storage spread all over the Cortex

Psychological research studies confirm that memories are made up of so-called mental pictures that consist of scents, colors, shapes, tastes, words, sounds, etc. as well as associated bodily sensations, such as heartbeat, trembling, tension, pressure, nausea, itching, etc.

GET THE PICTURE

* When we say, "What do you see?", we refer to a **mental** picture

* This includes every sensory experience in your brain

* This means that everything you:

See
Smell
Taste
Hear
Feel (touch + emotion)

is a mental picture

These mental pictures are not stored as a single unit in just one location of the brain. Instead, they are stored in separate fragments located in different brain cells that have a specific task. For example, there is a part of the brain that only stores color and another part that stores movement and scents. The Visual Cortex has more than a hundred different layers that can each store only one specific type of data. Each of our senses has its specific location in the Cortex. Therefore, a complete memory has to be collected from all the different regions of the Cortex.

The comparison process

All incoming new data has to be analyzed in order to become meaningful to us. To do that, the subconscious analyzes on several levels that gradually build up the whole picture (all in a fraction of a millionth of a second):

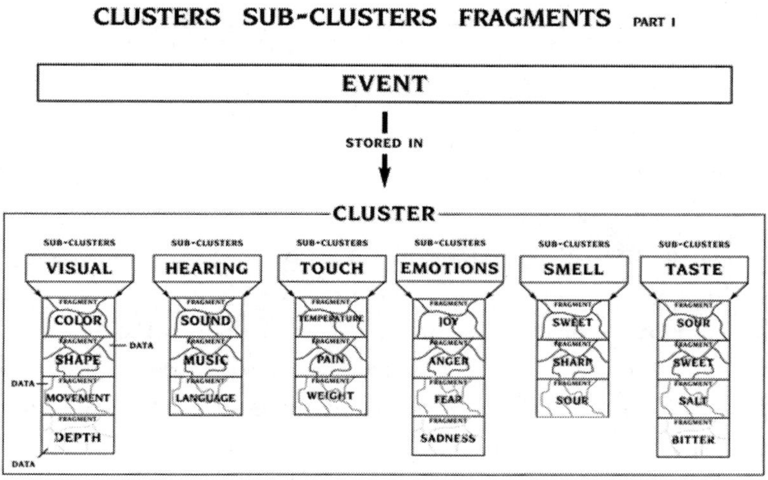

CLUSTERS SUB-CLUSTERS FRAGMENTS PART I

EVENT

STORED IN

CLUSTER

VISUAL: COLOR, SHAPE, MOVEMENT, DEPTH
HEARING: SOUND, MUSIC, LANGUAGE
TOUCH: TEMPERATURE, PAIN, WEIGHT
EMOTIONS: JOY, ANGER, FEAR, SADNESS
SMELL: SWEET, SHARP, SOUR
TASTE: SOUR, SWEET, SALT, BITTER

Level 1 - Fragments

We compare fragments of new incoming data with fragments of previously stored Clusters. Fragments are specific: color, movement, facial expression, shape, smell, sound, words, etc.

Level 2 - Sub-clusters

After the analysis of the fragments, we then compare on a larger scale. Now we compare parts of the 'picture' with the already existing parts of the Clusters. We compare the combination of all fragments of one specific sense with complete "pictures" of that same sense. These "pictures" of just one of our senses are called Sub-clusters. Examples of Sub-clusters are: visual images or objects, combinations of sound, taste compositions, touch sensations, smell combinations and the physical symptoms of emotions.

Level 3 - Clusters

In the next step, the subconscious compares the whole new event with previously stored events. In other words, we compare the present situations with previously stored Clusters that contain similar events. This time it's not a matter of fragments or Sub-clusters. Now our brain is looking for bigger similarities.

These three levels are processed all together in the subconscious. But, we have no factual awareness of this process. If you were aware of this process, you would experience thousands of mental pictures at the same time. It would drive you crazy! The final analysis of all this work will be delivered from our subconscious to the conscious part of our brain. The speed of processing this new data and then comparing it on three levels with existing material is tremendous! Just ask yourself how long it takes for you to understand what you see after you've seen it? We are not even aware of the fact that there is a time difference between the point of seeing it and recognizing what we see! Keep in mind that we have five senses (the sixth sense is what we refer to as emotion). For each of our senses we make comparisons from one second to another! Now, let's assume there would be only 10 mental pictures per sense, per second, that we always compare with new incoming data. This would result in only 50 pictures per second that you would consciously become aware of. As a result, you would not be able to function at all! In reality, the subconscious doesn't only process 50 times more data, instead, it processes a **million** times more data in order to make us aware of what we experience.

Factual data is always connected to physiological aspects

This is the reason that all these processes take place in the subconscious and outside our awareness. It is just the comparison of sensory factual data. Each piece (*fragment*) of comparison material also has a physiological attachment to it, which represents the physiology that caused your emotions at that specific moment when you stored the factual data. These physiological components are attached to each single piece of sensory data that enters the brain. These attachments are not stored in the Cortex, like the factual data, but stored in the Limbic System. Why are these attachments necessary? They show us the value of a specific piece of data and enable us to make distinctions between the same pieces of data in several distinct situations. To understand this, let's use a visual object as an example:

> **Example**:
> While you drive on the highway one of the many things you see is the "big M" of *McDonald's*. But this time you are not hungry at all! Therefore, at that moment, the "value" of the "big M" is very low for you. You hardly notice it. However, two days later, when you're driving through the same road, you are very hungry and you also love hamburgers. This time, seeing the "big M", activates a totally different feeling (physiology) in your body. The value of the "big M" is now completely different than the first time. However, a month later you make an appointment with a very important client. This could become your biggest account ever, and you really need this level of success at this point in your career. This person does not know the area, but he does know this particular highway. You are aware that there is only one *McDonald's* on this entire highway, so you choose the "big M" as a landmark to meet with the client. The meeting was a huge success! Now, whenever you drive pass this "big M", you experience a very good feeling,

the same powerful feeling (physiology) you experienced when you closed the deal there.

In total, you've experienced three events with the same object, the same "big M", but connected to three completely different feelings. If we did not have this physiological attachment to the factual data (in this case the "big M"), then this factual data would have the same meaning regardless where we would see it. This is because we always attach the physiological status of our body to the data that is present at that specific moment. We can compare it to a puzzle. Each piece of the puzzle has its own shape. Together they form a complete memory. The different shapes of the pieces represent the physiological status at the moment that this piece was stored. It is like the subconscious took a picture of all the present physiological commands and attached that picture to each of the pieces of sensory data.

Your past determines your conscious awareness

If all is functioning well, these fragments will be connected to each other by a code to form a Cluster. When you remember something, your conscious mind compiles the picture by joining these fragments back together. It can only do that if the data is properly encoded. You will know when or where something occurred because you will hear the music or the voices that you heard, you will smell the same scents and you will feel the same physical responses and emotional sensations. In this manner your brain is constantly busy with reconstructing your past. All of these memories are stored in your brain cells. The Fragments of these memories, or Clusters, are used as comparison material for the data that comes in through your senses in everyday life.

Did you ever wonder why, for example, when you see a banana you not only recognize the object as a banana but you also know its taste and that it must be peeled before you can eat it? It all seems so instant and 'normal', but to do so, your subconscious mind has to make a lot of comparisons between the new information (in the case of the banana) and the material that has already been stored in your brain cells. Your consciousness of the present (what you know now) is completely determined by the stored data from your past. This data is your only available comparison material. For every thousand bytes of awareness, your subconscious has to compare, analyze and process more than a billion bytes of data. Where does this data come from? From previously stored experiences collected during your entire life. Therefore, your present awareness is always based on already stored data from your past, regardless of when it was collected, fifty years ago or two minutes ago.

Comparison material needs to be encoded

To make previously stored data usable and valuable as comparison material it needs to be approachable. If our subconscious can't find it in the Database, or can't properly process it, the data is of no use to us. Once found, it has to contain specific information that helps the subconscious identify the similar, new incoming data. Last, but not least, the subconscious needs data that tell us what the importance of the new incoming data is for us individually! How does the subconscious manage this huge task? It would be totally impossible if there would not be strict rules and order on how we store and retrieve data. We already know that each cell has its own specific task. A nerve cell that stores the color red is never capable to store a smell, taste, shape or even another color other than red. To make this more understandable, just assume that every cell has a specific number. This means that one memory is stored in millions of different cells spread out all over the Cortex, each cell with its own specific task, and each with its own specific number. The content of a memory is determined by the amount and sequence of the numbers. Together they form the specific "code" of that memory. Depending on the incoming information, the subconscious can use the whole code or just bits and pieces of it (as a process, it is similar to the readings of DNA). There are different kinds of codes, but we can separate them into two main groups:

The absolute code

The relative code

Let us now see how these two codes determine the meaning and power of all our comparison material.

The absolute code

Each piece of data in a Cluster receives an absolute code. This process takes place in the Cortex, the upper layer of our brain, in cooperation with the Thalamus and Hippocampus area. In the Cortex we store all incoming sensory data (scents, tastes, colors, shapes, etc.). This absolute code determines the identity of the new incoming sensory data and is independent from the circumstances surrounding the data. A simple example will clarify this:

> ***Example*:**
> You are looking at a table. How do you know it's a table? You know this through several different Clusters that also contain tables that you previously stored. By comparing all these different (Sub-)Clusters, the subconscious concludes (stimulus/response) that it is a table. The absolute code of the object is, therefore: a table. It will remain a table whether it's in a room, set outside, or floating in water. The

circumstances in which that table finds itself do not change its absolute code. A table is, and will remain, a table. That is its identity.

This is true for all data that is evaluated. A glass is not a book and a watch is not a bicycle; a desk is not a car and a monkey is not an elephant. Each item has its own specific code, its own identity. The moment that the subconscious makes the proper connection with existing comparison material, a code is given to the new incoming data. This code is its absolute code. This way, every new incoming picture of a table will derive its code from already existing similar data (other tables). In reality, one object has a whole series of codes.

How do you know it's coffee?

Subconscious analyses take place so naturally that we never give it thought. If someone offers you a cup of coffee, you drink it without giving it a second thought. It may be that you never consciously think about it, but in reality, your brain is subconsciously working at a tremendous speed to determine if it truly is coffee. Ask yourself, for a change, how you know if what you're drinking is actually coffee? How do you know it's not old dishwater or even worse, hydrochloric acid? Many would indignantly respond, *"The answer is totally obvious!"* Yes, of course it's coffee. But we know this only because our brain does a lot of work *under the hood* to make this obvious to your conscious brain. With this kind of situation, there is always more than meets the eye. Let's break it down: First, you were asked if you wanted coffee. The word *coffee* immediately activates several Clusters that deal only with coffee. Those Clusters do not only contain information about the appearance of coffee, but also information about the taste, smell, color, and the sensations in your mouth and throat as you drink it. As soon as the coffee is served, you have a cup full of brown liquid (with a special warm aroma). The incoming data activates the comparison material of coffee. If that were not to occur, then you would never know if the liquid that what served was indeed coffee. With PMA, you can make your subconscious processes visible to your conscious! You can test this for yourself. Let us use, as an example, a chair:

> ***Exercise***:
> Look at a chair. How do you know it's a chair? Look at the chair one more time and then, after you finished reading this paragraph, close your eyes. Can you now see in your mind what this chair looks like? Now come up with other pictures of chairs. What pictures come up? All sorts of different chairs may now come to mind. These are some of the other images that your brain used in order to conclude that the object you were observing was indeed a chair.

If you were successful in performing this experiment, then you have experienced how you can become consciously aware of what happens in your subconscious brain. In the beginning, some people may need a little bit more time with this exercise. You can, of course, do this test with any object in your environment. Don't just do this one exercise. Please, try it out for yourself over and over again! It will help you understand how things work in your brain and it will teach you to trust your subconscious. And best of all, it's fun! It will also serve you later because you will have experienced, first hand, how your brain works through this sort of little experiment. Being able to spontaneously 'call up' comparison material plays an important role later on in your self-help sessions. In everyday instances, when you see a chair and the subconscious determines that it is indeed a chair, and fittingly informs the conscious part of the brain, you won't see any other chair images flashing before your eyes. These images remain hidden in your subconscious.

How the subconscious works

To understand where things go wrong we must try to understand how the subconscious works and how it creates emotions.

If you see this picture of a dog, does the word D-O-G appear in your mind? Many people may say: *"I see nothing in my mind; I just know that this is a dog"*. But what is going on in the subconscious to make you *know* that this is a dog? To let you *know* that it is a dog, a lot of comparison work has to be done in your subconscious. Let's take a look at this, for we have already experienced that it is possible to make the comparison material in the subconscious visible. This is a very amusing and captivating experience!

Exercise:

Look again at the picture. Now, how do you know this is a dog? Close your eyes and ask yourself of which other dog it reminds you? Please give your brain the opportunity to come up with pictures. What do you *see* in your brain? If everything is all right, you'll see a picture of another dog. If pictures other than dogs come up, don't worry. That is totally normal. Actually, it means that you are already ahead of the game, but we'll talk more about that later in this book.

This exercise showed again you how to make some of your subconscious comparison material visible for the conscious brain. But, what if you see an object that you've never seen before?

Unknown objects

Recognizing an absolute code becomes very difficult when the object (or other sensory data) is unknown to us. No matter how much the subconscious searches the Database, it cannot find anything that has enough similarity in order to serve as comparison material. It becomes difficult to determine the identity of the object. This probably occurs most often when we hear unknown words. For this moment, let us limit ourselves to objects. In our life, we all have seen an object that was completely unknown to us. At that point, the subconscious searches diligently for comparison material. It simply cannot find any comparison material because this is the very first time you have ever seen an object of this kind! The subconscious then tries to compensate by providing data that tell you something about its shape, the material, the color, the weight or its location. It will provide data about parts of the object that it's able to recognize. Often times, this may not really help you. In some cases, we can consciously make an educated guess from the context in which the object is set, and sometimes this guess is correct. However, in most cases, this doesn't work either. Then we have to settle for the identification of an 'unidentified object' and give it a place of its own.

You connect it to what you do know

If the object does interest you, however, then your interest and/or desire will provide the impetus for you to continue asking until someone finally reveals to you what it is. When that happens, not only is your curiosity satisfied, but also a new Cluster is formed. As soon as the explanation about the object begins, the ingredients of whatever is being explained will call up all kinds of related Clusters. The subconscious connects the details of the unknown object with already existing (Sub-)Clusters and Fragments of Clusters from the Database.

> ***Example*:**
> You are visiting someone who takes you to his garage. There, you see a machine that is 1'x1' and about 4' tall. It has an AC cord and a sack is hanging from the back. On the top of the machine there is a strap long enough to hang it around your neck. It is unclear what this contraption is used for. Your subconscious cannot find one single Cluster with similar content to use as comparison material. You ask your host what the object is. He explains that it is a kind of vacuum cleaner. As soon as the word *vacuum cleaner* is used, the subconscious immediately activates various 'vacuum cleaner' Clusters. He continues to explain that it is used primarily in the autumn. Clusters about autumn come up. In your mind's eye you see and feel the bleak autumn weather. Then he relates that this vacuum cleaner is

specially developed to suck up leaves. At that moment, your subconscious calls up all sorts of Clusters dealing with leaves. The leaves are sucked up and land in the sack, which can be removed by a simple hand movement. The contents are then dumped into a compost pile. Your subconscious relays Clusters dealing with compost piles and gardens. The identity of the object is now clear. A new Cluster has been formed, a *'leaf-vacuum cleaner'* Cluster.

If you see the same object six months later, then its absolute code can be quickly determined now that you have comparison material available to you. Even if the leaf-vacuum cleaner were to vary in shape or color, you would still be able to determine that it was indeed a leaf-vacuum cleaner because of the rational connecting ability of the conscious brain and the additional data provided by the subconscious. In this manner, we can determine the absolute code of all the things we perceive by making subconscious comparisons.

The relative code

We can now understand that each new incoming piece of data is immediately assigned its absolute code. This lets you know, for example, that in a certain room, a chair is a chair, a table is a table, curtains are curtains, lamps are lamps, and so on. What it does not tell you, however, is the relative code of the data. What is meant by the relative code? Why do all pieces of data also need a relative code? This is necessary to allow a specific meaning to be attached to a certain piece of data for you personally. The same piece of data that has already been assigned an absolute code can have a different relative code depending on the situation, as we have already discussed in the case of the “big M”. This relative code places the object in its appropriate context. Let’s look at another example:

> ***Example*:**
> You are present at a dinner party. A steak knife is lying on the table. The relative code of this knife is limited. The delightful dishes served and the content of the stimulating conversation are of much more importance to you. If sometime later someone was to ask you what was on that table, you would describe the beautiful dinnerware, the silverware and the aromatic dishes. You probably would not even mention the knife. After all, it is a very ordinary object that had no effect on your perception of the evening. A week later, the same people invite you to another dinner party. Once again, the same tastefully set table and the same knife appear. Now something happens that you will not quickly forget. Two of the other guests begin having a violent quarrel. One of the two grabs the knife and threatens the other with it! Fortunately, the quarrel ends after the intervention of others. The knife is taken out of his hand and laid back on the table. Shocked, you look at that knife as you realize what could have happened!

The relative code of the knife has now been drastically changed by this event. Yet, we are still speaking of the same knife! The next time you see a knife like that, you will experience a totally different feeling about that knife compared to the first time you saw it. This feeling is activated because of the relative code, or value, you connected to the knife during this scary experience.

The conscious part of the brain determines the relative code

How does the brain determine this relative code? In fact, it is not the subconscious that determines it, but the conscious part of the brain! The determination of the identifying absolute code is a question of comparing similar data in a way that's similar to how a computer does. It can be done effortlessly in the subconscious. Nevertheless, the determination of the relative code is a conscious process and is dependent on a number of factors. First of all, it is determined by what relative code has been given to similar data in the past. This is nicely stored in connection with the various Fragments of Clusters and will be delivered to the conscious, by the subconscious, after processing. The relative code will be solely determined by your feelings. Feelings or emotions can only be experienced in your conscious brain.

How does this work in the subconscious?

An emotion, or feeling, is always the result of physiological changes. These changes are created by subconscious messages that activate cells and organs. These messages come directly from our activated comparison material. "Activated" means that based on the stimulus/response rule, specific pieces of (Fragments, Sub-clusters) of Clusters, as well as Bad Clusters, are selected to use as comparison material. The moment this material is selected, we refer to it as "activated". We consciously notice these activations because we feel the physical results of the connected physiology in our body. Our brain has a module to feel emotions. We also have a module for many other things, like for instance: music, language, special skills, etc. However, if we stick to the example of language, we would not be able to understand the whole meaning of language if, first, we do not learn and fill our Database with words. This works exactly the same with emotions. The module for emotion is there, but we have to feed its Database with experience in order to connect different emotions to different events and the Fragments in those events. We can make distinctions between our various emotions because we experience them differently in our body. For example, there is one emotion we will feel in our stomach, another mainly in our throat, and the next one in our heart. The genetic program combined with our personal experiences will determine where, and to what degree we feel a specific emotion in our body. We acquire the different levels of intensity of an emotion throughout our life.

We are all the same and yet so different

All people share the same kinds of emotions, but definitely not the same intensity of emotions. Neither do they feel the same emotions for the same reasons. Therefore, the reason why and how strong we feel emotions is something we learn, and it differs from person to person. This is the result of the fact that we all have different comparison material. We store the type and the intensity of an emotion as a physiological code. This code determines the relative value of each single piece of data in our Clusters. The codes that create the most intense emotions are the codes given to the most powerful emotions in our life. As soon as comparison material is selected, the codes will activate specific cells in the Limbic System to carry out the connected physiology. The conscious mind will immediately feel the effects by the physical symptoms that the activation of the physiological code will cause in the body.

Physiological codes are not the same as emotional symptoms

The physical symptoms are also stored in the Cluster, together with all the other sensory data that is present at that same time. Keep in mind that physiological codes are <u>not</u> the same as the physical symptoms they cause. As a simple example, think of the effect of adrenaline. The physiological code activates the adrenal glands to produce more adrenaline. This part of the process you do not feel. You actually start to feel this at the moment that the adrenaline affects the heart rhythm. Now you start to feel that your heartbeat is rising. The heartbeat is the physical symptom, which is the result of the physiological code. Why is it important to differentiate between the physiological (relative) code and the emotional physical symptoms? Because they are stored in two different areas of the brain! The content of Clusters is stored in the upper layer of the brain, the Cortex, but the physiological codes, or commands, are stored in the inner part, the so-called Limbic System. We feel our emotions through physical changes and store them in a separate area of the Cortex as a part of a Cluster (or Bad Cluster). This means that the physical data from inside our body is processed and stored in exactly the same way as sensory information from outside. We call our emotions our sixth sense. Please understand this has nothing to do with some sort of telepathic sense that is also commonly referred to as the *"sixth sense"*! In conclusion, we can say that every single piece of sensory data inside a Cluster, regardless if it comes from the outside through our five senses or from the inside through our sixth sense, the physical symptoms of our emotions and/or each piece of data is always unbreakably connected to a specific physiological code in the Limbic System. Let us now see how the knowledge we obtained so far looks like in a practical example:

Your Clusters determine what you perceive

Every person on Earth is unique! Every person has accumulated his/her own quantity and content of Clusters. The amount and combination of Clusters and connections he/she has is also unique. No one on the face of the Earth has the same collection of Clusters, or Bad Clusters, as you. That is also why each individual has his own memories, his own perception of the environment, and his own interpretation of events. We all have our own set of belief systems based on our relative codes or values. That is why you can witness the same event as someone else but afterwards, as you compare notes, you will be surprised to find that you experienced it in a completely different way than your companion. This is because each one of us can only make his/her own individual interpretation based on their unique comparison material!

Let us examine an example of a group of four people. They are at the same location and witness the same event. In spite of the fact that they see and hear the exact same things, they all experience it differently. This is caused by the differences of their previously stored experiences in life and the emotions connected to them. As a result, each person developed a totally different set of belief systems, which in turn determines their individual reality:

> ***Example:***
> A group of people talked about what they have just witnessed together. They all saw how a young man was pulled out of his car rather roughly by the police and was subsequently arrested. The group is made up of several types of people: a very objective observer, a young man that used to be a drug addict, a police officer, and a 70-year old Jewish man.
>
> ***The objective observer***
> The objective observer witnessed the event and assumed (belief system) that the police had a good reason for this arrest. However, he does not know why the young man was arrested. Nor does he know if he was armed or dangerous. What's more, he doesn't really know if the

policemen really were police, or if they were simply dressed and acting like police officers. As he was observing all of this, he couldn't add too much more information to what he had seen. He can form an opinion about what he saw, but not about the reason why it happened. In order to do this, his subconscious selected the appropriate Clusters as comparison material. These could be Clusters that have to do with policemen in daily life or police activities watched in scenes from films, Clusters about arrests, Clusters about the mistakes made by the justice system, as well as numerous other Clusters.

The ex-drug addict

How did this young man perceive the event? Obviously he witnessed the same thing, but which connections were made in his brain? He used to be addicted to drugs and in the past was repeatedly picked up by the police. Different Clusters are now called up from his Database. He immediately feels sympathy for the young man who was arrested. He knows how it feels to be suddenly picked up. He doesn't have much to say on behalf of police in general. To him, their attitude is one without feeling for the problems of others (belief system). All the Clusters and Bad Clusters containing his bad experiences with police are activated.

The policeman

The policeman present with the group is also confronted with his different Clusters. He knows very well how it feels to have to arrest someone. He feels and knows the dangers and risks from this kind of an arrest. He immediately empathizes with the officers making the arrest. He can vividly recall an occasion when his partner was unexpectedly attacked and knocked down by a person being arrested in a very similar situation. He identifies the detainee as a villain, a criminal that deserves even worse treatment than just being picked up a bit roughly (belief system).

The Jewish man

What does the 70-year old Jewish man experience? Watching the man being grabbed by the police calls up Clusters, and most definitely Bad Clusters, that recall his past experiences of being Jewish. He immediately labels the demeanor of the police as "arrogant". *"Just like the Gestapo... Insolent power-hungry cops, without the decency to treat someone with dignity! Cops can be so cold-hearted* (belief system)*! People never learn!"* He is completely upset by what he has seen.

The activation of their own Clusters, along with their individual experiences, leads to each one experiencing the events in his own way, colored by their own belief systems. The activated comparison material causes each individual's assessment of the situation to be vastly different from others in the group. Even though all four individuals were present in the same place, each of them had entirely different impressions of what happened. That, which they saw, of course, was exactly the same! What led to the differences in judgment? Indeed, it is the difference in their comparison material and the attached emotions (relative code) that were called up or activated. If a few days later you were to ask each of the four to write down what they saw, you would get four entirely different stories! Although they all objectively witnessed the same reality, the differences in their personal comparison material and especially the connected emotions (relative code) to this comparison material, created a totally different set of belief systems for all four people and it also created their individual reality, <u>their</u> "truth".

Automatic selection of the material with the highest relative code

Incoming new sensory data will activate existing comparison material in the Cortex, always based on the automatic stimulus/response rule. Our subconscious will make a selection from all the activated Cluster fragments, based on their relative code. It will automatically select the data with the higher relative codes. This will be used as comparison material. It will deliver its analysis of the new incoming data to the conscious part of the brain, based on the highest relative code of the comparison material. This relative code creates a feeling in your body that reflects the importance of the new incoming data.

> ***Example 1***:
> You expect nice guests for dinner. There is a candle on the table and you take a match to light it. In your subconscious, several Clusters are activated with a content of a nice dinner by candlelight. They have Physio-clusters attached to them that give you a good feeling.
>
> ***Example 2***:
> In the windowsill is another candle, exactly the same kind as the one on the table. You look at it and instantly your feelings change. In your subconscious several other Clusters are activated. One of them was created five years ago when you lighted a candle in a window. But the candle was too close to a curtain. A few minutes later someone left the room and slammed the door too hard.

> The curtain started to move, made contact with the flame of the candle and caught fire. It was a scary situation, but not scary enough to create a Bad Cluster because, in this case, the fire was controlled within seconds and no further harm was done. However, the feeling of fear at the moment the fire started was attached to the information that is stored in the Clusters.

These relative (physiological) codes are carried out immediately after the subconscious accepted the connected Cluster as legitimate comparison material. If the brain always selects the data with the highest relative code, then why did you not feel the same negative emotion with both candles? Because of the different context you saw them in. It was this context that mainly determined the selection of the kind of comparison material. The overall physiology that was attached to the candle on the table differed strongly from the one on the windowsill. In conclusion, we now understand that every single piece of sensory information receives an absolute code in the Cortex that determines the identity of the data (scent, taste, color, shape, etc.) and a relative code in the Limbic System that determines what this piece of information means to us individually.

Find the answers in yourself

During the last years, a lot has been written about Emotional Intelligence (EQ). Emotional Intelligence comes down to recognize and properly value our feelings, and the feelings of others, and has the ability and capacity to deal with those feelings in an effective and proactive manner. Over the years it became more and more clear that feelings, or emotions, drive us in all our decisions and actions. If we want to expand our possibilities, energy and effectiveness, we have to look at the source of our drives: *our emotions*! EQ is not something you have to learn. It's already present when we are born! We just lost the courage to listen to it and use it properly. By practicing the *Progressive Mental Alignment®* technique you will experience how the freedom of using your genetic program of emotional intelligence will reveal itself. Then, you will also recognize that it was always there in the first place. You just blocked it and were afraid to listen to it and apply it.

The most basic measuring system: Pain – Pleasure

How do we start to learn and fill our Database with experiences? A newborn isn't able to reason. To be able to reason, you need language! A baby does not speak any language when it's born. Yet in this first period of our life we learn many of the most fundamental facts of life. How does that work? How do we know what to remember and what not to store? How do we determine the importance of incoming sensory information? We have a basic measuring system for that purpose. This measuring system determines whether or not the incoming data interrupts or improves the survival and quality of life. So then what is this basic measuring system based on?

FEELINGS!

We are all genetically equipped with this mechanism and its connected sensors. This is the most basic mechanism available for the baby to learn, differentiate information and gain experience. Even to a hundred-year-old person, it is still the most elementary mechanism determining all of our decisions. Some might think that we are also able to make 100% rational decisions. Well, here is the news:

<u>There is no such thing as a 100% rational decision!</u>

Our choices and decisions are always based on feelings (emotions)! Even if you are convinced that your decision is purely based on rational fact, you will discover that your decision is based on the emotional, or for that matter, the relative code of those facts! Even a simple decision like *"Shall I have a salad instead of a sandwich, or not?"* is an emotional decision based on the relative code of your subconscious comparison material. If you easily gain weight you will feel totally different about that extra sandwich than when you are the type of person that can eat what you want and never gain one ounce of weight. PMA results in great self-confidence. It will be fun to experience the amazement when you discover, through PMA, how your subconscious shaped your emotions and how that, in turn, controls all your decisions and actions. It is even more fun and exciting to discover how easy you can change that process and use it to your own benefit!

Ingredients of a decision

At birth we are equipped with everything we need in order to live. Now, how are we going to load this vast computer, our brain, with our personal comparison material? As you may already know, as a baby we cannot reason. In order to be able to reason we need language. Language creates the abstracts that our reasoning process operates on. Try, if you can, to reason without language. It's virtually impossible. Reasoning helps us to understand things faster and better. Language and reasoning are important parts of "learning" and "gaining experience". But if as a child we do not have these capabilities, how then, do we learn? Learning and gaining experience is directed by our most basic measuring system:

PAIN/PLEASURE

From the beginning of our life we store all our experiences in our Database.

THE MOST BASIC MEASURING SYSTEM

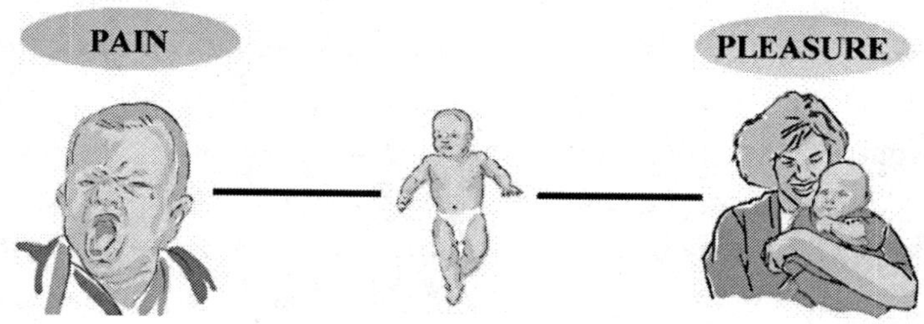

If everything goes right, all the data in our brain will be properly encoded with correct, absolute and relative codes. But, as we will see, some of the subconscious data is <u>not</u> encoded correctly, that's why we call these Clusters: *Bad* Clusters. Nevertheless, the content of our Database is the only comparison material we have to compare new incoming data with. Every decision that we make now – in the present – is directed by:

1. ***Previously stored comparison material (Clusters, Bad Clusters, both connected to Physio-clusters)***

2. ***Our feelings based on the pain/pleasure principle***

Although language is very important, it is just one of the many modules we have. None of the words we learn would have any meaning if they were not connected to other subconscious mental pictures. We must realize that we all learn and store very important data from the very first day of our life without the ability to use language. This early data becomes the foundation of our Database, and therefore, the foundation of our values and standards. In this manner, step-by-step, we develop the ability to reason, among a lot of other wonderful capacities. Nevertheless, even when the child reaches an age that it can speak, it can still be difficult to reason with the child. Why is this so? This is because the child does not have enough stored data, and hasn't made enough connections between words and other mental pictures to give the words their full meaning. So your wonderful arguments do not make sense to the child. Did you ever try to reason with a youngster (in some cases, an adult) by telling them one of your personal experiences in order to protect them from the same mistake you made and trying to prevent them from feeling the same pain? Did it work? It often doesn't work at all! How come? Even if the older child (or adult) has enough factual data to compare your experience to, but has not lived through the same negative experience, your argument will probably not convince the child. In other words, the child doesn't have enough powerful negative physiology (emotion) attached to its factual data. Experience only becomes powerful if it is attached to a strong emotion! Our judgment is all a matter of the relative value of our comparison material.

Consider the ordinary things

We experience the capability to evaluate our daily surroundings in the right way as very normal and automatic, but isn't it amazing how it all works in our subconscious?

> ***Example*:**
> It is a warm summer day and you take a dive into a swimming pool. Afterwards, you dry yourself off with a towel and lay out on the grass to enjoy the sun. An ice cream vendor comes by. You decide to buy one and you are refreshed.

How did you know that it was water that you dove into and not a glass plate? How did you know it was a towel you used to dry yourself off and not a sheet of sandpaper? How do you know you lied down on the grass and not in the middle of the street? How did you know it was an ice cream you ate and not a piece of white marble? *"What stupid questions"*, you may well say, *"I can see, smell and feel it!"* Even though the questions may seem to be senseless, they truly are not.

There are numerous things that we consider obvious and ordinary, when in fact they are not. We consider the above things as normal because we have learned them. Offer an African Aboriginal an ice cream. He doesn't recognize it and may not even want to taste it until he is completely convinced that it won't cause him any harm. We can only evaluate what we see, feel, hear, smell and taste if we already have comparable data in our Database. Nevertheless, if the African Aboriginal decides to eat the ice cream, he will not make that decision based on cognitive facts and reasoning. He will make that decision based on his feelings! Before we continue, let us do a small exercise to experience the connection between cognitive facts and their connected physiology:

Surfing the subconscious

So far we have spoken about Clusters and Bad Clusters. The majority of our memories are Clusters. They contain pleasant, as well as unpleasant, moments. Many of them are related to very happy, successful and energizing experiences. PMA will help you to regain those memories. This is pure fun! While doing this, you practice PMA and you learn to apply the very same tools that you need to eliminate the Bad Cluster physiology. How does this work?

***Exercise*:**
In your mind, please go to a happy or pleasant event of your life. Now, find the most pleasant moment and the detail by paying attention to your body. It is not your conscious controlled rational memory, but the result of the physiology in your body, which will tell you what the moment and the detail is. Be there again and feel it. After you find the most pleasant or happy detail, focus on that detail and your feelings. Become aware of what it is you exactly feel at such a moment and where you feel it in your body. Now let your subconscious brain go and allow it to come up with as many pictures as it wants to. Whenever a new picture pops up, find the most pleasant moment and detail in that event by paying attention to what your body is telling you.

How does that feel? Discover the connections between factual data of a memory and the physiological symptoms of your body. Let us now go to some other topics.

***Exercise*:**
Go back to your childhood. Try to remember in detail all the houses and all the rooms in those houses were you lived before. In your mind, walk through the houses and look or choose one of the following topics to go back to in your mind:

- Your teachers
- Your schoolmates
- The favorite places where you used to play
- Your vacations
- Your first date
- Your first kiss

- Your first car
- One of the happiest moments in your life

You will come across of a lot of details and events you did not think about for a long time. You will have a lot of fun doing this. It will show you the joy and the power of the PMA method and will enrich your present life. Develop enjoyment in experiencing how your brain works. If you understand how your brain works, you will better understand the behavior of the people around you. Every time you succeed in bringing up a very good moment from your past, you will not only have a nice memory. You will also activate very positive physiology! This will have a positive effect on your mood and health.

Step-by-step comparison

We have to realize that this exercise was about encoded Clusters with a happy content. None of these Clusters are causing us any problems. However, what we are really looking for are the neurophysiological 'jamming stations' in our Database, our Bad Clusters! Our mind is like a huge library where every Bad Cluster that we eliminate is the key to a whole room full of books (Clusters) we didn't have access to anymore, because they were blocked by the power of the Bad Cluster, as we will find out. This is another enriching effect of PMA, and it is a great exercise to prepare you for the real goal of PMA: the finding and eliminating of negative physiology connected to Bad Clusters. To bring us closer to that point we first need to deepen our understanding of this whole process. Let's observe, step-by-step, what happens during the processing of incoming sensory information. As an example, we will use visual information. This process mechanism works the same for all our senses. Plainly put:

- An object is perceived through your eyes.

- It's transmitted to specific brain cells. For instance, the horizontal lines in what you see will activate cells that can only perceive and store vertical lines. Each of the specific colors you see will be transmitted to the same amount of specific cells that are only capable of receiving and storing this specific color. Every single piece of data will go directly to the connected cells that are genetically programmed to perceive and store that specific piece of data.

- All incoming sensory information (except a main part of our smell) also has a second route. The same information that goes directly to the Cortex cells, where it will be processed and stored, also goes through a separate route to the Thalamus with its variety of nuclei. For a long time scientists did not understand why we have this "miniature brain", the Thalamus, inside our big brain, the Cortex. Now we've unraveled a part of its mystery. It is obviously one of the main centers that play an important role in creating the absolute as well as the relative code of new incoming sensory data.

- Almost instantly we become conscious of the object we see, but do we also instantly understand what we see? Just imagine that someone behind you shouts at you: *"Look out!"* Quickly, you turn around and you see that something is coming at you. Immediately, in a reflex, you dive away to avoid the object. At that precise moment, do you know what the object is that, in a reflex, you tried to avoid? In most cases, you would not know. This shows you that the subconscious did not have the time to properly analyze the data and inform your conscious brain what the object was. This is because analyzing takes time.

- Your subconscious is a stimulus/response machine. Contrary to the conscious brain, the subconscious cannot think, reason, argue or feel. Therefore, it is not able to make distinctions between new incoming data and previously stored data. Just imagine what a mess it would be in your conscious brain if the subconscious would have no mechanism to make this distinction at all! You would constantly see thousands of mental pictures in your conscious brain and would not know if the pictures are previous memories or of the present situation. Remember, the subconscious processes more than a million times the amount of data than you will ever become aware of in your conscious brain. You would be unable to understand your environment, or move in it if your subconscious wasn't able to make a difference between the present and the activated material!

- How does your subconscious manage to make the differentiation between new and old data if it cannot think or reason? It is all based on an insignificant time-difference. Let's recall the two separate routes that information takes:

    - Direct route to the appropriate preprogrammed cells in the Cortex
    - The detour through the Thalamus

- The information that reaches the Cortex cells through the Thalamus arrives there in just a tiny moment later than the data that goes directly to the Cortex. The Cortex receives the real picture of the present, and a fraction of a second later, it receives the codes of the Thalamus that activates similar previously stored data as comparison material. It is this insignificant time difference that enables your subconscious to differentiate between new incoming data (present) and previously stored data (comparison material).

- Now the real comparison process can start. The Thalamus codes will activate several connections of colors, shapes, movements, etc. that are similar to the new incoming data. We have millions, if not billions, of Fragments, Sub-clusters and Clusters nicely encoded and stored in our subconscious Database, ready to use as comparison material in order to create our reality. Finally, after analysis, these codes, derived from our comparison material, will together form the total sequence of the code of the new Cluster.

- However, this is not the end of the process! The most important part still has to come. Every part of the Cortex has a connection with the center of the brain, the Limbic System, where our physiology is controlled. What kind of code will be stored in connection with the new Cluster? The physiological codes that are already attached to the different pieces of the selected comparison material to form the new code and sequence of the new Cluster. Later we will discuss the function of the ligands and the neuro peptides in this huge process of inner communication between the cells. Then, we will understand even better how the subconscious can perform this huge task.

- How does the subconscious make its selection of the appropriate comparison material, even though it cannot think or reason? Your computer cannot reason either, and yet it is able to select and analyze a huge amount of data at high speed. All the subconscious needs is a program and encoded data. The program is genetically delivered and the encoded data we collected throughout our total life is there in abundance.

- How does the subconscious make the selection out of so much material? Based on the codes. The first step is to assign the absolute codes to determine the identity of the new incoming data, based on previously stored Fragments and Sub-clusters. Once the identity is clear, it has to determine how important this data is for your conscious brain, or in other words, for you. This is not difficult because already, in the past, your conscious brain assigned a relative code to a large amount of similar objects. Now, the task of the subconscious is to put the identified object (absolute code) in the correct context of the new incoming information by comparing it to the bigger picture, to similar events (Clusters) in its Database. It will select the most similar events with the highest relative value (partly activated by the Thalamus) and combine this with the pieces of comparison material of the object that have the highest relative code.

- The selection of this comparison material means that it stays active just a moment longer than the rejected comparison material. This little time difference results in the execution of the connected physiology of the selected material to a level that we consciously become aware of the physical symptoms that are caused by that physiology. These feelings, regardless of how significant or insignificant they may be, determine our belief systems, and therefore, our thinking, decisions and actions.

- At this point, the conscious brain receives the analyzed information of the subconscious that will grant us awareness of what it is we see and receive, at the same time the signals from our body tell us the importance of the new incoming data.

- Process complete!

We now start to understand, more and more, why the subconscious needs so much data to process in order to make us consciously aware of what enters through our senses. Keep in mind that the subconscious performs all of this not only for the visual part, but also for the other four senses we have. On top of that, it analyzes the physical symptoms of our emotions and all of the above at the same time and during a split of a second. Quite impressive, isn't it?

Old codes become handy

A new event that finally will be stored as a Cluster consists of thousands of details. For instance, let's say that you have dinner at your home. The table, the dining room, the silverware and many other things are a part of this new event, that will be stored as a new Cluster. The majority of the incoming data of that event already has a code in your Database from the many times you ate dinner in your dining room. In that case, it is a great help to the subconscious that it receives all those old codes that are already set from the Thalamus. Now it only has to create new codes for the things that are not the same as previous experiences. It is like typing a word in a computer index and immediately after you typed the first letter, you have a hit. The more letters you type, the closer you get to exactly the same word. This way, the Thalamus will hand-out a general code to the subconscious that automatically activates every piece of data in the Cortex that, more or less, looks like the new data. The subconscious doesn't reason, it uses an elementary stimulus/response mechanism that leads to the selection of suitable comparison material! It only compares the present incoming "picture" to similar "pictures" from the past that are already stored in your brain. The similarities that determine the absolute code are found in the amount of similar codes of Fragments and Sub-clusters, not in the emotional meaning or the interpretation, which belong to the conscious part of our brain.

Suddenly, I was thirsty

How does this work in our daily life? Let us first consider a normal situation without any extreme emotions or threat. An example will serve to clarify the workings of this mechanism:

> ***Example*:**
> One warm evening you are watching television. Your body is not producing any special signals of thirst, hunger or other desires. On the television there is a commercial where you can see a beer as it is poured into a glass and you can hear the sound of the glass filling up with beer. You see the bubbling, foamy yellow liquid in the glass. At that point, you want some beer. You get up and grab one out of the refrigerator. As you are thinking about what you are going to do, you can already feel the coolness of the glass; you can almost taste the beer, feeling the foam on your lips and how the beer slides down your throat all the way to your stomach. The only thing left to do is to actually pour the beer in the glass and drink it.

Do you recognize this kind of experience? It is a textbook example of the functioning of the subconscious processing and executing the physiology connected to the activated comparison material. The beer on the television activated several Clusters. It happened by the things that you saw and heard on the TV. The commercial can show the picture and project the sound, but cannot project the taste, smell and feel (cold, wet and foamy). But, it is not even necessary. The missing data is already in the existing Clusters. The subconscious receives this incoming data and activates Clusters that have a similar content. But of course, you cannot quench your thirst with a TV commercial! You need real beer to do that. Remember, before you saw the commercial you were not thirsty. The Clusters that served as comparison material were originally made when you had actual beer in front of you and drank it. These Clusters have all the physiological commends that create 'thirst' attached to them. Hence, you feel the thirst (result of physiology) that is present in these Clusters. In order to completely satisfy your present desire, you will have to stand up, walk to the refrigerator, get a beer, pour some in a glass, bring it to your lips and drink it. As you are doing all of this, you will experience the familiar coldness, aroma and taste. Then your thirst will be quenched. All the pieces of data belong together and form one unit.

You fancy yourself in Spain

Millions of small and large Fragments, Sub-clusters and Clusters make your life what it is today. They serve life. Let's view another simple example of the processing power of the subconscious:

> ***Example***:
> You are on vacation in Spain. You enjoy a pleasant evening out on a terrace. Spanish music is playing in the background. Everyone is drinking *Sangria*. You have a date with someone you find extremely attractive. The entire evening is

a great success. The Clusters that created that evening are stored in the Database. Six months later, you are visiting someone in the neighborhood. He has music playing in the background. You recognize the music as Spanish music, and indeed, it is the very same song that was playing on that wonderful evening during your vacation in Spain! What do you now 'remember' from that evening? Was it just the music? No. For a moment, you can feel the warmth and the Spanish atmosphere. You can see the face of the one that was with you that evening. You can hear the voices and certain words that were spoken. You can even 'taste' the *Sangria.*

The full extent of that evening comes to your mind in a flash. It is all the work of reactivated Clusters. What reactivated the Cluster? A memory moment: The Spanish music. Sometimes only a few memory moments are needed to reactivate a Cluster. The greater an impression the experience made (relative code), the fewer memory moments are needed to reactivate the Cluster. If the particular experience was not very impressive to you, then you will need more memory moments to reactivate the Cluster. Did you ever notice that if, later in your own home, you drink the same kind of *Sangria* it tastes different, even if you brought a bottle with you from Spain? How come? Because the surroundings of your own home activates also many Clusters related to other things that happened at your home, each connected to their own physiological load. Your taste is a physiological process that is strongly determined by the kind of comparison material, or more important, the physiological load of that material. What you experience now is not the similar feeling and taste to when you were in Spain because the subconscious will mix this information with a large load of other information, in this case related to your home.

The miraculous sensitivity of our sensors

It's obvious that we determine the individual meaning of new information solely by feeling, or in other words, by physiological changes (relative codes)! Many times they are just minor physiological changes too insignificant for the conscious brain to notice, but not too tiny for the subconscious brain! The subconscious has the capability to register and process even the most insignificant signal. To describe how extremely sensitive the registration system of our cells are, some scientists use the following metaphor: *"If you would drop a teaspoon of sugar in the ocean in Florida, the subconscious antennas (sensors) in our body-cells would be able to register the change in sugar level as far away as the beach in Main."* To better understand the sensitivity of our subconscious and physiological processes, we have to go a little deeper into how information is transported and processed in our body. But before we do that, we have to understand some of the basic principles of our physiology.

Chapter 3 – Physiology

What is meant by physiology? *Webster* dictionary defines it as, *"the organic processes and phenomena of an organism or any of its parts, or of a particular bodily process."* What exactly does this mean? To put it simple: It is the total of all physical and energetic processes in our body that make it possible for us to stay alive. Without physiology we would die! It is made up of numerous bio-chemical and dynamic processes. The processes of osmosis, energetic impulses, digestion, hormonal balance, enzymes, hydration, heat regulation, respiration, blood circulation and many other processes are included in keeping your body alive. All together they form the physiology of your body.

Physiology is not a coincidental process

It is easy to accept that such things such as hair, skin and eye color, as well as height, many diseases and specific character aspects, are usually static and unchangeable because they are genetically determined. The physiological processes, on the other hand, are anything but static. They are always in motion. It is logical to assume that processes, which are dynamic, must be steered and driven by something. But, if they were not controlled, then it would be left up to chance whether or not your heart was in the mood to beat, or if your kidneys, liver or pancreas felt like working slowly, quickly or not at all today. So what really controls and steers our physiology? As we will see, the human body is consisted of a conglomeration of mechanisms that constantly reacts and responds to signals of our surroundings. If we are able to find what controls our physiology and if we are also able to influence and change things in our control center, we definitely can easily achieve goals we thought we weren't capable of reaching and we can perform on a whole new level. Let us discover together how this is possible.

Don't blame it on your genes

Since 1953, when James Watson and Francis Crick discovered the DNA helix, people tend to believe that our genes control our life. Actually, you can still find these teachings in every textbook, and, unfortunately, it will take a while before professionals in the healthcare industry understand that this belief system of the last five decades is wrong! It's so convenient to have this belief system because it takes away any burden of responsibility. Based on this wrong assumption you may ask, *"If my behavior and all kinds of diseases are mainly controlled by my genes, why would I put energy in trying to change it?"* So then, let me ask you a question: Does the operating system of your computer control the performance of your computer, or will the response of your computer mainly depend on how *you* use the operating system of your computer? The operating system of a computer cannot act on itself. Neither can your genes! Genes are like little "computer chips" that only act after something has activated them. If they are not first activated from outside, they will do nothing at all!

No response without stimuli

Genes contain, among other things, the blueprint of the basic programs of our physiology. But if nothing activates them, we'll die. The human body is made up of approximately 50-70 trillion cells. Each of those cells is a living unit with an internal genetic operating system. Like a computer chip, the operating system can only produce and act within the boundaries of its program. But if it does not receive a demanding activation to do so, it will sit still and do nothing. To put it simple, if you don't eat or drink, if there is no sensory input, your cells will not receive signals and will not act nor grow, regardless of how perfect your genetic code may be. Your computer operating systems will not do anything unless you start to type on your keyboard or use your mouse. Without stimuli the operating system will not produce any response, just like your genes.

Without input, no physiology

We can use a computer's operating system and its programs by connecting all kinds of sophisticated sensors to the computer, such as sensors that are able to observe movement, sound, temperature, pollution of the air or any type of change in the surrounding. Each of these sensors can create input that activates the programs that analyze the input and respond to changes, as programmed. The programs use the basics of the operating system. We can compare these sensors and programs to our five senses: eyes, ears, smell, taste and touch. As soon as they receive information from the outside, and not a moment sooner, the operating system will start to respond. So what activates our physiology? It is the input or stimuli from outside! Regardless of whether this concerns food, drinks, oxygen, medication, radiation, chemicals, light, energy or what we see, hear, feel, smell, or taste. The physiological processes will not start without first receiving input.

Our most powerful drive

Many of us have learned that the most powerful drive in the human body is "the power to survive". This is not correct! If this were true then hundred thousands of people would not commit suicide each year. I do not mean to deny that "the power to survive" exists as an important drive. However, it is subjugated to a stronger force, the most powerful drive in the human body:

away from pain

This tremendous force controls everything we think, believe, decide and do in life. It's the force that usually inspires the power to survive. This force operates at all levels: biological, physiological, mental, emotional, and overall, as well as at a cellular level. It will always steer us away from pain: physical as well as emotional. Even if someone commits suicide, '*away from pain*' is the drive that caused it. But suicide is never *away from pain*, is it? Unfortunately, it is if your present situation and/or expectations of the future are experienced as more painful than death itself! A belief system like this is very powerful (that our present situation, or expectation of the future, is more painful than death). The reason for these kinds of belief systems differs from person to person. This leads to the thought that this tremendous power of the '*away from pain*' drive is not always healthy and objective. More will be discussed regarding this aspect later. We have to understand that the *away from pain* drive will push us, if possible, always in the direction of 'pleasure'. Unfortunately, we do not always have that option. Many times there are just two options: pain and less pain. If those are the only options, then this innate force will always push us in the direction of 'less pain'.

The two main operating systems of our physiology

We have two main operating programs that regulate our physiology and therefore, our existence. Both are controlled by the '*away from pain*' drive. These two are:

- **Proto-physiocluster**
- **Physio-cluster**

Let us now discuss these two main operating systems of our physiology.

Proto-physioclusters

The physiological processes are not just for creating emotions. There are numerous other physiological processes that have nothing to do with emotions. Actually, we would still have a perfect physiology even if there were no emotions! On the other hand, our emotions determine who we are! All emotions, literally, *everything* we feel in our bodies, are always caused by physiological processes. We are all born with a program for basic emotions. They are regulated by already existing innate physiological programs. Step-by-step we increase the intensity of our emotions during the things we experience in our life. Physiological functions such as heart beat, our water household, the regulation of hormones, respiration, circulation, and other processes must continue, regardless if emotions are involved or not. The vast majorities of our physiological processes continue to function automatically and are built into a type of genetic Proto-physiocluster. They are inborn and already begin to function as early as in the egg and sperm cell (before conception).

Proto-physioclusters maintain balance

Proto-physioclusters contain the necessary information to keep the body in existence. To ensure the continuity of our physical existence we depend on physiological processes. In our body, there are many different ‘antennas’, or receptors, that monitor if our body is still in balance and if the physiological processes are functioning in a correct way. These receptors register if there is a shortage or an excess of certain substances such as hormones, oxygen, sugar or digestive particles. They relay the results through different centers in the brain as well as in the rest of the body. These centers react to the information and make the needed adjustments by sending out specific signals to restore balance.

We can compare Proto-physioclusters with a relay, a switch. The antennas capture signals that show there is too much of a certain substance in the body. As an example, let's use sugar. This will result in an automatic response of the physiological control centers. A "switch" will be turned on, which sends out a signal that will activate specific organs to lower the amount of sugar. If there is not enough sugar the "switch" works the opposite way. Proto-physioclusters don't think; they just follow the basic stimulus/response rule. They have only one purpose: to maintain physiological balance. They can only cause problems if they are genetically damaged. They are never the cause of psychosomatic complaints or behavioral problems. This on/of switch mechanism not only works at the level of our total body (always under supervision of the brain) but also at the level of each single cell. Each cell has its own "brain" with on/of switches. It's not located in the nucleus of the cell where the genes are located. This is because it is not the genes, but thousands of little antennas that function as the control system of the cell. They are located in complicated proteins in the skin of each cell.

Physiology – starting at the beginning

The Proto-physioclusters exist since the moment we were first conceived, especially at the cellular level. We do not need to learn them; they are all inborn. They deal with the most elementary physiological reactions, such as the heartbeat, the heart rate, regulation of the oxygen levels, release of digestive fluids, maintaining fluid levels, regulation of the hormone levels, and respiration. Without these Proto-physioclusters, we would not be able to live. Our will has no control over these automated stimulus/response processes. The Proto-physioclusters keep us alive from conception onward, and serve as the basis of all our later physiological reactions. As soon as we, as newborn babies, are conscious of the outside world, we want to be a part of it.

This demands action. Action can only take place thru physiological changes. The action then demands more oxygen, more energy to be burned, and numerous other physiological reactions. As soon as there is a shortage or excess in the body, special antennas, or receptors, sense it. All the physiological changes are registered with these receptors on a continual basis. As a result, the registrations are immediately directed to the different areas of the brain.

Away from pain, our most basic drive

All of our Proto-physioclusters maintain the physiological balance in our body. This entire amount of Proto-physioclusters acts as a system in the exact same way as every single cell in our body. To maintain balance, every cell will always stay as far away from "pain" (imbalance) as possible. Again, this is because they are all driven by this fundamental power: *away from pain.* The most threatening "pain" of the cell is to degenerate and die, cease to exist! The existence of the cell is, therefore, protected by the *away from pain* drive. This force becomes active whenever the existence, or the balance, of the cell is in danger. Its actions are always based on the stimulus/response rule. The *away from pain* rule is the dominant ruler of all our biological, physiological and emotional processes. It is active on all levels in order to drive us away from all sorts of pain.

Cells are like people

To grasp the importance and the impact of this process, we have to understand how our cells function. Cells are like little humans, all 50-70 trillion of them. They each have a structure that, in general, is equivalent to the human body. Figuratively speaking, you can say they have a circulation system: lungs, reproductive organs and a digestive system. Humans love to associate and live together with other people that have their similar backgrounds and structure of life. Cells act just the same. They also live in and are attached to specific groups with a similar structure. We usually call them organs or organ systems. To survive emotionally and physically, people need each other and a healthy environment to live in; so do cells. People communicate; so do cells.

Our communication and response system

Our entire body originally develops from one single cell, the combination of an egg and sperm cell. This one cell duplicates into more cells that each, in turn, duplicate until the genetic code tells the cells to differentiate. However, before this process of differentiating takes place to its full extent, the cells create a structure of three layers, the endoderm (inner layer), the mesoderm (middle layer) and ectoderm (outer layer). All the organs and parts of our body will develop and grow out of these three layers, each of them out of their specific layer. A very interesting point is that from the outer layer (the ectoderm), only a few major organs develop: The skin, the epithelial (outer layer) of our sensory organs and the brain. Together they represent our system of perception, communication and understanding of our environment. This system determines our behavior. The basic structure of the cell is exactly the same as the body's structure! All its systems that communicate, understand and act are in the ectoderm, or outer skin, of the cell.

Your genes do not control you

So what about our genes? Didn't Watson and Crick, more then half a century ago, make it very clear that our genes control us? No, in fact they did not, but we did embrace such a belief system. If this were true, then it would be so convenient! Why? Because if our genes control us, then there are many things we cannot change or control. We can blame a large variety of things, like health problems, character, criminal behavior, immoral sexual behavior, etc., on our genes and comfort ourselves believing one day science will discover how to change these. *So, in the meantime I'll just continue living as I always do since my genes determine, anyway, when I will become sick and what kind of person I am or will be!* Well, here's the good news! You are <u>not</u> ruled or controlled by your genes.

Genes can change

Biological experiments show us that even the simplest life form we know, bacteria, is able to change its genes. *Scientists used the genetic defect in a specific bacteria and proved it is possible to do this*. Bacteria must eat, like all life forms do, in order to survive. However, their genetic defect made it impossible for them to digest milk sugar (lactose). To be able to digest lactose they have to be capable of producing the enzyme lactase. Their genetic defect made that impossible. Scientists put these bacteria in a Petri dish. The only food they added to the Petri dish was lactose. It was the obvious expectation that the bacteria would die because they were unable to digest the lactose. Surprisingly, this did not occur! Later, research proved that the bacteria were actually growing because they changed their genetic structure in order to be able to digest lactose. The bacteria followed the most powerful drive in living creatures: *away from pain*! Therefore they survived. This drive, *away from pain,* is already present, at a biological level, in the sperm and egg cell we originate from. Its survival mechanism is based on the simple Proto-physiocluster rule: stimulus/response.

Without environmental signals there is no life

If bacteria were able to change their genetic code, would it not be reasonable to assume that the higher life forms, like animals and humans, can do the same? Individual cells act a lot like humans. But the sum of cooperation and interaction between all our 50-70 trillion cells create a few miracles that make humans unique! The total process of their functions and interactions are accountable for human awareness, conscience and our free will! The configurations of our genes are unique for every person on this planet. This configuration determines your talents and capacities, but it depends on your input and free will if they will ever become manifest. However, genes do not create your belief systems, decisions or behavior. In turn they determine, to a certain degree, the innate weakness of specific organs or organ systems. The development of serious health or behavioral problems, will only be determined by the genes for a very small percentage, probably not more then 10%. The majority of what we develop will be determined by incoming environmental signals. The understanding of these biological principles and rules are vital to understand the mechanisms that control our health, belief systems, decisions and behavior. If there are no signals (stimuli) from the environment then there will be no motion, no change, no physiology, no emotions, no belief systems, no behavior, …no life!

The nucleus, our Database of potentials

The nucleus of the cell (where the genes are located) can best be compared to an office where the blueprints of our physical body are stored. The genes in the nucleus are the storage room of all the visible and hidden possibilities of our physical system. The nucleus never stores behavioral patterns or belief systems! It is not the "control center" of your behavior, but just the Database of the blueprints and possibilities. The Database of your computer will never become active unless first there is a signal from outside activating it. The same applies to our genes. The nucleus holds all the instructions and blueprints of shapes and textures that are needed to keep the system (physical body) going. It will only deliver those blueprints when a signal from outside the cell reaches the nucleus and incites it to do so. A computer can only respond to those things that it's programmed to do. This is the same with our genes. They contain a unique program, but it will never act unless it gets activated from outside. For example, many of us use a computer, but how many of us actually use all the possibilities, or full capacities, of our computer? Probably no one! This works the same with our genetic potentials.

The gate guard of our cells

Genes cooperate closely with the stimulus/response mechanism of the outer layer (the skin) of their cell. The genes will only respond and act after they receive a signal. But what or who determines if a signal is allowed to enter the cell? It is controlled by a magnificent mechanism based on stimulus/response. On the surface of each single cell floats thousands of proteins, and in the case of some cells, even several hundred thousands of proteins. They function as guards, constantly searching the area for signals. Each of these guards, or antennas, can only detect one specific type of signal. What kind of signal are we talking about? Any kind! This could be food particles, biochemical, medicines, hormones, and peptides, even energy such as light, magnetism, color or sound. If the antenna detects the specific signal that it is made for, it will attract this signal. In the next step this antenna, this guard, gives an impulse to another protein next to him and that protein functions as a gate and opens the door. The gate has a specific shape that fits the shape of a specific signal perfectly. This means that the antenna will only respond to this signal. It is only this signal that is able to open the gate and is allowed to enter the cell. This whole process is stimulus/response based and operated. No thinking or feelings are involved! This wonderful mechanism keeps us alive and if the signals do not overload or poison us, this system will always keep our body in balance. This is all a part of our Proto-physiocluster system. This mechanism will never harm us because it obeys a genetic program that keeps balance and keeps us as far away from pain and damage as possible.

Proto-physioclusters can be misled

However, like any system, any person or any computer, it can be misinformed, misled or overloaded. Because it cannot think, reason or feel, it will always follow its genetic stimulus/response reflexes. As a result, it can technically act perfectly to the signal, but this leads to the result that the cell, or even a total organ or organ system can be severely damaged. How is that possible? There are two main reasons for that:

1. *Environmental signals*

2. *Signals from other cells inside our own body*

If everything would be perfect in our environment and inside our body, our Proto-physioclusters would always keep us healthy and balanced. However, we all know that the environment is far from perfect! But what about the interaction between cells caused by the signals coming from our own body cells? The understanding of this leads us to the second operating program of our physiology: the Physio-clusters.

Physio-clusters

Physio-clusters are a group of physiological data that together form a unity. What are they made of? Originally, they are combinations of little genetically determined Proto-physioclusters (On/Of switches). You can compare some of the Proto-physioclusters to the letters of the alphabet and some

Physio-clusters to specific letter templates. Templates are usually basic documents with specific words and sentences that we create in order to avoid writing the same text repeatedly. We use templates as a basis for letters with different contents but with the same ground pattern. For instance, when we write a letter, we use the same opening words and conclusion, but in between we write different messages. This is the same with our Physio-clusters. Our Proto-physioclusters never change. They always have the same meaning and same shape. They are like the letters of the alphabet; we can create many words and sentences with them. Proto-physioclusters are independent little 'antennas' and 'switches' and they are only activated by signals from incoming sensory information or from signals of other cells in our body.

Physio-clusters are always connected

If we would be controlled solely by our Proto-physioclusters we would never develop psychosomatic diseases. Regarding the effect on our body, the difference between Proto-physiocluster activity and that of Physio-clusters becomes more visible during sleep or even better, during anesthesia or Alzheimer (in its severe state). During sleep we still activate large amounts of Physio-clusters through our dreams, but during anesthesia or severe Alzheimer, the amount of activated Physio-clusters decreases drastically. Let us, before we describe the effects of Physio-clusters first discuss how we create them.

At the very beginning, when our Database is still empty, it does not contain Clusters. We have to first experience things in order to create them. The moment we start to experience things, we not only store the sensory facts of the experience but also how we feel at that moment. If we would not store it that way, then all the stored data would have the same personal value to us and we would not be able to remember how a past event felt. Our feelings are always the result of physiological changes. The neuro-physiological commands that cause that feeling will be stored in connection with a Cluster. The Clusters are stored in the upper layer (the Cortex) of the brain and the Physio-clusters are stored in the Limbic System. Physio-clusters are always attached to either Clusters or Bad Clusters. Hence, there are no Physio-clusters that exist alone. Physio-clusters are only executed when the Cluster or Bad Cluster they are attached to is activated. Conversely, if no part of a Cluster or Bad Cluster has been activated, then no Physio-cluster will be activated either. This means that not one single Physio-cluster will ever be activated without a signal from the cells in the Cortex. Those cells are only activated by environmental signals or by our thoughts! On the other hand, thoughts will never come spontaneously. They first need a signal from the environment to activate them. The content of that signal will determine the contents of your first thoughts. From there on you can continue your thoughts, but only as far as your Database can deliver previously stored data. Of course we are able to combine all kinds of activated data as much as we want, but whatever we create that way will always consist of pieces of data that we already previously stored. As an example, try to think of how you could combine a *kramouktra* with a *snoeksoma* to create a *poemala*. Did it work in your brain? No it couldn't, because you have no such words in your Database… I made them up.

Physio-clusters never happen on their own

The emotional experiences that we have during our lifetime cause specific physiological patterns that we store in these Physio-clusters, freeing the subconscious from not having to search through the Proto-physioclusters for all the information it needs every time. You might say that we also learn at a physiological level. Remember, a Physio-cluster never happens on its own, but is always attached to a Cluster or a Bad Cluster. Does that mean that every Cluster and every Bad Cluster has a Physio-cluster attached to it? Yes, always! But is the body always in movement? Yes, even if we are not working and asleep, our bodies still have physiological activity; otherwise we would die! In the procedure itself there is no real difference between the physiological processes of maintaining normal bodily functions and physiology needed when feeling emotions.

We all possess the right tools to feel and experience emotions. As soon as those tools are used, more energy is needed and that includes changes in the physiology! At that point the body cannot just continue with the normal physiological status but must make the necessary changes and adjustments in order to create a situation that we consciously can detect the physiological changes and feel the emotion that it will cause. You can compare it with a car. Instead of having an idling motor you need a functioning car that is ready for action. If you want to drive, then more combustion must take place, certain parts need to get rolling and action is needed to do all of this.

The same rules apply for our body. The status of the physiological processes that is present at moments when there are no emotions can be compared to an idling motor. As soon as there is emotion, changes are needed in the motor speed! Now there is emotional action and physiological changes are needed! The intensity of an emotion is just a matter of the amount of activated cells, similar to the activation of muscle cells. The more muscle power you need, the more muscle cells will be activated. Keep in mind that the Proto-physioclusters are "switch" mechanisms. Like our muscles, they have only two possibilities: on or off, 100% active or 100% inactive.

Nature vs. nurture

Besides emotional situations, there are many times when we are in a state in which there are no great adjustments needed. Of course, our muscles are also in movement when we are just sitting. We are always breathing, our intestinal muscles are working and the heart muscles are continuously busy. These are all included in the usual processes of life, to the autonomic physiological processes that are built into our bodies and are set into motion from the very earliest moments of life. It is only after the activities or emotional experiences surpass a certain level that a different kind of physiology with a different intensity takes place, all caused by our emotions. Many of the physiological processes in our body are controlled by a combination of Proto-physioclusters and Physio-clusters. This process is already set into motion in the case of a newborn baby. The functioning of the Proto-physioclusters keeps the fetus alive from the moment of conception onward. After birth, the inborn sucking reflex is a prime example of this. The way that this mechanism works can be better understood by analyzing an example from daily life:

> ***Example*:**
> You are drinking a glass of water. While you are drinking, numerous physiological processes are in operation, such as your salivary glands, the peristaltic muscle action in your esophagus and other processes as well. But before they begin to function, there must be a stimulus from the outside. This would be the cool glass in your hand, you looking at the glass, how it touches your lips, and how the water goes down your throat as you drink it. This is pure sensory data. For certain, there are numerous Clusters and their connected physiology. By calling up these Clusters, physiological reactions are automatically set into motion!

However, the reflex to drink and all the related physiological reactions were already genetically present in the form of a Proto-physioclusters. How do we know that? This is apparent from the fact that a newborn baby, without any previous experience, already has this mechanism in place and it's functioning. When she is put to her mother's breast, she knows instinctively and immediately what to do. As soon as her sucking reflex is executed and milk is in her mouth, the next Proto-physiocluster comes into play, namely the swallow reflex, and all the physiological actions that are needed to get the liquid swallowed. After each swallowing experience, the child creates a Cluster. All the factual data of the previous swallowing experiences are also stored in Clusters. These Clusters are the sum total of all her experiences thus far. However, with each new experience, she learns, and if there are enough similarities between those Clusters and new incoming sensory data, she will use these Clusters as her personal comparison material to analyze the new event.

Taste is a matter of experience

If you stick a finger into the mouth of a hungry baby, immediately she will begin to vigorously suck. The child still does not have the experience (Clusters) needed to make the distinction between the mother's breast, a pacifier, her own finger, or any other object that can be sucked on. If, however, you tell a three-year-old child to close her eyes and open her mouth because you are going to give her a lollipop, and instead you place your finger in her mouth, she will know immediately that it is not a lollipop. Why does the three-year-old know, yet the baby does not? Because the three-year-old has many more Clusters with information on taste and feeling shapes with her tongue and lips. In short, she has the necessary Clusters to deal with this topic in order to make the distinction. As soon as the data regarding your finger comes in, she gets a disgusted look on her face and will not suck on your finger. This happens solely because of the sensory perceptions. The sensory perceptions did not match the Clusters that she called up when you promised her a lollipop. Her subconscious had already activated “lollipop” Clusters. The data regarding the lollipop did not match the new incoming data.

The physiological data is packaged separately

How can we picture the Cluster and the physiological data being attached together? Is the physiological data actually inside the Cluster? No, this is not the case. The physiological data is packaged separately. They are stored in Physio-clusters. Nonetheless, they are each inseparably attached to their connected Cluster! You might say that, figuratively speaking, the data in a Cluster is stored in a white ball and the physiological data is stored in a grey ball. As such, it could be depicted in the following diagram:

CLUSTERS & PHYSIO-CLUSTERS
ARE STORED TOGETHER

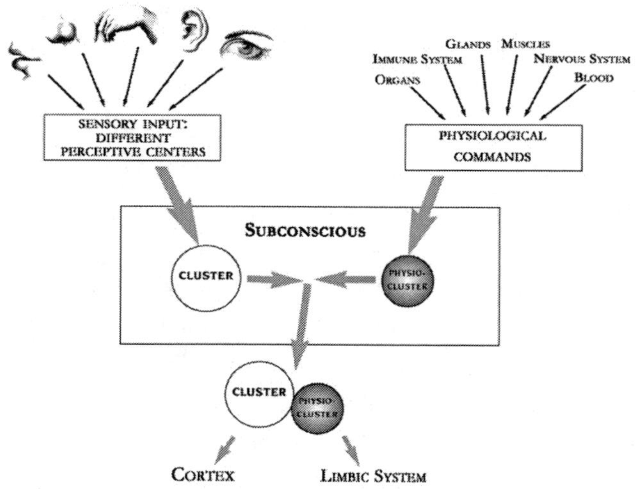

SENSORY INPUT:
DIFFERENT
PERCEPTIVE CENTERS

GLANDS MUSCLES
IMMUNE SYSTEM
NERVOUS SYSTEM
ORGANS
BLOOD

PHYSIOLOGICAL
COMMANDS

SUBCONSCIOUS
CLUSTER
PHYSIO-CLUSTER

CLUSTER
PHYSIO-CLUSTER

CORTEX
LIMBIC SYSTEM

Incoming new sensory data is processed, meaning that it is thoroughly compared to similar previously stored data. After the process is concluded, the analyzed (encoded) sensory data is stored in the Cluster (white ball) and the commands causing the physiological status of the body at that time, in a Physio-cluster (grey ball). This principle not only functions at Cluster level but also on parts of the Cluster, called Sub-clusters, or even at the level of Fragments. The white and the grey balls are now "glued" together. Just like the subconscious is able to distinguish the different types of sensory data from each other, it can also distinguish the 'grey' from the 'white' balls. How? It does this by codes. The subconscious determines that the white ones contain sensory data, needed for the comparison process, and the grey ones contain the connected physiological commands. How does it know that piece of data got into a grey or into a white ball?

The separation of factual data and physiology

This is less complicated as it might look. It is a totally automated program, based on the stimulus/response rule. How does your video camera know where to store the incoming sound and where to store the picture? They are two totally different signals. The same applies to the physiology and sensory data. They enter the subconscious as totally different signals. The subconscious takes care of the proper encoding of both and stores the sensory data in the Cortex and stores the physiological data in the Limbic System. A code to activate the connected Physio-cluster is added to each piece of data. Whenever that piece of data will be selected in the future as comparison material, this code will activate the connected physiology. Described in detail, it works like this: The Cortex cell, activated by a new incoming piece sensory data, is the exact same cell where that specific piece of data will be stored after processing and encoding. That also gives us the explanation as to why data is always activated as comparison material when there is enough similarity between the new and previously stored data. The subconscious cannot do it any other way because of the stimulus/response rule. If a specific color enters the eyes, it will be passed on to that one cell (or group of cells) that can only store that specific color. It is not that color in itself that activates a complete memory, but the combination with other sensory data. Every piece of sensory data activates its own specific cell. Therefore, a total event activates thousands, yes, millions of cells! These cells start the "fire" and connect with each other. However, if their combination was already present in previously stored events, the data of these events will be used as comparison material. There will never be a 100% similarity between two events. This is great, because now the subconscious activates all kinds of data which similarity come close to the new incoming data. We derive our awareness and thought processes from this large variety of activated comparison material. In performing all of this, the subconscious itself does not think or feel, but follows strict stimulus/response rules. At the same time, the different physiological data, which cause your present feelings, comes in from the different parts and sensors of the body. The subconscious does not analyze the physiological commands; instead, it accepts them as they are! It just connects the present physiological commands, or codes, with the analyzed pieces of sensory data. It stores the sensory data in the Cluster and the physiological commands (codes) in the connected Physio-cluster.

The reversed process during the comparison

The last diagram showed us how Clusters and Physio-clusters are stored together. What happens if they are later used as comparison material? The opposite of what happens during the process of storage. Incoming sensory data activates the cells that perceive that specific piece of data. A number of cells, activated by the incoming data, connect automatically to the size of a Fragment and from there, to a Sub-cluster. This (in connection with a general code mainly coming from the Thalamus) activates all previously stored Fragments and Sub-clusters with similar content. The combination of several Sub-clusters determines which Clusters will be activated as the most similar comparison material. The subconscious now has a large amount of Fragments, Sub-clusters and Clusters to its availability. Now it will start to select the most appropriate ones. Based on what? Based on the highest level of similarity between the data of new incoming events and similar events in the past.

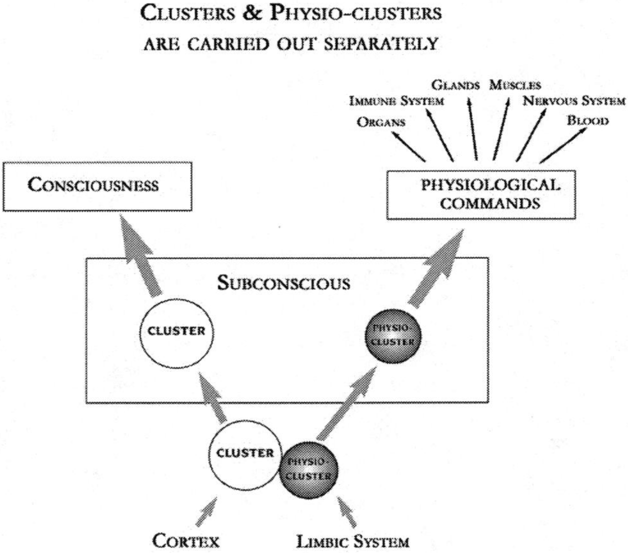

CLUSTERS & PHYSIO-CLUSTERS
ARE CARRIED OUT SEPARATELY

From the most similar material, it selects the data with the highest relative code. The final analysis from all that (Cortex) is sent to the conscious brain and the commands in the connected

Physio-clusters (Limbic System) are sent to the several organs and organ systems in the body. The speed of all this is tremendous! To better understand this, just remember the last time you saw something that frightened you or evoked another strong emotion. After you received the sensory information, lets say a visual one, how long did you have to wait to feel the emotion in your body? It was just a split of a second, right? What you almost instantly felt was the result of all the combined processes we have discussed so far. Pretty amazing, isn't it?

The subconscious makes it easy for itself

The subconscious stores the physiological data from a particular emotional event so they can be used again later. You might compare this to how standard letters or templates are used in a word processor. Imagine that you have a bunch of letters you have to send on a regular basis. You store the letter in your computer. Each time you have to send this template, you open it up, change a few details, such as the name or date, and then print it out for mailing. If you later discover that you could improve the template itself by altering a few words, then you make the necessary changes, save them and then the new template will be ready for the next time. That's exactly what the subconscious does. Why should it continuously create new Physio-clusters when certain emotions can simply be repeated to the same effect? The subconscious follows the same routine in the Limbic system as it does in the Cortex. It stores the 'templates' on Fragment, Sub-cluster and Cluster levels. This makes the templates very easy to use.

Compassion must be learned

A newborn baby is only equipped with its inborn potential in the form of its primary physiological programs and basic emotions. Neither of these is developed in a newborn child. Of course, it learns very quickly to express anger and sadness when she does not receive the care or nourishment when she wants it. How often have you seen a very young child poking the eyes of a cat or pulling its tail or hurting it in some other way? As adults we often say, *"Don't do that... that hurts the kitty, it doesn't like it."* Not only the words, but also the tone of our voice that is used makes the most impression. As a result, compassion for the poor animal is beginning to form. Is once enough? No, we all know that this same process must be repeated over and over before the child ever begins to understand what she is doing. Some may excuse the child's behavior by saying that she means no harm but is only playing with the cat. Also, she has little control over her muscles and that is why she is a little wild. Of course, these arguments are correct, but it is not the end of the story. The child is following its desire as it plays with the young animal. It wants to have it, to hold it and to snuggle with it. The child doesn't know that the animal has a completely different idea about cuddling!

Gathering comparison material

Do the warnings of the parents make up enough Clusters in the child to create a feeling of outrage, anger, and compassion towards animal abuse? No. As you know, many more Clusters and emotional experiences are needed for that. Some of them are formed by the behavior of others. The young child sees his parents or other adults responding to the pain of animals. She observes their outrage at the abusers and compassion for the injured animals. Clusters are made from all these experiences and are nicely stored in connection with the existing physiology that represents the present emotions at the time of storage. When the child is stubborn and simply doesn't want to be gentle with animals, then she will be punished by either parent or by the animal itself. Step-by-step the child learns why it is unjust or cruel to act that way towards a defenseless animal. Another facet that plays a role is the desire to earn the approval of the parents. The child earns approval whenever she treats the animal with care and love. *"It's wonderful the way you are treating the puppy, so gently and carefully, darling!"* The warm feeling of acceptance and approval from the parents is attached in the form of physiological data to the Cluster that is stored. In this way, the child slowly learns to develop his basic emotions. These emotions are stored as physiological data in Physio-clusters. In this way, the Database is slowly filled with the Clusters and Sub-clusters needed to later be called up as comparison material. Of course, attached to all these are the Physio-clusters.

Physio-clusters determine our emotions

Emotions are always the result of physiological reactions. How do we know this? Every emotion is the result of changes in the body. Every change in your body is the result of a physiological process. To transport the information about these changes from several parts of the body to our brain is also a physiological process! At this point we have to make an agreement about the word "emotion". In PMA we call everything that we feel an *emotion*. Love, anger, fear, sadness, shame, jealousy, disgust, etc. are some of the well-known emotions. However, in PMA we also refer to pain, hunger, thirst, desire, and feelings of recognition, etc. as emotions, or feelings. Everything we experience as a change of feeling, regardless how strong or slight the feeling is, is called an emotion. Emotions provide every piece of sensory information with meaning... but more about that later.

The development of your emotions

Scientists agree that we are all born with a set of basic emotions. Nevertheless, we see a large variety in the way different people develop how they experience and express their emotions.

Although we are all born with the same set of basic emotions, we develop them differently. How we develop them is due to two aspects:

1. Our genetic determined constitution

2. The things we experience during our life

Although there are many differences in how, when and why we experience emotions, the genetic programs that control our emotions are, for all people, the same. Our experiences during our life shape our emotions and their intensity. We always store the sensory information of events in connection with our emotions in our subconscious brain, our Database. We need this Database to understand and give meaning to later incoming sensory data. Without our Database we would still be in the same state we were in when we were born. If we would have no comparison material, we would not know where we are, who we are and what we are doing. We would still have the same basic emotions of a baby and we would judge everything we hear, see, smell, taste and feel on that basic level. To understand our mind/body relationship it is very important to know what scientists agree on:

An emotion or feeling is the result of physiological changes in the body!

Individual perception

Let us look at an example that demonstrates how this subconsciously works:

***Example*:**

You really love animals. You see a group of rebellious teenage boys hitting and tormenting a puppy. Increasingly, you feel anger at the boys while feeling pity for the poor animal. What just happened in your brain? The pictures and sounds came in through your senses. It activated numerous different Clusters of young puppies. A lot of them have a physiological load that can cause you to feel emotions. Think back to the time when you saw a little puppy jumping around and you laughed so much. Not to mention the pleasure you had in playing with this kind of an animal. You can still remember how you snuggled with the furry little thing. Among those Clusters you have called up are some Clusters that were made when you once accidentally stepped on the paws of a puppy. The puppy's whimpering made you feel so sorry for it. What you are now seeing can also call up Clusters that have to do with unfair treatment. Clusters wherein include the strong oppressing the weak. This deals with power and justice. When these Clusters were being made, outrage also played a big role. These emotions will activate physiological changes. This physiological baggage is attached to the Clusters that were called up. To top it off, you have your Clusters about justice and injustice. Based on the differences in size (the big teenagers and the small puppy) your anger about this injustice intensifies even more. Through prior experiences, you've developed several belief systems about justice and injustice. A little baby would never react like you at this point. But you will, and solely based on your existing comparison material, its physiology and the belief systems that are formed out of that.

Let us now look at how all this sensory and physiological data is transported inside our brain and the rest of our body, and how cells communicate with each other.

Chapter 4 – The language of our subconscious

You really need this

You might ask yourself at this point: *"Do I really need all this information in order to understand and practice PMA and to become more happy and successful in life? Is it also necessary to repeat certain aspects so often?"* Yes, it is necessary because you need it for your own intellectual persuasion and insight. Why? As you will later see, your innate protection mechanism (called the "Friend Mechanism" in PMA) will try to withhold you from going to the content of the Bad Clusters.

As soon as you understand some of these technical aspects, and what's more, you experience the reactions in your own body, then you will be even more convinced that this is how the mind/body connection really works. Only then will it feel "safe" to use the PMA technique and let go of your protection mechanism and enjoy the process! With this knowledge you have already started programming yourself to be able to cooperate effectively with your *Friend Mechanism.* In this case it is directly true that knowledge is power. If you wouldn't have that intellectual persuasion and insight, you would not allow yourself to go to the Bad Clusters. You might ask, *"Is this mechanism that strong?"* As you continue reading, you will find out in this book how strong it really is!

The subconscious does not make mistakes

For every thousand bytes of data that will reach our subconscious, it has to process at least a billion bytes of data. This gives us a deep respect for the capacity of our brain and even more respect when you start to realize that this huge process only takes a fraction of a second! The most remarkable part is that the subconscious, like your computer, never makes mistakes. However, a computer can be treated and programmed wrong and so can our subconscious. Just like a computer, even when wrongly programmed, your subconscious will never fail in following a strict program of rules. Although the outcome may not be what we want or need, the subconscious always follows its stimulus/response rule.

How the processing of that huge amount of data in the subconscious can lead to weird and unrealistic pictures is proven by our dreams and nightmares. How do you like the fact that 75% of all your decisions and behavior is dictated by comparison material similar to the content in your nightmares? As we will see, when we discuss the activity and power of Bad Clusters, this assumption is not as crazy as it might sound. Do you like exciting movies? Well, by applying the PMA technique you are about to see some of the most exciting movies you will ever see: the *movies* you stored in your own head! These "movies" control a large portion of your existence! It is a fun and exciting process. You will enjoy it and you will gain more out of it than you can ever imagine up to this point!

The capacity of the brain

How much of our brain do we use? It is a widespread misconception that we use only a small part of our brain. In actuality, we use the full 100% of our brain! Only, we do not use it to its full capacity! This is an important distinction. Brain cells that are not used will die! *"Use it or loose it"!* Compare this to the capacity of a Ferrari.

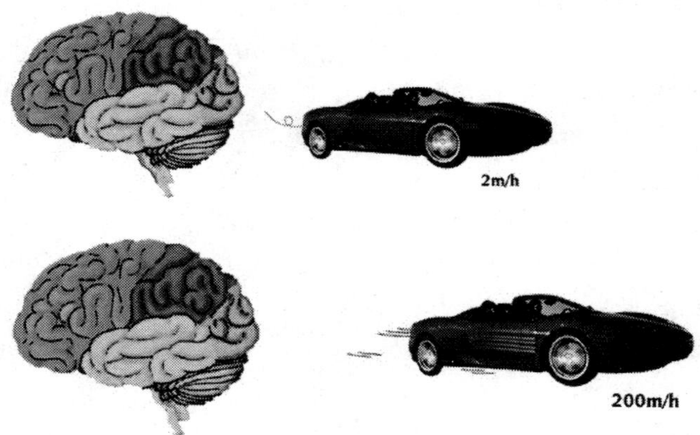

If you drive it at two miles per hour, how much of the car do you use? All of it, right? How much of its capacity do you use? You can compare the capacity of your brain with a Ferrari. You can drive the Ferrari at two miles per hour although it can easily reach 200 miles an hour. The whole car is being used, but only a small percentage of its capacity!

Some facts about our brain

Our subconscious has an enormous capacity, but we block many of its possibilities by our own thoughts and fears. If you get rid of these blocks, you will enormously expand in your own growth! We will not go too deep into the function and science of the brain, however, let's look at some interesting scientific facts about the brain:

- The weight of the brain is 2% of the body weight
- 78% of our total body is water!
- Each cell (neuron) of the brain has a specific task. Each one is specialized to store one specific fact or type of data. If a cell, for instance, is made to store

only the color red, the brain will only use this cell when needing to store the color red.

- How many times can the brain use this cell for that purpose? As many as you need, there is no end! It is just like using the letters of the alphabet as often as you want and in millions of combinations.
- But how can the brain distinguish between one memory with the color red and another memory with the same color? By the combinations with other cells! For instance, you can see a red shirt right now and later a red car. They have the same color, but all the rest of the sensory input is different. This way the combination of cells for the red shirt will completely differ from the cell combination of the red car.

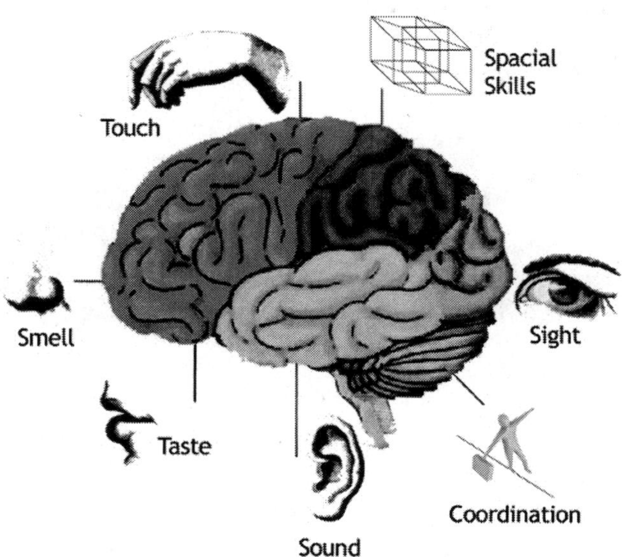

- For each shape, color, taste, smell, sound, feeling, etc. we have specific cells that can only store them.
- Specific cells can make a sound stronger and other cells can make it weaker; one cell makes the color darker and the other brighter, etc.
- Every cell is specific and can be used in unlimited amount of combinations and as often as needed, much more than the number of molecules in the universe.
- How many of these cells do we have? The brain consists of 100,000,000,000 (one hundred billion) nerve neurons. We have about the same amount of these cells spread throughout our entire body. A large portion is found in and around the spinal cord.
- Each neuron has 10-50 glia (glia=glue) cells.
- Each neuron has several dendrites that split like the branches of a tree. Each cell can make its way up to 100,000 connections with other cells.

The smallest contribution to the transport of information

We've probably learned that nerve cells communicate through a complex "wiring system" called dendrites and axons. They are connected to each other by synapses. An electrical impulse will go from cell to cell passing the synapses. Before that, an electrical impulse arrives at the end of a dendrite and will be translated into bio-chemical agents called ligands or peptides. (Ligand: *ligare* - to bind or tie). These ligands act as messenger molecules, or signals, that carry the message of the impulse over the synaptic gap. These messenger molecules are captured by a type of umbrella on the other side of the synaptic gap and are again translated back into an electrical impulse. This electro/bio-chemical path was assumed to be the main route of transporting information from one cell to the other.

- The possible numbers of combinations of synapses the brain can make are more than the amount of molecules in the entire universe!

The Synaptic Gap

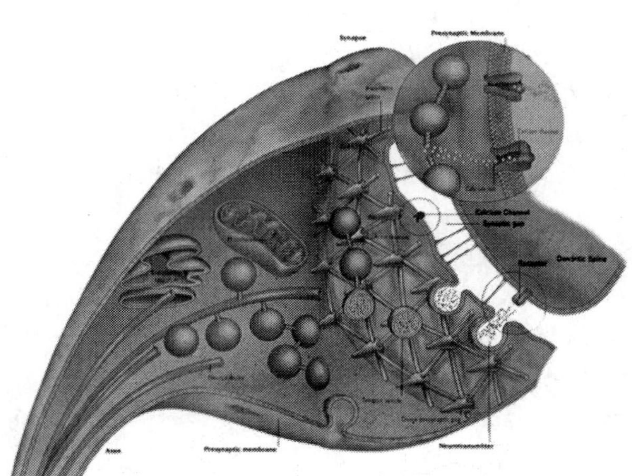

However, recent scientific research shows that, in reality, this is the smallest route for transporting information. It is only responsible for approximately 2-4% of the total communication in the human body.

The bigger route of transporting information

There is another process based on a large variety of bio-chemical substances (ligands or peptides) that will go directly from cell to cell without using the synaptic clefts! Just imagine: Although it only takes care of 2-4% of the total communication in our body, the electric/chemical synaptic route already has a larger amount of combination possibilities than there are molecules in the whole universe (according to scientists)! Then how much of this enormous capacity of the brain do we really use? Can you imagine what your possibilities are if you would use the full capacity of your brain? By taking away your fear-based inhibitors, your Bad Clusters, you will open the road to expand your full capacity, health and energy.

Don't vegetate but live with passion

Today, most people just work, eat, sleep, make money and spend it. They just vegetate! They don't feel the real power of life! They might look successful, but most of them feel an emptiness and inner disappointment because of the constant returning of a daily routine. Why do we stick to those routines that do not give us the satisfaction in our personal and professional life? What stops us from changing and having great relationships, vibrating energy and successful fulfilling careers? It is not our rational thoughts that stop us, but our feelings! Nevertheless, feelings like happiness, satisfaction, joy, etc. are the determining factors whether we are successful or not in work and life!

Ligands: the messengers between our cells

Sensory information determines how we feel! As soon as information (data) reaches the sensors of the body, an explosion of energy takes place at lightning speed on a cellular level.

> ***Example*:**
> Imagine yourself walking through a quiet lane in a park. Suddenly a big dog breaks out from the bushes next to you and crosses your path. Immediately all the hairs on your body stand straight. It takes no noticeable time to give this instruction to all those thousands of hairs on your skin. All of this happens with incredible speed!

The moment external stimuli reach our sensory cells (cells that perceive smell, taste, sound, touch and pictures), they immediately respond by transporting the stimuli, or signal, through an electrical impulse, or through direct cell-to-cell contact by producing ligands. Ligands are the bio- chemical messenger molecules (signals) that send messages from cell-to-cell throughout our entire body. All active cells of our body produce a large variety of ligands that spit them out and into the body fluid (Remember, 74% of our body is water). Then, 'antennas', or receptors, on the surface of the cell attract them. Every specific ligand has its own specific antenna that it's attracted to, based on their mutual positive or negative electrical charge. The moment that a ligand binds to an antenna, it results in a reaction of the connected cell. A special class of ligands that are used in the processes of the brain is called neuro-peptides. Ligands are not the only signals that are captured by those antennas. We have antennas that can capture all kinds of signals from our environment. Food particles, chemicals, and yes, even light can be a signal that is captured and create a reaction in the connected cells.

Instructions from cell to cell

Consider those ligands as specific instructions that one cell sends to the other. Depending on the incoming information, these ligands are produced by the cells in different types and amounts. All our cells are covered with a variety of receptors that will attract and bind the ligands that have the matching code or vibration frequency and translate their binding into actions that create new ligands inside the cell. These ligands are then passed on to the next cells. This takes place in two ways:

1. *Through the synapses (2-4% of all communication)*

2. *Directly from cell to cell through the body fluid – blood and lymph – (96-98% of communication)*

Endorphin

A few years ago scientists discovered the morphine antenna (receptor) in the body and found that this receptor is primarily there for a type of morphine that is created inside our own body, called endorphin. Scientists always assumed that endorphins were only produced in specific parts of our brain. Now we know that several cells in our body produce and receive endorphins, as well. Among those cells are the cells of our immune system! Understanding these processes opened up a whole new perception of the mind/body connection. What is the essence of their discoveries and why is it so important to have an understanding of the process of the mind/body connection? In the context of this book, the most important implication of these discoveries is that we are now able to understand how our emotions and perceptions are formed. Although many details of this complex process still remains to be discovered, we can already see the relationship between sensory impulses, memories and emotions. It becomes clear how psychosomatic complaints are formed and the enormous importance of our subconscious interpretation of incoming sensory and environmental signals. This knowledge leads to a new level of understanding of our health, belief systems and behavior. We begin to comprehend the mechanisms of the subconscious and that it operates through strict rules. We discover that this level offers us pathways through the subconscious and enables us to communicate with the subconscious in its own language and based on its natural rules. Through this process of understanding, PMA was shaped, and we have been able to discover the nature of Bad Clusters, their origin and how to reach them and change their negative influence into positive energy. Also, it has helped us to learn the language of the subconscious and its rules. By having this knowledge, we know what the structures of Bad Clusters are and how their content can influence and dominate our feelings, thoughts, belief systems, decisions and actions. But what is more important, we will also understand how it is possible to change all of that to the better, just by tracing and revealing the contents of these wrongly stored memories (Bad Clusters) and change their harmful physiological influence on our system and into desirable power.

Ligands, the fundament of our feelings and actions

As already mentioned, our body exist for 74-78% out of fluid. It flows around and inside the body cells. Each cell is a miracle of activity in itself. Neurons, blood, muscle and organ cells are all capable of receiving and producing ligands. Estimates are that 300 different ligands exist in our system (Some scientists even assume that there are more than a thousand). We can compare ligands to keys.

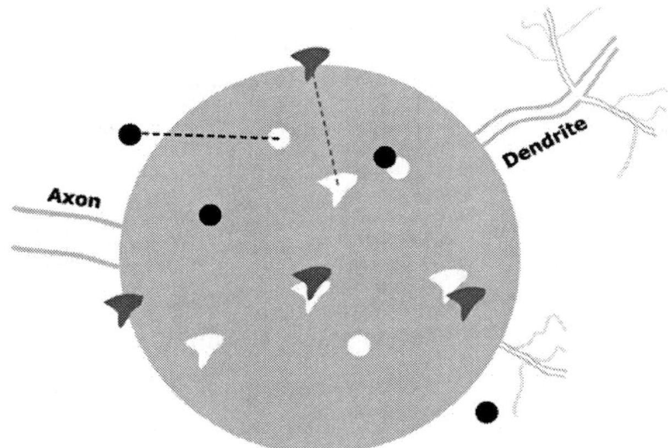

A single cell has several thousands and up to even a million “keyholes” in its skin. If this is true and there are only about 300 different ligands (keys) but there are thousands or even a million “keyholes” in each cell, then this means that there are large amounts of the same keyhole in just one cell. We now know that each cell has its own specific configuration of keyholes. For instance, one cell can have 20,000 of type A and 5,000 of type M, etc., and the next cell can have 1,000 of type A and 150,000 of type M. Each cell has its own specific configuration in amounts and in types of "keyholes". Some cells have 20 different keyholes and others have 200. This leads to almost an endless variation of ligand combinations, capable of transferring the most detailed piece of information in any amount. It also provides the cell with the capability to store endless amounts of codes in order to connect its own specific piece of data with millions of different combinations with other cells, while in the process of storing all the different events and memories we have.

Limbic System

Each sense has its own area in the Cortex of the brain. Each area is connected with the inside part of the brain, the Limbic System. The Limbic System stores physiological content. All parts of a specific memory (Cluster or Bad Cluster), stored in the Cortex, are through ligand codes, individually connected to a specific area in the Limbic System. As soon as the Incoming sensory information activates comparison material in the Cortex, the selected Cortex cells will release millions of ligands to the Limbic System in order to execute the connected physiology. Based on those messages, the Limbic System will now send messages to release impulses and ligand configurations in several organs and muscles. This process, among other responses, is responsible for the physiology in the body that we feel as emotions. This basic process is the same for everyone. The effects (of the unique ligand/receptor combinations) will differ from person to person based on their individual comparison material. Our senses deliver their signals continuously, so this is an ongoing process during every second of the day. The combination of incoming data will always determine what kind of comparison material will be activated.

The kind of selected comparison material will always determine how we feel about this incoming data. This process is purely based on stimulus/response without thinking, without feelings. As long as we only use Clusters as comparison material, we are fine and we feel okay.

Physio-clusters related to Bad Clusters

If, in turn, a Bad Cluster is activated as comparison material, our body will then be flooded with a ligand configuration that instantly changes our feelings and actions in a negative way. Your belief systems, decisions and behavior depend totally on how you feel. How you feel depends on the incoming information and the activated comparison material with its physiological load. The combination of the ligands will 'tell' the body cells what is the physiological load of the subconsciously selected comparison material.

Activated comparison material activates physiology (ligands)

The ligand configurations determine how you feel. How you feel will then be reflected in what you say, decide and achieve. This whole process has nothing to do with thinking, planning or arguing. You have no control over it. It's purely based on stimulus/response! Because, you cannot control the world outside of you, you will never know what combination of data will enter your senses the very next moment. And because you are not aware of the content of your Bad Clusters and have no control over the subconscious stimulus/response activity, you will never know when a Bad Cluster gets activated or to what level it will affect you. But the one thing you will always become aware of is *after* a Bad Cluster is activated; you will feel its activation in your body and it will affect your feelings, thinking, actions and health! This leads us to the realization that our functioning is to a large extent controlled by the Physio-clusters that are attached to activated Bad Clusters!

Physio-clusters never act by themselves

As we already know, Physio-clusters will only become active if the attached Cluster gets activated. They never act by themselves! This always occurs by incoming sensory data from the outside! When incoming data activates normal Clusters, the physiology it produces is proper for the occasion, but in the case of Bad Clusters, those physiological connections are always negative and not logically related to the situation you are in. To illustrate this, let's go to a moment when you came into a cozy room with a lot of friendly people:

> ***Example:***
> You feel comfortable among all these joyous and laughing people. The music and the candlelight create an atmosphere that makes you feel relaxed and happy. You observe the interior of the room. The antique furniture, the red plush curtains, the silver candlesticks, the tastefully set table, the Persian rug on the floor, and you take in all these things. Your host invites you to take a seat at the table. Someone sitting next to you is talking with the person across. They are discussing the death of one of their fathers. The dinner is about to start. A lovely fish soup with dry white wine is served. You take a sip of wine. After that, you taste the soup. Suddenly you feel very sick. You have the feeling of falling into a deep pit, as if you are going to faint. Was it the wine perhaps? Did you drink it too quickly, or was it the soup? Every possibility runs through your mind. You cannot understand how you suddenly feel so bad and for no reason at all.

Nothing threatening happened

What just happened? Why do you suddenly feel so bad? All the other guests appear to be just fine. It can't be the soup or the wine because all the other guests ate and drank as well. That's true, so it isn't because of the soup or wine, it's because a Bad Cluster was activated. But how? Everything seemed to be going along just fine. There was nothing there to call up a bad memory! That is precisely the problem with Bad Clusters! Nothing bad has to be happening for one to be activated; in fact, Bad Clusters are usually activated in perfectly harmless situations. It is not necessary to remember bad events. You may be as happy as a fish in water, when suddenly, there it is! The only thing needed is a trigger moment. And they were definitely present in this occasion. Which Bad Cluster was activated? Let us take a look into the subconscious mind to see which Bad Cluster was activated and why this happened.

> ***Bad Cluster*:**
> Nine years ago, you were invited to a dinner party at your best friend's house. He has a beautiful old home decorated with antiques. There are red plush curtains on the windows. Tomato soup was served with a glass of sweet white wine. Afterwards, fish was served with dry white wine. While you are taking advantage of the fine meal, the telephone rings. You see your friend looking with concern in your direction as he is talking on the telephone. As soon as he hangs up, he looks at you seriously and says he has some bad news to tell you: *"The telephone call was about your father"*. You ask, "*What is it? What is wrong with my father?"* Your friend sadly replies, *"He had a fatal car accident."* Your throat closes up, your heart skips a beat and you feel like all the

blood drains from your head. It's almost as if you are going to faint! In an instant, a Bad Cluster is created.

But it was an entirely different situation

How can such a Bad Cluster bother you after being silent for nine years? And on top of that, the current situation involved someone entirely different, a different house, different furniture, different food and the table was laid out very differently. You would have never associated this evening with the previous one. Apparently, there isn't anything around to remind you of the previous frightful event! Besides, that event took place nine years ago. You would think that after nine years you would be somewhat recovered from what occurred. Perhaps you had indeed worked through your grief over the death of your father, however, the Bad Cluster that was created at the time has remained untouched in your Database. Then what activated this Bad Cluster? Just as with all Bad Clusters, it was called up by trigger moments, basic similarities! What were the similarities in this instance?

Nine years ago	Now
Antique furniture	*Antique furniture*
Red plush curtains	*Red plush curtains*
Soup with white wine	*Soup with white wine*
The taste of fish	*The taste of fish*
The taste of dry white wine	*The taste of dry white wine*
The news about an accident causing your father's death	*A conversation about a father's death*

The similarities are clear. Yes, but back then there was tomato soup with sweet wine and now there is fish soup with dry white wine, and the news about the accident came from a friend and now there is only the discussion of a father's death between others, and about a man I don't even know! To refresh our memory: why are Clusters and Bad Clusters activated? To be used as comparison material in order to assign the correct value to new incoming data. The subconscious does not think or feel when doing this. It merely takes the data stored in the Database that shows the greatest similarity to the new incoming data. The Bad Cluster will be one of the many pieces of comparison material that was activated. The specific data that the Bad Cluster contained showed enough similarity to activate it as comparison material. From this experience you might develop a belief system that white wine is not good for your health, or that the combination of white wine and soup is bad for you. These are relatively innocent belief systems, but many of our most fundamental belief systems are also dictated by Bad Clusters! As long as Bad Clusters reign in your system, new incoming data will determine your feelings, decisions, opinions, functioning and success in a negative way!

Emotions

Our processing of the new incoming factual data of an event forms our emotions. In other words: emotion is not created by some external emotionality of the event itself, but purely by our personal subconscious comparison process that dictates our conscious interpretation of the incoming sensory data of the event. We would not be able to make any interpretation if we would have no emotional material to compare the new data to. This means that the emotional load (physiology) of the activated comparison material will determine what type and intensity level of the emotion will be that we will feel as a reaction on the new incoming sensory data. The ligand configuration will determine what kind and the intensity of our emotions. Just compare our adult reaction to the reactions of a very young child. You can start to cry after seeing an extremely emotional scene on television but the child feels nothing at all. It has no comparison material with enough physiological load to cause such emotions. We are all born with a basic operating system for our emotions. This basic operating system needs to be programmed in order to be able to feel the variety and intensity of emotions an adult can feel. We program our emotions based on the pain/pleasure scale:

- *Do we like it, or not*
- *Pleasure / more pleasure*
- *Pain / less pain*

Our experiences throughout our life will determine to what level of intensity we program our emotions. One occasion will build its emotions on top of the previous one. Together this creates our individual comparison material! Over time we will have more and more nuances and intensity in our emotions. We do not feel our emotions out of the blue. The physiological load of previously stored factual data that we use as our comparison material shapes our emotions. The activation of that data creates our present emotions, all nicely transported through ligand combinations. Your reality is the final conclusion of the comparison process of factual data and the activated emotion (physiology) attached to that data. Your decision and actions are always based on your reality! The main drive is not your factual analysis but the attached emotion.

Ligands determine the relative value of data

So far, we have focused on how ligands control our feelings and the intensity of our emotions. However, through this unique Ligand system, even the slightest physiological change is perceived, encoded, stored, and ready for use as comparison material. Through the endless possibilities provided by the Ligands, our subconscious is able to systematize and rubricate our feeling. This is very important in daily life. It enables us to experience the relative value of information through the slightest physiological change (for instance, if we recognize previous observed data). We usually don't consider this as emotions or feelings, but actually they are and the subconscious will read and process these neuro-physiological codes therefore the same way. Lets look at an example to illustrate the importance of this process:

> ***Example*:**
> You are working on your computer. You put your cup of coffee next to your keyboard. You've done this many times before. The relative value of the fact that your coffee is next to your keyboard is very low. However, regardless of how low the importance is, it is determined by a relative code. This means that this fact will activate a certain combination of ligands that transport and register this relative value. Suddenly a child runs by and hits the cup. The coffee is spilled all over your keyboard. Your keyboard is damaged and you have to buy a new one. The very next day someone puts a cup of coffee next to your keyboard. What will you do? Do you feel nothing, or will you immediately put the cup somewhere else, at a safe distance from your keyboard? Of course you would! Why? The Cluster containing the negative feelings you created the day before has been activated. This Cluster contains the accident with the coffee connected to the Physio-cluster that stored the physiological codes that caused the symptoms of your emotion when the coffee was spilled all over your keyboard.

It was the same cup, same location next to your keyboard, but a totally different feeling. You recognize the activated physiological code as a feeling in your body. But to the subconscious, which cannot feel, it is just a matter of relative codes. It does not matter to the subconscious if the code is low or high. It acts on the stimulus/response rule and will always activate the highest code if there is enough similarity between new incoming information and the existing Clusters in its Database. Even if we do not consciously feel the effect of the executed physiological codes (in case of a lower relative value), the subconscious - or more precise - the related antennas on each cell, will register, process and act on it! The emotions we clearly feel follow this exact same process. The only difference is they are stronger, with more ligands and more cells involved. The strongest emotions of all with the highest relative codes originate from Bad Clusters. We already mentioned several times the existence and the enormous power of Bad Clusters. But what actually are Bad Clusters? How do we get them, and even more important, how do we get rid of them?

Chapter 5 – The activation of Clusters and Bad Clusters

The subconscious sees no difference

To understand how Bad Clusters are created, activated and control us in so many aspects of our life, we first have to understand how a normal encoded memory, a Cluster, is used as comparison material by the subconscious. We store normal processed information in Clusters. We have billions of them, small Clusters and big Clusters. If you didn't have these you wouldn't even be able to understand where you are or what you are doing at this very moment. You would not be able to think, reason or make decisions. This also means that literally every decision you make is based on and dictated by the comparison material in these Clusters and Bad Clusters.

So far, we understand that we have a huge Database in our brain and that we need this Database to interpret new incoming data. In other words, to understand everyday events we need the already stored comparison material. The subconscious activates and automatically processes data that resembles the new incoming data. Data is data, regardless of whether it is found in a Cluster or a Bad Cluster. The subconscious does not care about the difference between a Cluster and a Bad Cluster! It can not feel or think. It just reads and processes codes, without judgment, just executing its genetic stimulus/response program. The activation and processing of comparison material is an automatic stimulus/response process. If enough similarity exists between the present observations and the contents of the Cluster, or Bad Cluster, then the Cluster or Bad Cluster will become active whether you want it to, or not, and whether you are consciously aware of it, or not. The data of the Bad Cluster is stored in the same brain cells as the data of the conscious (Cluster) memories. The emotions that come from Bad Clusters are very powerful and always negative.

Emotions are individual

A great deal has already been written about emotions. It is a topic that for ages has held the attention of psychologists. Many theories have been developed describing what emotions are and how they come to be. None of these theories, however, have ever been proven and what's more, they do not even agree with each other. However, one thing is agreed upon: emotions are very individual. An emotion is something that must be experienced by only yourself. There is no universal standard for the degree of an emotion that we should feel in a certain situation. Neither can you convey the intensity of your emotions to others. The other person can never feel your exact emotions! They can try to, based on their own comparison material, but it will never be the same emotion just as you feel it. This can be compared to trying to explain the color red to someone who is colorblind, or to explain to someone deaf from birth what a violin sounds like. But doesn't everyone get the same basic emotions from the moment of conception? Of course, but that genetic program does not define the intensity and the degree of the emotions! All people, regardless of race, religion, and no matter where they were born, have the same innate program for their basic emotions from the earliest moments of their lives.

Emotions are inborn

Every baby has the same basic emotional program that allows the expressing of sorrow, joy, pain, disgust, and anger. On the other hand, the intensity of your emotions and the fine tuning and variation of feelings are a different matter; it depends on what you experience in your life. You can easily detect that your personal emotions clearly differ from the genetic basic emotions that all babies share. What is more important is to discover what role emotions play in our existence and what could be the results of extreme emotions. One thing is certain, every human being has received the potential and the equipment to feel emotions and to further develop. The fact that each person feels emotions in a personal way is due to the fact that every individual has his/her own experiences.

Intensity is learned

Why do people react so differently to the same stimulus? Why does one person get angry at something, while another just shrugs their shoulders at it? Why does one person become very emotional and starts crying in a certain situation when another feels absolutely nothing? Why does one person feel disgust or horror whereas another has absolutely no idea why? The fact that there are such great differences cannot be denied. We see this difference around us everyday. How does this come about? It has even become a cliché to say, *"Everyone is different."* Are we different because of genetic reasons? Certainly! No two individuals are born with the exact same genetic structure. Is that why we all react emotionally different? This is highly unlikely because every person is born with the same basic emotions! It is certainly possible that people appear genetically different in their energy reserves and in how much stress they can handle. One family is more emotional than the other. Is this inherited or is it caused by what we have learned and experienced in our life? The difference in how newborn babies express basic emotions, regardless of where in the world they were born, shows no great difference. Regardless of whether the baby will turn out to be highly intelligent or not, will be black, white, red, yellow or brown, if his parents are rich or poor, all healthy babies in their first phase of life react in the same predictable emotional pattern. As the person grows, the difference in the way we experience and express emotions becomes more distinct. These differences are learned. Although a certain part certainly depends on genetic aspects, we would like to get an idea of how emotions are determined by acquisition or learning. When our emotions are influenced by acquired or learned things, then it should be possible to make changes in our emotional life. Every person is unique because no one on Earth has experienced the same things that another person has. Every person applies his/her own combination of individual experiences and then stores this in Clusters and Bad Clusters. On account of this very individualized collection of Clusters and Bad Clusters, every person is unique in his/her emotional reactions. A very substantial portion of our emotional experiences is accumulated in our youth.

The neuro-physiology behind emotions

What is the neuro-physiological the process behind emotions? First you perceive something through your senses. Then this activates comparison material in your Cortex. Connected to that comparison material is the physiological load stored in the Limbic System. This gets activated after the comparison material is selected. The Limbic System receives the signals from the Cortex and sends out its ligand combinations to several cells in the body. The cells instantly respond. The effect of that creates the symptoms of your emotions. The body has millions of little antennas (receptors) that register these symptoms, or changes, and sends a signal to the Frontal Lobe of the brain where an important part of the conscious is located. These symptoms are recognized by the conscious brain because they are incoming data and they are already present in the Database from previously stored experiences. These symptoms do not enter the subconscious through one of our five senses, but come from our sixth sense, our emotions. Why do we call emotions our sixth sense? Because they follow the exact same kind of neuro-physiological route as smell, taste, sight, sound and touch. Like the other senses, emotions have their own specific area in the brain in the so called Frontal Lobe, where they are perceived and stored. The incoming signals, this time from inside our body, are processed and compared with previously stored comparison material in exactly the same way as the sensory information that enters the brain from outside of our body through our five senses.

Your perception is your reality!

What creates our assessment, our decisions, our opinions, and our reality? Some people think that just one objective reality exists and this reality represents the truth. This might be right, but what purpose does this serve if nobody can recognize this "objective" reality? Each one of us is only able to bring into play our own personal collected data to compare with new incoming data, because that's all we have!

> ***Example***:
> If you would show a knife to a little baby, will it recognize the knife as such? Or will it try to grab it because you're moving it and it looks shiny? Does the baby realize how dangerous a knife is? No, the baby does not even realize any of this! In the reality of the baby, a knife represents no danger until it actually cuts a finger and feels the pain.

This simple example lets us understand that our reality is always 100% based on our previously stored comparison material and the belief systems we've already derived from that material. This leads to the following conclusions:

- Your reality is not what you see, hear, feel, smell, taste or experience.
- Your reality is <u>your interpretation</u> of what you see, hear, feel, smell, taste and experience.
- Your interpretation is exclusively based on your comparison material.
- Your reality is shaped by the relative code that you previously assigned to your comparison material.
- Out of this individual reality, you develop your belief systems.
- Your belief systems determine your assessment, decisions, actions and behavior.

The technical process of comparing new information with existing data is a universal operating system that works the same for all people. However, there are two major aspects that differ from person to person:

1. *No one has the same combination of sensory stored data in the Cortex.*
2. *Even if two people have some of the same type of data, no one has the same physiological, or relative code, connected to that same data.*

This is the reason that we are all different. You are unique, like everybody else! Although the conscious, the subconscious and physiological mechanisms are the same for all of us, no one has the same factual Database and no one feels exactly the same about each thing. If we all did, life would be rather boring, don't you think?

Feelings override thoughts

As a human being we can think and reason. This process leads to decisions that decide our future. What are the ingredients for our thoughts and reasoning processes? These are everything we have already stored; and if this is not enough, we do research and add the necessary information to our Database. This is all factual data! We need that to come to final conclusions and decisions. However, the final conclusion and decision will always be based on our comparison material, and more precisely, on the attached feelings. Some people are convinced that they make many of their decisions in a purely rational way. Especially in the corporate world, many managers have the belief system that there is no place for emotions. How wrong they are! If they don't change that belief system, then their company will not be around in fifteen years. There is no such thing as a rational decision!

> ***Example*:**
> You have to make an important decision in your company. The company is doing okay the way it operates at present, but a new approach would make more profit. You have the choice to continue your marketing approach just as it is, or to try a new approach an advisor suggested. This new approach will make an older employee who has worked for the company many years, obsolete. His skills are not needed anymore in the new approach. What will you do?

You could reason that the decision for the above example is only a matter of rational facts! You have to run a company and that company has to make profit. If that employee is not needed anymore, he has to go! You could say: *"See, this has nothing to do with feelings. This is purely rational!"* Is this really so? You could also argue: *"Of course, if feelings would play a role, I would never fire a loyal, elderly employee that worked for us for so long!"* Let us look at the drive behind the "rational" reason that you chose for better profit. Is that just a rational matter of numbers: more profit? What if you would choose to keep him and continue the old approach?

Your "rational" arguments can be:

- *It is expected from me that I make the maximum profit. If I do not make enough profit, I will lose my job.*
- *It gives me a kick when I create more income for the company.*
- *I need this because I want get a promotion and feelings only get in my way.*

And you can probably think of many more arguments. Is the nature of these arguments rational or emotional? What about the fear of loosing your job and the "kick" you experience, and the desire for a promotion? Are they rational arguments or emotions? You have no bad feelings towards that elderly and loyal employee. Nevertheless, you decided to let him go. Not because of the rational arguments, but because your emotions regarding the fear of losing your job, the "kick", and the desire for a promotion are stronger than your feelings for the older employee!

All our decisions, assessments and judgments are emotional!

Try to find one single decision that you have made that was not dictated by what you feel. You will not find them, not even one!

The lemon

There is another example from daily life that we can all relate to and will show how physical reactions are evoked by incoming sensory data. In this case it is not even a decision you are forced to make, but is simply caused by becoming aware of sensory data and you cannot stop your body from responding to it physically.

> ***Example*:**
> Are you familiar with the taste of a lemon? Now imagine yourself observing someone take a bite into a lemon. Aside from the puckered face that you may make just thinking about it, there are also other physiological reactions. Try to really imagine this happening! What are you feeling? Everyone who is familiar with the taste of a lemon will probably feel it in their salivary glands. You can feel the reaction in your mouth, almost as if you had taken the bite into the lemon yourself.

Why is that?

This is caused by all the times in the past that you tasted the sourness of a lemon. Each time, a physiological reaction was activated. You know what a lemon looks like, what it feels like in your hand, and how it tastes. All this data is stored in Clusters, and the Physio-clusters connected to them have all the physiological reactions stored in them. The appearance and the fact that you see someone biting into the lemon are memory moments that stir the Database to activate the "lemon" Clusters. The physiological data attached to these Clusters are mindlessly executed, whether you are the one eating the lemon or someone else is. The Cluster was activated, so the connected Physio-clusters are executed! Actually it is not even necessary to see the lemon being eaten. Just reading the word *lemon* and the fact that someone might bite into one, can stimulate a physiological reaction in you, while in your mind you see the entire event happening.

The dentist

Our lives are scattered with numerous examples that demonstrate the coupled reactions between Clusters and Physio-clusters. Let's dig somewhat deeper into this.

> ***Example*:**
> A child goes to the dentist for the first time. Excitedly, he climbs up into the chair. Now the child looks around and begins to find all the strange equipment as a bit intimidating. *Hey! What is that guy doing now? He's picking at my teeth with that sharp thing! What is that thing? A drill? Ouch, that hurts!* Various physiological reactions are set into motion. The child pales, lets out a wail, feels frightened and gets a curious knot in his stomach. Six months later he is told that he has to visit the dentist that very afternoon. Immediately the child pales, lets out a wail, feels frightened and gets a curious knot in his stomach. You can understand it well enough. All the data from the previous visit was stored in a Cluster. (We are assuming that the pain was not so bad that an actual Bad Cluster was created, although this can be true for any event we experience as extreme). The physiological data is also connected to this Cluster. The Cluster was activated when the child heard the news that a visit to the dentist was imminent (*dentist* being the decisive activating word). The particular Cluster comes up and the physiological data attached to it is executed.

Clusters and Bad Clusters

Everything we experience is nicely stored in our memory in Fragments and Sub-clusters that together form Clusters. We have millions, probably billions, of them. So far, we have discussed how we process and store Clusters. To understand the way these Clusters are stored is essential to the techniques that PMA uses to achieve its results. But under certain circumstances the brain does not store the Clusters in the normal analyzed, encoded way. By means of protection at the moment they were formed, some experiences are stored wrongly and therefore not available for later retrieval. We call these wrongly stored Clusters: Bad Clusters.

All the sensory data has the same relative code

Bad Clusters are, just like Clusters, collections of pieces of data that together form a unit. The greatest difference between the two is that the data in Bad Clusters is unanalyzed. This means that the absolute code (identity) has not been assigned and all the Fragments are individually connected to the same relative value. Therefore, all the pieces of data have the same high relative value. The associated physiological codes are also the same. A relative code of a Bad Cluster is the highest code possible! If the Bad Cluster is activated, then its physiology is replayed and re-experienced without us even being aware of the content of the Bad Cluster.

Why we call it a "Bad" Cluster

We call these wrongly stored Clusters a "Bad" Cluster because it resembles the bad Cluster on a computer storage device that contains data that cannot be retrieved by the operating system. The name is fitting because the effects of Bad Clusters are always bad; they limit our abilities, cause negative behavior, damage our health and hide a lot of energy that we could use for positive aspects in our lives. We will learn a lot about what a Bad Cluster is, how it comes into existence, the negative influence it has on our life and, more importantly, how we are able to change its negative power into positive energy!

Imagine a huge library with millions of books

There is a considerable difference in how we store a Cluster and how we store a Bad Cluster. To deepen our understanding about this, we can compare the storage and processing of data in our subconscious with a huge library. A library building has at least 20 stories loaded with books. All the books have written on the back a number, title and name of the author. In the basement of the building there is a computer. It contains the data of all the books. If you know the title, the author or a number, it will tell you exactly where in the library you can find the book. It also has a brief summary of the contents of the book. You can compare these to how your Clusters are stored. However, there are some books that have no name of author, no number or title! You cannot find them in the computer. These are your Bad Clusters! The huge library is your Database - the Cortex - where all your “books” (Clusters and Bad Clusters) are stored. The computer in the basement is the Thalamus. All the Clusters are registered there. It will tell you their code and where they are stored in the Cortex. However, you will not find any code for the Bad Clusters. The subconscious is a sophisticated computer with its own language based on strict rules and programs. It does not think, reason, argue or feel. It just acts, based on the stimulus/response rule.

Bad Clusters

Similar to Clusters, Bad Clusters are stored events as well as a collection of data that together form a unity. However, the content of a Bad Cluster has not been correctly analyzed and coded! The data in a Bad Cluster has not been assigned the correct codes to store it as usable comparison material. They were stored during an event that caused an emotional overload for the conscious and therefore, it was not able to assign the proper relative codes. This overload also effected the subconscious assigning process of the absolute codes. Bad Clusters are responsible for all the existing psychosomatic symptoms, unreasonable fears and destructive behavioral patterns.

How and when are Bad Clusters created?

Bad Clusters are only created during an event that you experience as traumatic. This can happen during moments of humiliation, physical violence, rejection, betrayal, incest, sexual abuse, torture, an accident, or a disaster. Even things like an angry parent, being locked in a small room, receiving a shocking message, staying in a hospital, and similar painful incidents can form a Bad Cluster. Whether you create a Bad Cluster or not will differ from person to person, and from event to event. It depends on the situation, your background, constitution, health, age and several other aspects. Does that mean that there is no rule to determine when, or when not, you will create a Bad Cluster? If you are expecting a list of events that create Bad Clusters, the answer is – no! However there is a rule that describes exactly when a Bad Cluster will be formed:

A Bad Cluster is the unavoidable result of the feeling that you lose total control.

What exactly do we mean by loss of control? Some psychologists tell us that the biggest fear of all people is to go crazy. What they actually mean is "losing control". If a situation becomes too scary or painful that you panic and you have the feeling that you fall into a bottomless pit without anything to hold on to, that's when you lose control.

A matter of perception

The determining factor is not how traumatic an experience is to objective outsiders. The seriousness of the trauma is solely determined by how <u>you</u> perceived it at that time. As a result of that extreme fear that exists in our body at the moment we feel that we lose control, our brain stores the experience, but it does not give the correct relative code or label to the incoming sensory data. The absence of the correct codes will make it later impossible for your conscious mind to recall the complete picture of that event. Maybe years later, at a given moment or place, you suddenly experience fear or an uncomfortable feeling, but you don't know why. Your heart starts pounding without any apparent reason. You suddenly feel emotionally blocked or your mood suddenly changes (mood swings) but you can't find a rational reason what's causing those feelings. This is all produced by the activation of a Bad Cluster. The feeling will remain as long as your senses perceive a combination of sensory signals, enough to activate the Bad Cluster. If this happens over a longer period of time it will have an enormous impact on your health and well being. Activated Bad Clusters are always strong and harmful "jamming stations" of your daily functioning and they damage your relationships, overall health and prevent you from improving and progressing in all aspects of life. That's why it is so important to get rid of the negative power of these Bad Clusters and release their huge amount of energy for positive ambitions.

An extreme physiological state during rest

As we already mentioned, every Bad Cluster has a Physio-cluster as an attachment. Inside the Physio-cluster, we find the entire package of physiological codes that were present in the body at the time the Bad Cluster was stored. Since the normal processing of the subconscious was blocked at that time, nothing contained in the Bad Clusters was assigned an absolute code and therefore, all the data is equally loaded with intense and painful physiology. Consequently, a simple thing such as a color, scent, shape, word or taste can activate strong negative feelings. The more Fragments (or even Sub-clusters) of the Bad Cluster become activated, the more the negative feelings will intensify.

Obstinate physiological reactions

What are the consequences of an activated Bad Cluster? Why is the Physio-cluster that is attached to a Bad Cluster always executed as soon as that Bad Cluster is activated? Isn't a Bad Cluster useless comparison material for the subconscious? It can't read it, right? If a Bad Cluster cannot be read, then why isn't it just rejected by the subconscious as useless? Well, precisely because it is unreadable! In order to be able to label a Bad Cluster as unreadable, its codes must first be determined. In order to do that, it must be readable. Because it is not, the Bad Cluster is "stuck" in the subconscious. As a result, the subconscious keeps executing its attached Physio-cluster. How long this lasts depends on the continuity of the incoming data. As long as the incoming signals are still there, the Bad Cluster will continue to be active. The physiology that is attached to the Bad Cluster will continue to be executed until the Bad Cluster has been pushed aside by the subconscious because the incoming sensory data that activate the Bad Cluster disappears. But why won't the subconscious simply reject the Bad Cluster as comparison material since it causes such negative feelings?

There are two important reasons why the subconscious cannot not do that:

1. *The subconscious cannot feel.*
2. *It cannot reject comparison material with such a high relative code.*

The subconscious is a sophisticated stimulus/response machine. It does not think or feel. It just acts and reacts on incoming signals by carrying out its genetically determined comparison program. Keep in mind that the subconscious program is based on codes. It can read and process all kinds of data that is properly encoded. This does not mean that its restricted to the absolute codes. The subconscious can read relative codes, as well.

It cannot reject it

We know that the subconscious processes a million times more data than what can ever reach the conscious brain. So, what does it do with all that extra data? Well, for selecting the most usable pieces out of it for comparison and to process new incoming data in the most save and healthy way for our body. By following its genetic program and rules it finally selects the data that is important to analyze the identity of the incoming sensory data to give it the most precise absolute code. It also selects the data based on the highest relative code. Once selected, the attached physiology of the data is carried out. The feelings that this creates in the body are perceived by the conscious brain and are the underpinning in which the conscious brain assigns the new data its relative value. As soon as incoming sensory data activates the content of a Bad Cluster, the subconscious has to deal with its content. The subconscious will try to separate the data with the highest relative code in the Bad Cluster, as it always does with normal encoded Clusters, and separate the more relevant from the irrelevant data in the Cluster with a lower relative code. That's when the problem starts. All the data in this "crazy" Bad Cluster has the same extreme high relative code. Nevertheless, to select, analyze and connect it to the new incoming data, the subconscious needs differentiation, even if it is just the smallest distinction between the pieces of data. But there is no distinction in the relative codes in a Bad Cluster, not even the smallest!

"Houston we have a problem"

If astronauts are in outer space and their spaceship suddenly shows a defect, they often don't know what to do other than just call their home base with the message: *"Houston we have a problem!"* Unfortunately, the automated stimulus/response machinery of our subconscious has no *Houston* to call and solve its problems. Now, what do we do? It is bound to its natural rules of stimulus/response and selecting the data with the highest relative code. Tied to its rules, it cannot make the necessary differentiations to pass its analysis on to the conscious brain. It cannot pass through its filters nor reject this data, either. Consider the following metaphor:

> ***Metaphor*:**
> You receive an envelope from the IRS and immediately open it because you know the letters I-R-S have a high relative value. You start to read the letter, but to your surprise, you realize that there is no logic in the wording of the letter. It is just a bunch of randomly chosen words without any meaning in the sentence. In other words, there is no absolute code (identity) given, and therefore, all the words have the same relative value: this letter is from the IRS! You cannot derive its clear message and as a result, its content is totally useless to you. Would you throw it away? Of course not! It is from

the IRS. You will carefully keep it as proof for later (in case the IRS contacts you) to show that nobody was able to understand the content of their letter. You don't throw it away because it has a high "relative code, or value"!

The value of an activated Bad Cluster has a similar high value for the subconscious. Its codes make absolutely no sense to the subconscious mechanisms. But one thing is clear, it is unable to just throw away data with such high relative codes because its genetic programs don't allow it! It is not able to make logical connections between the Bad Cluster data and the new incoming data. Keep in mind that the subconscious cannot feel. It just reads codes! In this case, it just reads the high relative codes. After the execution of those types of codes, we consciously start to feel the symptoms of the emotions that are caused by the physiological changes.

Clusters with negative physiology

From time to time we all experience unpleasant events. We store these negative experiences as Clusters because they were not scary enough to make us lose control and create a Bad Cluster. Do we also experience negative energy from them? Yes, actually we do, but their physiological power is not nearly as strong as that of Bad Clusters. Why is that? In storing Clusters, the subconscious always follows its program precisely, as set forth in its genetic rules. One of the basic rules is that it will always connects new incoming data with existing data that has a physiological code that is as far *away from pain* as possible. This means it will always select similar previously stored data with the lowest possible relative code. After selecting the most suitable comparison material, the subconscious sends its analysis to the conscious brain and carries out the physiology that was attached to the selected comparison material. The physical symptoms, as a result of that process, will be registered by the conscious brain. Based on these registrations of these symptoms (feelings), the conscious brain assigns the new incoming sensory data its relative code. However, the subconscious cannot just select any single piece of data purely based on their lowest relative code. In this process, the subconscious has to obey the stimulus/response rule and the rule that it always selects the data with the highest relative code while keeping perfect harmony with the *away from pain* rule.

Based on the stimulus/response rule, the Clusters that display the largest amount of similarity with the present situation will be selected as the most fitting comparison material. If there are no Clusters that qualify, the subconscious will then choose comparison material at a deeper, more detailed level and select the Sub-cluster with the most similarity to the new incoming data. If they, too, are not available, it will go again at one level deeper and activate Fragments with similar content. Nevertheless, if Clusters are available with an overall content that equals the present event, it will always follow its rule of stimulus/response and select that Cluster because of its largest amount of similarity to the present event. In the case that there are several Clusters that display an overall picture that equals the present situation, the subconscious will choose the one with the higher relative values over the one with lower relative values. Ultimately, in the case of an activated Bad Cluster, this way of processing has a far-reaching consequence!

When a Bad Cluster is activated, its physiology creates strong physical symptoms, together creating an emotion. These strong physical symptoms are now consciously registered and as such stored in a Cluster. Let's say the Bad Cluster activation takes place in your living room. This experience in your living room is now stored in a Cluster, including the negative symptoms caused by the activated Bad Cluster physiology. If at a later time you enter that living room again, this specific Cluster of that activated experience will be included in the comparison material that is selected by the subconscious to analyze the incoming data. It has no choice! It can only follow its rules, and this specific Cluster has so many similarities, because it is the data of the same living room that enters your brain, and on top of that the data contained in it has a very high relative code.

It is a matter of speed

Due to the strict language rules of the subconscious, it is unable to connect every new incoming sensory information to just any piece of comparison material, solely based on the *away from pain* rule, for a*way from pain* is not the only rule that controls the subconscious language. If the combined incoming data of the present picture automatically activates (stimulus/response) entire Clusters with a similar overall content, then the subconscious has to use the data of that Cluster because of its large amount of similar data. However, this leaves unimpeded that the subconscious will operate according to what its rules allow it to do and it will still store the new data as less painful or as less negative as possible!

In this process Clusters with a negative content will not cause us nearly as much problems as an activated Bad Cluster! The main reason that we do not experience so much negative physiology from negatively loaded Clusters as from Bad Clusters is because the Clusters are processed at such high speed. As we already know, an activated Bad Cluster gets stuck in the process because the subconscious cannot read its content and is unable to reject it. Because this occurs, its physiology will be carried out for a longer period of time. Because of their proper codes, Clusters are activated and selected at a tremendous speed. The moment we start to feel their physiology, the next group of Clusters are already activated by new incoming data. New Clusters are now activated and processed and the previous set of comparison material, including their Physio-clusters are cleared. You can clearly experience the difference between these briefly activated Clusters and the ones that stay active for a longer period by performing a little experiment. To do so we chose a topic with positive physiology, for we want to prove that the intensity of the physiological symptoms are determined by the amount of time that it stays active in your subconscious. And why take a negative memory if we can prove this with a positive memory that will give you a good feeling!

Experiment:

First: Try to remember a recent dinner that you really enjoyed. Just remember it, don't relive it, don't focus on it! Immediately after that memory pops-up, think of something you have to do at your office or in the house, or anything else along those lines. What do you feel?

Second: Now try to relive that same wonderful dinner. Where was it? What did you eat? What did you taste? Who was there with you? What did you hear? Be there and focus longer on the event and focus on the most enjoyable moments.

Did you feel the difference? If the data of that same 'dinner' Cluster would have been activated as a part of a large number of other similar comparison material, you would feel the same thing you felt when you just briefly remembered the dinner. However, if you do not process it in such a high speed, as it normally would, and give it time by focusing on it, you feel its full physiological load. A Bad Cluster always gets stuck because it cannot be processed and therefore it will always carry out its full load of physiology.

No logic in a Bad Cluster

The Physio-cluster is executed as soon as the Bad Cluster is activated. It is activated only because separate pieces of new incoming sensory data show a similarity, and not because the situation as a whole is similar. This is very important to understand. Why? Because there is similarity in color, shape, taste, scent etc., that activate pieces (Fragments and Sub-clusters) of a Bad Cluster with each of them having its own connection to the Limbic System where the connected physiological commands are stored. Considering the above fact, if a Bad Cluster is activated, then we cannot expect to be able to logically understand the contents of the feelings caused by the Bad Cluster. The only thing we can be sure of is that the combination of single pieces of data in your surroundings have somehow served as triggers to repeatedly activate this Bad Cluster. However, the original circumstances in which the Bad Cluster was created has absolutely nothing to do with the present circumstances that later activated this Bad Cluster, for it are not really the circumstances that activated the Bad Cluster, but a combination of particular pieces of incoming data. That is why it is crucial to completely understand the following fact:

There is no logic in the contents of Bad Clusters! There is no rational connection between the present event and the event stored in a Bad Cluster.

If they are not just a few Fragments, but a whole Bad Cluster that's activated, then the emotions can reach extreme proportions. If it are just a few Fragments that are active our innate protection mechanism will hide the activation of a Bad Cluster for our conscious brain. To understand how that is possible we have to realize that a specific physiological reaction is not limited to just one emotion, nor does it appear in just one emotion. Consider for a moment how the heart rate can increase! It may increase during totally different emotions like excitement, anger, love, fear, but also during physical exertion. In the case of the latter, emotion is not even involved. Therefore, we must conclude that it is not only one single physiological reaction that determines that sort of emotion felt. Nor does an emotion consist of simply one physiological change. An emotion consists of a collection of different physical symptoms. The physical symptoms can also overlap in different emotions. One specific musical note doesn't make a tune although that same note will be a part of many songs. Before we can understand how our protection mechanism hides Bad Clusters for our conscious brain, let's examine some examples to get a feeling of what the effect of a Bad Clusters is.

WHAT IS A BAD CLUSTER

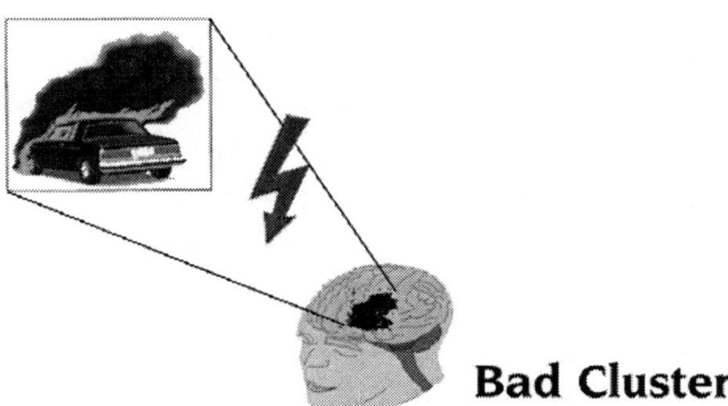

Traumatic experience that creates a short-circuiting in our brain, and therefore is stored different

Graphic example:
Imagine that you saw your best friend, child, parent or someone else you really love, getting into a car just before it catches fire. Before you can reach the car to pull your loved one out, the car explodes. You're freaking out! You will never forget this horrible event!

However, some moments in that event were so hard to emotionally grasp, that your mind went into 'protection mode'. In this mode the pictures that you could not cope with were excluded from your consciousness. Your brain did not process them in the normal way. It created a Bad Cluster of the moment your loved one was in that car. Can you remember the event? Yes, but what about the details? You absolutely do not know the ones that occurred at the time the Bad Cluster was formed.

Why are Bad Clusters created?

What aspect in a scary event causes our brain to go into overload and create a "short circuiting" that results in storing incoming information as incorrect encoded data? It happens at the moment we think we lose control, in other words, we panic! Our subconscious programs has the genetic programmed task to deliver enough information to the conscious brain so that we stay in control over our life. If we reach a state that we feel we lose control, we lose our grip on our existence. That is just too much! We are not made to handle and process that feeling correctly. The strongest force in us – *away from pain* – becomes active and will give us back the control. How? By narrowing down the world to a size that we can control.

How do we manage that? By using the innate module of our brain that enables us to concentrate. The result of that is the blocking of other incoming sensory information from getting through to the conscious brain. Unfortunately, the fear of control-loss is so powerful that it forces the actions of the "concentration" module to be totally out of proportion. It will block the conscious awareness of every incoming sensory data outside that "little world" we created and completely focus on at that moment. However, our ears, eyes, nose, taste and touch are technically in tact. This means all the information captured by our senses enters the brain as usual. The only difference is that the conscious part of the brain does not "examine" this data. However, the conscious part is the only part of the brain that can feel. It is the only part that can give incoming data its relative code. Isn't that also the case in a normal situation of concentration? But what about a non-threatening event where we concentrate? Is there not also a lot of data that enters the brain without any conscious awareness? Absolutely! But the *entering* of data is not the problem.

The existing physiology is the real problem

The real problem is the existing physiology at that time of the Bad Cluster event. In order not to lose control, we end up in an extreme state of alert, the highest state of *fight or flight*! This is the highest negative emotion that we as humans can experience, which, in fact, is not very healthy for our body! Just imagine what the subconscious will store. During a Bad Cluster event, all the incoming sensory data will be stored in the cortex connected to the physiological commands existing at that time. But that is the most negative emotion, or in other words, the most negative physiology that exists in the human body! Exactly! This is the real problem. The data is not the problem, but the physiology. The conscious brain is totally blocked at that time. The consequence of this is that every single color, shape, scent, taste, sound etc., will be assigned the exact same high negative level of relative code.

Emotionally loaded data is remembered better

Recent scientific findings have taught us that all the factual sensory data, that is stored in the Cortex, has a direct connection to the Limbic System. This shows us a new understanding of how we store and remember information. Without going into details it has created an insight that we can summarize in the following conclusion:

The more emotion we attach to sensory data, the better we remember that data

Therefore, the more emotions a teacher connects to its teachings, the better we remember the facts of what was taught. Now we know why! This is due to the neuro-physiological connections between the Cortex and the Limbic System. Based on this understanding, we could expect the data that enters the brain during a trauma, which contains the highest emotional load that we could ever imagine, be remembered in detail! Nevertheless, thousands of interviews have shown that this is not true! People that experienced a trauma were unable to recall a large amount of details. "*But isn't that normal, considering the situation*?" It is absolutely true from a human emotional point of view, but not from a neuro-physiological stand point! Based on the Cortex/Limbic System connection, combined with the fact that the subconscious always selects the comparison material with the highest relative code, we should be able to remember even the smallest detail. However, based on these facts we must conclude that during a trauma, during a moment that we are so afraid and shocked that we totally lose control, our brain goes into overload, into a short-circuiting! Let's look at a practical real life example of a man who practiced the PMA technique:

***Example*:**
Jake was a man who had a great career in sales and a promising future. But he had a car accident and was home for two years feeling sick, tired, depressed, having headaches, etc. He visited several psychologists and therapists; none of them was able to help him. Frustrated, he didn't want to spend any more time or money on discussing the accident, *"I remember <u>everything</u> about it and don't see the point of going through it all over again."*
Fortunately, he agreed to try PMA because he had been told it was different and it was a powerful technique. He was able to get initial assistance from an experienced PMA Coach. He indicated that he bumped into a car and another one crashed into the back of him. His PMA Coach asked him the following odd sounding questions:

- PMA Coach: *"What was the color of the car you bumped into?"*
  Jake: *"Blue ... um... no red, or was it white?"*

- PMA Coach: *"Was your radio on during the accident?"*
  Jake: *"I guess so, it usually is."*

- PMA Coach: *"Was it playing music or were you listening to conversations?"*
  Jake: *"I don't know. Does it matter?"*

- PMA Coach: *"Who was the first to approach you, a man or a woman?"*

Jake: *"Why do you ask? I don't know."*

- PMA Coach: *"What color of clothing was he or she wearing?"*

  Jake: *"What does that have to do with my complaints?"*

He couldn't answer any of the questions correctly. This indicates that a Bad Cluster had been formed during the event. He was not aware that a Bad Cluster was formed, but it was definitely there and it contained all the details, including the pain and emotion of that accident. The accident itself became a Bad Cluster, but the accident also contained many details that activated an earlier stored Bad Cluster. Because he kept talking about the part he did remember, he continued to constantly activate that Bad Cluster plus the previous one. This was the real cause of his health complaints. The PMA Coach was asking questions based on the subconscious language rules. The Coach wasn't interested in the *why* or *who* of the event, instead, in the *what* and *when*. He was looking for the elements that created connections through similarities at the subconscious level. Following these clues he could zoom into the event and easily trace the Bad Cluster. When they went deeper into the circumstantial details, gradually everything started coming back, not only the details of the accident, but also the earlier Bad Cluster that was activated by that accident. After both Bad Clusters were revealed, their harmful physiological influences instantly faded at that very moment. After the PMA session was done, all of the details had come back to him and, more importantly, the activated Bad Clusters had been traced and eliminated. As a result, the complaints had disappeared and he was able to get back to work. We all have experiences that we've stored as a Bad Cluster. They are not all as dramatic as this example, but we all have them, and they have a strong effect on our thinking, decisions, feelings and actions.

A Bad Cluster is not a suppressed memory!

In psychology we hear a lot about suppressed memories. This refers to negative events that you want to forget as soon as possible. It can be all kinds of things and you can have all kinds of arguments and reasons as to why you want to forget them. However, the force behind that process is always the same:

away from pain!

Our protection mechanism, the so called *Friend Mechanism* of which we will discuss in detail later on, is very powerful in shielding painful things from our consciousness. It can make us suppress memories that we have consciously experienced as if they never happened. Many psychologists and psychotherapists are satisfied if they succeed in bringing up suppressed memories. They discover that certain complaints of their client seem to be related to events they have suppressed. They try to discover these suppressed events because they live under the assumption that they are getting closer to the source, and therefore, to the solution of the problems. You might think, *"But, isn't that the same as what is done through PMA?"* The answer is: *"No, it's different in every aspect!"*

A fundamental difference

The first fundamental difference is that suppressed memories are the result of a conscious decision. This means that they are stored in Clusters and not in Bad Clusters! Our protection mechanism has forced us to do anything to help us suppress the memory. This can include lying to ourselves, imagining that things were different, etc. When therapists try to help their clients regain those suppressed memories, they are confronted with the same protection mechanism. This mechanism automatically tries to lead the person away from pain and guilt. To overcome the power of that mechanism, the therapist sometimes uses all available tricks, including suggestions and leading questions. Therefore, the outcome of this process often has shown to be very doubtful, and in some cases, even damaging. People may end up 'remembering' and belief things that never happened as to be true! Positive results are usually achieved by reasoning and conditioning to positively accept and review these regained memories. However, during this whole process, the Bad Clusters, which is the driving force behind suppressed memories, always stayed out of the picture. And as long as they remain undiscovered, they will keep giving the person hard times, in spite of any form of therapeutic conditioning. With normal suppressed memories and their common treatment, we see three unsatisfying effects:

1. People come up with, and start to belief in, incorrect memories, which can sometimes be quite damaging to themselves and others.

2. The root-cause of the pain is not taken away and remains hidden in the subconscious as a powerful neuro-physiological jamming station.

3. They now develop belief systems based on the provided rational explanation for their complaints and behavior. The belief systems comfort them but do not eliminate the root-cause of the problem. On the contrary! They empower and create a whole amount of incorrect belief systems that keep the Bad Cluster active.

Bad Clusters are totally different from suppressed memories! Bad Clusters have never reached our conscious mind, so to our awareness, they're not there and do not need to be suppressed. They are completely a matter of the subconscious. Remember, the subconscious does not reason and does not feel, therefore, it has no reason to suppress a Bad Cluster. It is just there and follows the strict rules of its subconscious program: stimulus/response. When you manage to trace it, it dissolves into a normal Cluster and its negative effects will disappear completely and forever. When you don't trace it, it keeps bugging you, no matter how hard you work on reasoning and conditioning yourself. With tracing and eliminating Bad Clusters we see the opposite effects:

1. *The root-cause will be revealed in a "non directive" way and with concrete results.*
2. *After tracing the Bad Cluster, their negative physiological effects will immediately be eliminated, completely and permanently.*
3. *Inhibiting belief systems disappear automatically or are easy to change.*
4. *It will unlock its large amount of energy for positive use.*

You cannot or you do not want to remember

If you cannot remember the content of a Bad Cluster, and you cannot remember the suppressed memory either, then what is the difference? The difference is caused by the way the subconscious processed both. To put it simple, a suppressed memory is a correct encoded Cluster that's accessible to the conscious brain. On the other hand, it is impossible to consciously access the content of a Bad Cluster because of its incorrect codes. You <u>cannot</u> remember a Bad Cluster spontaneously, but suppressed memories are stored in a Cluster that you don't <u>want</u> to remember! Let's look at an example to describe the difference between a suppressed memory and a Bad Cluster:

***Example*:**
Imagine a little six year old boy who witnessed a horrible crime committed by his own father. The child watched a confrontation between his father and an unknown man. His

THE MISSING PICTURE

father is always very kind and friendly. Our six year old never saw his father this angry. Both men are screaming and yelling. Suddenly, his father draws a gun. The child knows from T.V. what kind of damage a gun can do and is extremely scared by seeing the gun combined with the anger on his father's face and the fear on the face of the unknown man. At the moment that his father fires his gun, the child's brain goes into overload and creates a Bad Cluster.

After a while, the child slowly gains back his conscious awareness. The first thing he consciously notices is the devastating look on his fathers face and the unknown man on the floor in a pool of blood. The father did not notice his child was present until this moment. The father panics and grabs the child by his shoulders, shaking the child and yelling at him, *"You can never tell anybody what you saw here! If you tell anybody they will come and take me away from you and you will never see me again!"*

It is obvious that the child is terrified. He can't forget that horrible picture of the man on the floor and the fear on his father's face. Over and over the picture is coming to his mind and makes him feel terrible. Whenever this picture pops up, the child pushes it away, like he is adding a "stop sign" to that horrible picture. The picture in itself is terrifying enough, but every time the picture pops up, it activates the related Bad Cluster and its negative physiology. If this would just be an unpleasant "Cluster" experience, that did not create a Bad Cluster, then it will lose its unpleasant physiological load because our subconscious will follow its rules and connect it over time with a growing amount of other Clusters that have a more positive physiological load. The subconscious cannot do it any other way because it is genetically programmed to go as far *away from pain* as possible. The subconscious cannot make such connections with a Bad Cluster because it can't read its contents. The consequence of this is that the negative physiological load of the Bad Cluster will not diminish.

The cause of suppressed memories

Whenever a Bad Cluster becomes activated, its full negative physiological load will be carried out and felt. Just imagine what kind of impact this has on the child mentioned in our example! The child cannot bear that situation. He starts to push the memories (Clusters before and after the Bad Cluster) aside whenever they pop up, or in other words, he begins to suppress the entire event. How does that work in the subconscious? To understand this, we have to go back to the absolute and relative encoding of the data and the four basic rules of the subconscious language:

- *It is stimulus/response operated*
- *Away from pain*
- *Always selects the comparison material with the highest relative code*
- *If possible, it will always select the comparison material with the most positive relative code*

The highest relative code (physiology) that the conscious brain can give is the "panicking *fight or flight*" code during a moment we lose control and that is attached to every piece of the content of a Bad Cluster. But that is a short circuiting situation and it makes the data unreadable for the subconscious! The highest relative code that would still be readable is a code that will be assigned to the data of very negative events, but not that negative that we emotionally cannot handle it and lose control. As long as we are emotionally in control the data will be stored in normal encoded Clusters! We already know that the relative code represents the emotion we experience at that moment. What would be the highest emotion in the seconds prior and after a Bad Cluster short circuiting? It is a level of fear that comes very close to the Bad Cluster panic, but we are still able to normally manage and process the data of that event.

The mechanism of suppressing

Every time this horrible picture pops up, the child experiences strong fear because this picture (Cluster) has enough similarities with the content of the Bad Cluster to activate it. However, the situation he is in at such an activated moment is in itself not threatening or painful. Therefore, he will not create new Bad Clusters by these activated memories. He will store all those moments of activation, including the physical symptoms, in regular Clusters! If a Bad Cluster is activated as a whole, and not just as few Fragments or a Sub-cluster, the emotions will reach the maximum level of our capacity to process the data in a normal way and we will still be able to store them in a correct encoded Cluster. The conscious brain is not aware of the content of the Bad Cluster but does feel the effects of its negative physiology. The child does not want to feel this and therefore it consciously adds a specific relative code that notifies the subconscious that this picture is unwanted and that the conscious brain does not want to see it again, and then the suppressing process starts.

Based on the harmony between the rules of its language, the subconscious will automatically go as far *away from pain* as possible and select the data with the highest relative code. Whenever this includes specific comparison material to which the conscious brain added the "stop sign" code, then a conflict occurs. This "stop sign" material is stored in a Cluster, therefore, the subconscious can read and process it because it is correctly encoded and it is approachable for the conscious brain. But in the past, that same conscious brain added a special "stop sign" code to it that clearly states that it does not want to see this material! As a result of this dilemma, the subconscious will use these Clusters as comparison material but their content will not be delivered to the conscious brain. Nevertheless, it will carry out the attached physiology to this material. The activation of these specific Clusters in combination with the physical effects of their physiology is enough to activate the Bad Cluster.

"I lost the memory of several years of my childhood"

Normally you should at least be able to remember a lot of your childhood starting from the age of three, although some people remember many moments during their first year. However, many people complain that they have absolutely no memories before the age of eight, ten, or even fourteen, while others complain that they are only missing one or two years from their childhood memories. It is clear now that we cannot remember the content of a Bad Cluster. We also understand how we consciously choose to suppress memories, but how is it possible to lose several years of our memory? To understand this, let us go back to the example of our little six-year-old:

***Example*:**
The next day our little six year old boy goes to school. On his way to school the nasty pictures keep popping up activated by basic similarities, or triggers, in his surroundings. Whenever that happened, the child told himself ,*"I don't want to see that,"* and he forced himself to focus on other thoughts. However, the pictures do come up because of triggering similarities. Remember, one of the basic rules of the subconscious language is stimulus/response! This means that the location or event where the pictures were triggered will also receive the "stop sign" code. Why? Because the data of that present event or location caused the activation of the pictures. So, all the incoming data of that moment will receive that extra "stop sign" code of the conscious brain. Now imagine what this means. Wherever the pictures are activated (school, school yard, home, garden, playing with his friends, etc. etc.), the child will consciously focus on other thoughts and assign that special "stop sign" code to all the incoming sensory data in all those different circumstances and locations.

This process leads to a large amount of suppressed memories of all kinds of locations, people and events. By this, we are able to totally block a period as large as several years from our conscious memory! Keep in mind that all of these memories are Clusters and not Bad Clusters! This means that their content can be processed by the subconscious and is approachable for the conscious brain, for it was that part of the brain that put the "stop sign" on it. The good news is, it is that same conscious part of your brain, or in other words, you, who can override that code and allow the blocked pictures to come up again, if you really want them to.

It is all a matter of decisions and choices

Is it that easy? Technically, yes! However, humans are not machines and we will run into our protection mechanisms. Based on this mechanism, we create many inhibiting belief systems. We have to understand that as soon as we allow the suppressed pictures to come up, the Bad Clusters will automatically be activated, too. If you have no tools to undo the Bad Clusters of their powerful negative physiology, its symptoms will activate your protection mechanism. It cannot process the content of the Bad Cluster and is not allowed to deliver the suppressed data to the conscious brain because of its "stop sign" code. What could be powerful enough to override that code? Once again, it is always about the language of the subconscious, and its main rule is: *away from pain*! We discussed already that many times we do not have the option pain/pleasure, but only the option: pain/less pain. This insight can help us.

The first step is to fully understand that leaving your Bad Clusters untouched, and therefore, active in your subconscious, is way more dangerous and painful than tracing them and undoing them of their negative physiological load. Once you really understand that, you will activate your most powerful drive, *away from pain* to motivate yourself to find your Bad Clusters! The more you become aware of the physiological reactions in your body which leads to the understanding of how strongly Bad Clusters inhibit your success, relationships and health, the more you become motivated to find your Bad Clusters and dismantle them. On top of that, you will experience a large amount of positive energy whenever you trace a Bad Cluster. This motivation is also the result of physiological (relative) codes. The more you create leverage this way, the easier it becomes to override the "stop sign" code and make the conscious decision to allow all suppressed memories to come up in order to lead you to the related Bad Clusters.

You surround yourself with activating signals

Based on what we've discovered so far, it would be logical to conclude that we would stay as far away as possible from items, situations and people that activate, or trigger, our Bad Clusters. Since *away from pain* is our strongest drive, this sounds reasonable. Unfortunately, it is exactly this powerful drive that creates a situation that we voluntarily surround ourselves with triggers that activate Bad Clusters. We know by now how we store factual data attached to physiology. We also know how Clusters and Bad Clusters can both become activated material, purely because of the stimulus/response rule of the brain, without any control or awareness of the conscious brain. We also know that the strongest force in the human body is "*away from pain*". If we combine all this knowledge we are led to a peculiar conclusion. It leads us to the conclusion that we actually surround ourselves with signals that keep our Bad Clusters activated all of the time! Their negative physiology determines our total life. How is this possible? Why would we do such an insane and illogical thing? It is not as illogical as you might think. Let us see how that apparent illogical behavior is in reality very logical, if you understand the rules of the subconscious language.

Clusters, Sub-clusters and Fragments

Let us briefly go back to where we discussed the Clusters, Sub-clusters and Fragments and their connection with the Limbic System, where our physiology is arranged. Sometimes we remember an event but seem to miss a lot of details. Maybe we just remember a specific detail of an event without recollection of the whole occurrence. This is due to the way we store data. We store specific mental pictures (smell, taste, touch, feeling, sound and sight) in several divided levels. It can be a specific smell, taste, object, sound, or word, etc. We call that specific data a Fragment. If there are several Fragments combined into a bigger picture of the same sense, we call it a Sub-cluster. If several Sub-clusters are activated to form a complete memory, we call it a Cluster.

CLUSTERS SUB-CLUSTERS FRAGMENTS PART I

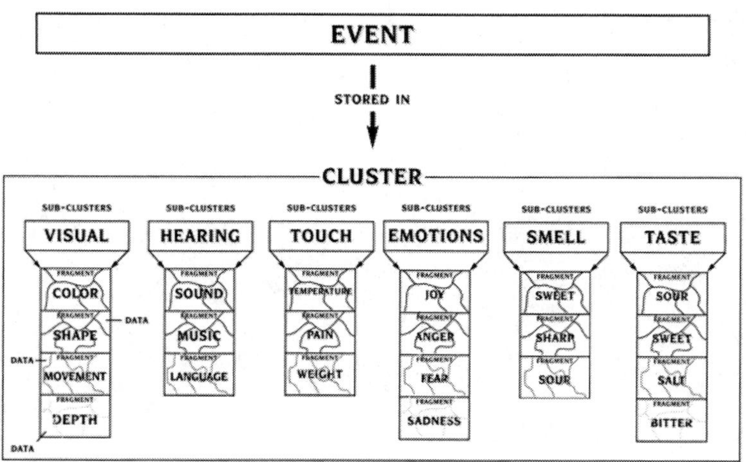

On each level, Fragment, Sub-cluster and Cluster, the brain activates the attached physiology. The physiology at the level of a Fragment is not as strong as at the higher levels of aggregation (for there are less ligands of a certain type produced). This works perfectly, because in this way, our mind can easily determine the relative code of each single piece of the comparison material. If there is a larger level of similarity between incoming new data and stored data, a Sub-cluster will be activated as comparison material. Now the intensity of the physiology becomes stronger! If the similarity between incoming data and a stored event is even greater, then the whole Cluster will be activated! The more Fragments and Sub-clusters become active, the more intense the physiology will become! This is still within healthy and normal boundaries because we speak of Clusters. Bad Clusters, however, are activated in the same way!

Activating Bad Clusters on a low level

As soon as a Fragment of a Bad Cluster is activated, its attached physiology will be carried out. The more Fragments become active, followed by Sub-clusters, the more intense the physiology will become. - See drawing -

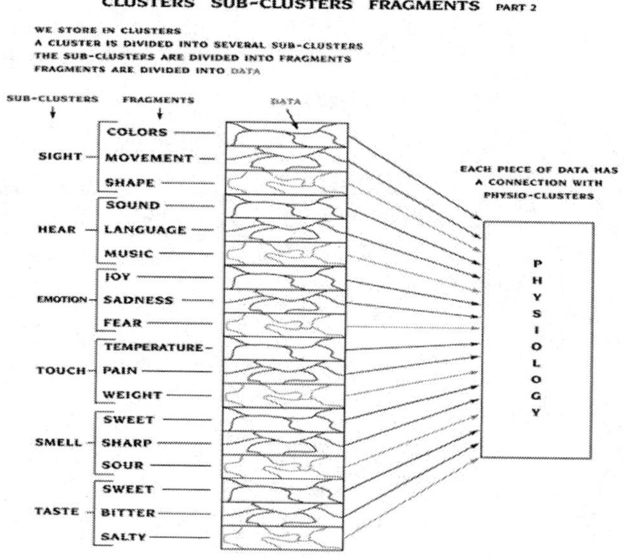

If several Sub-clusters are activated, the physiology will give us unpleasant feelings, even to a level that makes us ill! However, if only a few Fragments are activated, then the physiology isn't all that intense. We may feel a light increase of our heartbeat or a slight pressure in our chest or our belly. So, how will we interpret and perceive the undersized emotional symptoms that are caused by activated Bad Cluster Fragments? To understand that, we have to go back to our strongest force or drive: *away from pain*! The majority of all new incoming material will activate positive, as well as negative, comparison material. Keep in mind that we have the symptoms of all our emotions, positive and negative, stored in Clusters. Only the negative ones that are too extreme to deal with, originating from an overload situation, will be stored in Bad Clusters!

If large parts, several Sub-clusters, of a Bad Cluster are activated, we have no other choice than to recognize the effects of the attached physiology as a negative emotion! The emotional symptoms we experienced at a given moment where just a few Fragments were active, we do feel, but we do not interpret them as negative because our interpretation will go *away from* pain an if possible in the direction of pleasure! Just consider what you physically feel when you feel joy. What do you feel in your body if you are in love? Take for instance, the heartbeat. We feel our heartbeat when we are in love, but also feel it when we are terrified! We feel our heartbeat in moments of happiness and joy, but also in pain and fear. If the activation of the Bad Cluster is at a level of a few Fragments, the physiology will be insignificant, but still enough to notice. This leaves room for positive (*away from* pain) interpretation!

Likes and dislikes, a matter of physiology

A lot of our emotions, positive and negative, share some fundamental physical responses, like heartbeat, sensations in our stomach, chest, muscles, etc. If we feel those sensations in just a light way, we will interpret them as something positive! We do this because we want to. This sounds okay, doesn't it? Well, actually, it isn't! We previously discussed that our decisions are primarily based on our emotions. This has an important consequence! Our choices, decisions and actions are primarily based on what we feel. If the feelings come from just a few Bad Cluster Fragments, we will not recognize them as negative, instead interpret them as positive feelings. Our feelings will dictate who the people are that we associate with. These feelings also determine if we like or dislike certain foods, music, houses, colors, shapes, smells, art, objects, etc.! To like, or to dislike, are feelings caused by Physio-clusters. Which feelings will be dominant? The strongest! Where do we find the strongest feelings? Attached to Bad Clusters!

> ***Example*:**
> Imagine yourself in a furniture shop. You see a beautiful sofa. You don't know why, but the moment you see the sofa, you like it, yes, you even love it! This is the sofa that you want and no other!

Realize why you like things

This can happen with anything you like, or dislike, regardless of what or who. The problem is not that you like it, but *why* you like it! If you immediately have an explanation for this, such as: *"My grandmother had a sofa like that and I love her very much and that is why this sofa gives me such a good feeling"*, then everything is okay! But what if you have no idea why you like the sofa. You just do! Well…wrong! You never *just* do anything! “Everything we say, do, feel, decide, etc., has a cause and that cause is your comparison material!” If your comparison material comes from normal Clusters, you’ll remember. If your feelings originate from Bad Clusters, you will not be able to trace why you like this sofa so much!

Think of that for a moment. That, in itself, is shocking enough! But worse than that is the fact that these people, colors or items activate you constantly! Remember, the brain follows the stimulus/response rule. This does not mean that you are immediately activated from the very moment that those triggers enter your life. It can sit there in your surroundings for a long time before it actually activates some Sub-clusters, or even the whole Bad Cluster. Ask yourself, *“Was I activated when I bought this item or met this specific person?”* At least enough to create a certain excitement with regard to the subject or person. You could still interpret it as something positive, so the physiology won’t reach a negative level at that moment. That way, the physical symptoms don’t immediately harm you and you are not activated to a level where you feel a negative influence! Now these triggers are sitting there around you, just waiting for the moment to become fully activated. What is the difference between the Bad Cluster physiology that led to the decision to buy this item and the physiology that will occur when, in a later stage, this Bad Cluster gets activated? Just think of the previous example of the heartbeat that you experience when you are in love, but also feel when you’re terrified. The determinative factor is the configuration and intensity of the physiology. You will not suffer negative feelings from just a few active Fragments. If there are several fragments of the Bad Cluster that are activated, or even one or more Sub-clusters, then you will absolutely feel the effects of their strong negative physiology!

Things we love become unhealthy triggers

Then how do they become activated in a later stage, interfering with life in a negative way? This will differ from situation to situation, and from person to person. However, the fundamental reason why they get activated is always the same. Once again, it comes down to the stimulus/response rule. The moment there is enough similarity between the incoming new data and the existing content of the Bad Cluster, you will get activated! You can have a color or item in your surroundings for a longer period of time without getting activated. Then suddenly, it hits you like a sledge hammer! If you are unaware of PMA you will have no clue what happened and why you suddenly feel so horrible. The moment of activation can be caused by almost anything. Just imagine this next example:

***Example*:**
You have a beautiful painting that you bought a year ago. The very moment you saw the painting you felt attracted to it. You don't know why, but you really wanted that painting. It shows a house, and in front of that house there are two little children playing in the grass with a cat under a tree. After a while, you even believe you realize why you like it so much. The house kind of resembles your parents' house and you have great memories of those years when you lived there as a child. On top of that, one of the children in the painting looks a lot like your sister when she was that age, too. So, everything seems in order! You like the painting, and by now, you know why!

A few days ago you had visitors. They were a little upset when they visited you! On their way to your home they ran over a cat with their car. They stopped and tried to find the owner of the cat, and they did. It was a little girl. She was so upset to find out what happened! While your visitors were telling you their story, you glanced once in a while at your painting. You felt their emotion to a level that made you upset, too! Why? You don't know! But the real reason was an activated Bad Cluster.

More Sub-clusters become active

What was the content of that Bad Cluster? At the age of six you were playing with your sister in front of the house. Suddenly, you hear a car trying to do an emergency stop, followed by an awful sound of a screeching cat. You are both nailed to the ground! You think immediately of your cat. You and your sister loved that cat dearly. Yes, it was your cat that was hit and killed by the car. Your little sister was screaming and crying and totally upset. At that moment, you created a Bad Cluster. Nothing in the painting brought that memory to your conscious awareness. It just activated a few Fragments of the Bad Cluster. Ultimately, it was the story of your visitors that added the activation of several other Fragments of the same Bad Cluster while you were simultaneously looking at the painting.

So now several Sub-clusters of the Bad Cluster are active. This is simply too much to handle and no longer open for positive interpretation. You start feeling miserable while they tell their story. You tell yourself that it might be the meal you just ate or maybe you caught the flu, or it is simply your love for animals that caused this. (belief systems). You don't really understand why you feel as you do. In reality, you are activated, and that's the reason! You feel your heart beating very fast, you have nausea, you feel like crying and you almost feel like you are going to faint! The next day, when you enter your living room, you think of the story your visitors told you the day before and look at the painting. You suddenly feel the same symptoms all over again. You feel your heart beating very fast, your nauseated, you feel like crying and you feel faint! From now on, you won't need the memory of their story to feel this way. The painting in your living room is enough to activate you! Mind you, you are not yet aware that this feeling occurs whenever the painting comes to your sight. You just don't make that association and you don't notice the link!

How many people will have items, colors or persons in their environment that are constantly activating their Bad Clusters? And let me ask you something more: How many people have Bad Clusters? We know by now: **everyone** has Bad Clusters! So, how many people will surround themselves with activating items, colors or persons? <u>We all do</u>! Isn't this depressing? On the contrary! It is only depressing if you are unaware of how the brain works and how we surround ourselves with these signals. If you now know how it works, you can start to use it to your benefit! Let us find out if you can discover some of these items or people in your own life.

> ***Exercise*:**
> Write down items or colors in and around your house that you would never want to give up, or lose, but you don't know why you are so attached to them. Write down the names of people you associate with, although you don't even like them so much, or that take up a lot of your time and, rationally speaking, you would like to remove them from your life, but for some reason, you can't!

If you cannot come up with a reasonable explanation, then that should convince not only you, but also other objective people, that you can almost be 100% sure that these items, colors or people exist around you because of your choices dictated by activated Bad Clusters! Now let's continue our exercise.

Exercise: *Focus on one of your favorite items*

- Pick one of the items and focus on it.
- What do you feel?
- Where do you feel it in your body?
- What if you would intensify this feeling?
- Just focus on the item and allow the feeling to come. Don't fight it!
- Now let your brain do what it always does. Just look and feel until a new picture pops up spontaneously.
- Do not suppress any of the spontaneous pictures! Whatever pops up, go with it!

How to use the activating items to your benefit

After this exercise sinks in, people usually ask: Does this mean I have to throw away everything around me that is a possible activator? Well, what if that activator is your spouse? Usually it is not your spouse's fault, but there are some details about your spouse, like a certain facial expression, eyes, movements, etc., that activate you. These signals activate similar data of a person that harmed you in the past and who has nothing to do with your spouse. And you don't want to throw him/her away, do you? (Maybe you do, but then you really have a problem!) There is absolutely no need to throw away anything! Actually, these activations can help you tremendously if you know how to use them to your advantage.

A lifetime tool

Searching for Bad Clusters means looking for missing pieces in your consciousness. It is a search and discovery of the unknown. Practicing the PMA method is an experience that will serve and support you for the rest of your life. Better yet, the technique you learn through studying and applying PMA will create a whole new level of insight and motivating possibilities. If at any time in the future you feel an unpleasant emotion coming up, or you overreact and cannot explain why, using the PMA technique on yourself will trace where the emotion is coming from and will empower you to eliminate it. PMA is truly a technique to improve your lifestyle forever. When you finish the theoretical explanation in this book and accomplish its exercises, you can return to the items and people you wrote down in this exercise. And after you practice the PMA technique, you can use the objects and names of the people you wrote down to discover the related Bad Clusters and undo them of their negative charge and free the positive energy they hide.

Chapter 6 – The hidden Power Of Bad Clusters

The effects of eliminating Bad Clusters

What is the advantage of eliminating Bad Clusters? You may even wonder, *"What is the point of eliminating memories that you can't remember, anyway?"* Actually, you are not *eliminating* memories; you are bringing up data that is incorrectly encoded and removing its destructive, emotional (physiological) load. This means that you are actually eliminating the physiology that is connected to the Bad Cluster, not the data in the Bad Cluster. Progressive Mental Alignment leaves your memory intact while permanently disconnecting the negative physiological effects from traumatic experiences. As soon as the contents of a Bad Cluster have been discovered, your conscious will give each piece of data its correct relative code. Now these Bad Clusters are no longer an unrelated collection of pieces of data, but a story, an event that you once experienced. You can now remember everything all over again. Even if you have a strong constitution and barely consciously register the symptoms of activated Bad Clusters, your body will still pay the price.

A Bad Cluster is something your brain can't remember but your body cannot forget.

Pay attention to the activation of Bad Clusters

Are all Bad Clusters dangerous? They are only hazardous when they become active. How do we know when they are active? By recognizing what the symptoms activated Bad Clusters. What are those symptoms? Lets have a closer look at some of the most frequently noticed symptoms:

Do you agree that all of these symptoms mentioned above will have an effect on your behavior? If so, it is of vital importance

HOW DO I KNOW IF I HAVE BAD CLUSTERS?
We all have them!

HOW CAN YOU TELL?
* Any emotion that is out of proportion
* Any form of repetitive unreasonable behavior
* Lack of emotions
* All inexplicable complaints or emotion that appear unexpectedly and abruptly
* Inexplicable physical complaints
* Irrational behavior
* Dysfunctional behavior - to be able to get so much more our of life but being unable to do so
* Insomnia
* Fatigue without apparent reason
* Depression
* Fears
* Phobias
* Eating disorders
* All kinds of addiction
    * Alcohol, Smoking, Drugs, Work,etc.
* Fear of cold calls
* Fear of failure

that you get rid of the negative effects of the Bad Clusters and set free the large amount of energy for use to your advantage. In order to start the process, you have to first recognize your behavioral patterns. Therefore, we will discuss how Bad Clusters are activated, and later on, how they create many inhibiting belief systems and behavioral patterns that keep the Bad Clusters active. But first, let's discover how a Bad Cluster gets activated.

The activation of Bad Clusters

How does a Bad Cluster become active? Actually, in exactly the same way as Clusters! This is by way of "memory moments", also called "triggers". These triggers are made up of a combination of signals at a basic level. Signals that, for instance, form a scent, taste, piece of music, specific move, a pair of eyes, specific words or their intonation, etc. Let's clarify the activation and effects of a Bad Cluster by means of a visual example:

Picture 1

A 31-year-old woman hosts a marriage ceremony. She did this many times before and loves her job. However, at this time it is different.

THE WEDDING

As she performs the ceremony, she suddenly starts feeling awful. She feels her heart palpitating, she is sweating, her knees are shaking, she feels pressure in her chest and fears she's going to faint. She cannot find a reason why she feels so terrible. The people she speaks to are so friendly and are all in such a good mood.

Picture 2

Among hundreds of Clusters, one Bad Cluster became active in her brain. When she was a 16-year-old girl, she worked at a gas station and became the victim of a hold-up.

She was terrified and thought that the criminal would definitely kill her. In an event like that, it's absolutely understandable that she suffered palpitations, sweating, shaking knees, pressure in her chest and a fainting feeling. But why she experienced this same feeling at a very pleasant wedding ceremony is not so understandable.

Let's see what happened in her subconscious comparison processes. There's a Bad Cluster active because of basic similarities. If she went to a doctor, he would probably say she is hyperventilating or suffering from a panic disorder. He may conclude that she might be a bit overworked or had experienced a panic attack. He would most likely prescribes a tranquilizer and advises her to take some rest. The fact is hyperventilation or panic attacks are always activated Bad Cluster material. Stress is 100% the result of your personal perception, coming from your comparison material along with its physiological load. Nevertheless, it is still odd in her case. Based on the rules of the subconscious, in normal situations she would have remembered this holdup. But, first of all, this holdup was not a 'normal event'; it was a Bad Cluster situation!

Picture 3

The subconscious brain needs the correct codes in order to be able to process data. Because Bad Clusters do not have correct codes assigned to them, the subconscious cannot use its content for normal processing. However, the incoming sensory signals will activate the specific nerve cells based on similarity and the stimulus/response rule. The subconscious will try to read the relative codes of the Bad Cluster data. However, the relative code turns out to be the same for all the pieces of data of a Bad Cluster. They all have the same highest relative code possible! The subconscious cannot pass to the conscious brain the content of the Bad Cluster but it can, and it will, carry out its physiology in the same way it does with normal Clusters.

In our example of the wedding/hold-up, the Bad Cluster was activated, including the strong negative physiology, based on a certain amount of elementary similarities. Of course the Bad Cluster is not the only comparison material that is activated. Among the large amount of Clusters, this Bad Cluster was activated, too. Let's look at the similarities that activated the bad Cluster:

THE CONNECTIONS

Similarities

Wedding	*Holdup*
Red dress	*Red coat*
Blue jacket	*Blue pants, shoes*
Green curtains, flowers	*Green hat*
Color pedestal	*Color pedestal*
Black/grey gun	*Black/grey microphone*
Pointed at her	*Pointed at her*

As long as the incoming data carries similarities to the Bad Cluster content, it will stay active and have all the opportunity to manifest its physiology. Our lady will start feeling just as bad as when she went through the hold up, although she is unable to relate the two events because the Bad Cluster doesn't get through to her consciousness. Therefore, she has absolutely no idea why she suddenly feels that way.

The story continues

She managed to finish the wedding ceremony, but she still feels horrible. She tells her colleague about how she struggled to finish the ceremony. Her colleague is concerned and sends her home. The next morning, she feels better and goes back to work. Her colleague sees her in the office and asks: *"How are you doing today, do you feel any better?"* This immediately activates some Fragments or even Sub-clusters of the wedding, *"Oh, yes, thank you, I feel a lot better"*. A few seconds later, she enters the same room where the wedding took place. Instantly, she starts to feel horrible again. What happened? The question her colleague asked, combined with all the incoming sensory data of the room where the wedding took place, activated the total Cluster of the wedding in her subconscious. This Cluster contained all the basic data to activate the Bad Cluster all over again.

As a result, on the following day, she won't need her colleague to ask the same question in order to start the activation. By just entering the wedding room is enough! As a matter of fact, this is how phobias are created. Now she starts to develop belief systems to explain why she feels so horrible. She might tell herself: *"It's the building... probably the air-conditioning"*, or *"I'm sure it's the stress due to the lack of cooperation I experience in this company"*, or many other belief systems. None of them is actually true! However, because she keeps working there, she will be activated every day. She can either resort to ignoring the symptoms, or if the symptoms become too strong, she can take medications to suppress them. The medicine might make her feel better, but that won't change anything about the subconscious stimulus/response rule, and as a result, her body will continue to suffer from the negative physiology of the activated Bad Cluster. Over the weeks, months and years the results of that negative physiology pile up in the body and will create serious physical complaints. This is how psychosomatic complaints develop.

Bad Clusters get stuck in the process

It is crucial to understand that a Bad Cluster is stored in exactly the same cells as Clusters that contain similar data and is activated in the same way by incoming new data. The only difference is that, after activation, Clusters are processed normally, which means they will either be shut off as irrelevant to the occasion, or passed on to the consciousness to make us aware of its content. However, the Bad Clusters do not make it through this high-speed process. The physiology of the Bad Cluster stays active as long as the same type of new data continues to enter.

Keep in mind that the processing of normal encoded data is done at a tremendous speed. That's why the subconscious can process so much more data subconsciously than will ever reach the conscious brain. We usually do not concentrate on just one object. Normally, we move constantly and the incoming data of all our senses changes constantly. This means that not one of the pieces of normal encoded comparison material stays active long enough in the subconscious so that its physiology can be carried out at an extreme extent. Before that happens, another load of comparison material is already activated. Nevertheless, a Bad Cluster is not processed! It is stuck! Therefore, its physiology is carried out to an extreme level. Because it is stuck and the subconscious always selects the comparison material with the highest relative code, its physiology is carried out. It cannot reject the Bad Cluster because the subconscious cannot process it. Therefore, it cannot choose another normal encoded piece of comparison material with a positive physiological code to replace the Bad Cluster. To do that, the subconscious first has to process the content of the Bad Cluster, which, under normal circumstances is impossible, but it can be done through the PMA technique. Nevertheless, it will only be effective if we strictly follow the language rules of the subconscious! Why is it that we don't recognize the fact that it is a Bad Cluster that is activated although we are clearly feeling its physiology? After we learn how the mind and body connection works, the answer to this question will be clear. At this point we'll start by looking at two basic reasons why you don't recognize the activation of a Bad Cluster:

1. *The subconscious cannot process the content of the Bad Cluster because of incorrect encoding and, therefore, it will not be passed on to the conscious part of the brain.*

2. *The events that activate the Bad Clusters usually contain no fear, pain or danger. The emotional content of the activating event usually differs totally from the Bad Cluster event. The only similarities are simple unrelated factual data like color, taste, sound, shape, movement, etc.*

This last reason is especially what makes it difficult when you don't know the rules of the language of the subconscious. The PMA technique is in tune with these rules. To deepen our understanding of how Bad Clusters can suddenly damage our health in spite of the fact that there are obviously no apparent reasons to be sick or dysfunctional, let's look at the following example:

Example:
A woman, 44 years of age, is a manager in a big company. She is happy with her job and has a great family. All of a sudden, she starts to get terrible headaches. And at the same time, she experiences her first panic attack. This all happened at the company when she was in her office all by herself, sitting in front of her computer. The, next morning she has another panic attack in the same office. From that point on she feels horrible every morning at her office. After a while, she manages to control her feelings, but it costs her a lot of energy to do so. Her professional performance starts to drop. She tries to find out what's happening. Is it 'sick building' syndrome? Is there physically something wrong? There are no answers! Finally she learns about PMA and applies the tools. She's relived the moment when it all started to find out why she got her sudden headaches and her panic attack on that first day at her office. This is what she described:

It was raining heavily so I had to run from my car into my office. Once behind my desk, I started my computer like I do every morning. It always starts with a flashy light, then it turns dark, and finally it goes to a nice green screen. After my computer started, I had a discussion with an employee who under performed her job. It was necessary to talk to her, although she got very upset. She screamed at me and stormed out of my office slamming the door so hard that it scared me. I did not feel good when she left the room. My secretary, a blond, blue-eyed lady, came in and said: *"Did you hear that?"* She looked at me and asked: *"You are okay, right?"*

Then I freaked out! The headache had already started after the employee slammed the door, but now I really lost it!

What happened? Going back in her mind through some events in her past, she arrived at an event that occurred when she was 11 years old. She was in an open field when a thunderstorm suddenly broke through. It started to rain heavily. She ran for shelter as fast as she could. Lightning struck a tree about 100 feet away from her and it swept her off her feet. The last thing she heard was the loud bang of thunder before she hit the grass. She regained consciousness in a hospital where a blond nurse with blue eyes shakes her gently while saying, *"Can you hear me? Don't worry, you are okay now"*.

Obviously a Bad Cluster had formed at that occasion. What was it that activated this Bad Cluster? It is factual data that activated similar data that's already stored. So then, in her case, what activated this specific Bad Cluster? Basic similarities between the factual data! Let's compare:

Similarities

Then	**Now**
Rain	*Rain*
Running	*Running*
Thunder	*Slamming of the door*
Lightning	*Computer flash*
Green grass	*Green screen of computer*
Nurse blond/blue eyes	*Secretary blond/blue eyes*
Can you hear me?	*Did you hear that?*
You are okay now	*You are okay, right?*

Among a lot of other comparison material, the Bad Cluster was also activated. Because the brain could not properly process the Bad Cluster, it stayed active and the physiology was carried out. That first panic attack at the office that activated the Bad Cluster was stored in a normal encoded Cluster, including the unpleasant symptoms caused by the activated Bad Cluster physiology. As we can see, there is no similarity between the event of a thunderstorm and an office with a computer, but there are many similarities in elementary data! It was not the first-time activation of the Bad Cluster that caused her problems. It was the constant activation, day in day out, that caused this as a continuous complaint. How was that possible if it wasn't raining every day, nor did she have any angry employees slamming the door every time? Actually, the Bad Cluster does not need all of that to get activated.

Re-activation

The next day, just by entering her office and starting her computer was enough to activate the Bad Cluster again. The Bad Cluster did not get activated directly, but through the existing Cluster that she created at the moment she had her first panic attack. Where was she when that took place? In her office in front of the computer! The next day, when she sits at her desk, the incoming data about her office (the computer, the flash and the green screen), logically activated the Cluster that was created the day before. And, in turn, that specific Cluster contained all the data to activate the Bad Cluster all over again. Now she has two Clusters containing enough similarities, or connections, to activate the Bad Cluster. Sure enough, the next day, the same process will occur. She will develop a chain of Clusters that are all connected and are able to activate the Bad Clusters. When certain memory moments (signals) are constantly present (for example, a color, object or smell), they will serve as a constant memory moment, an activation moment, in your life. This definitely has a negative influence on your feelings, behavior and decisions. By finding these memory moments (signals) through PMA she could trace the Bad Cluster, which automatically got neutralized and she could now function 100% again at her job without health complaints.

Chapter 7 – The secret of psychosomatic health problems

Psychological or physical?

Perhaps all of us have heard before the term *psychosomatic*. It describes symptoms or illnesses that are felt in our bodies, but are caused by our minds, or psyche. How and why does the mind do this? Most professionals in the medical field agree that many of our illnesses are psychosomatic. What sort of symptoms are considered to be psychosomatic? It could be almost anything! Stomachache, headache, allergies, muscle and joint pain, intestinal problems, eczema, and a very long list of other symptoms. The most predominant, and always present before any chronic disease develops, is probably exhaustion. Which symptoms are not psychosomatic? The purely somatic or physical symptoms. We can divide these into two groups:

1. *Acquired symptoms*
2. *Genetically determined symptoms*

1. Acquired symptoms come into existence by something that happens to us in our life where irreparable damage has occurred. This can happen through bacteria, viruses, or when another living organism has inflicted permanent damage to certain organs. Take for example, a very severe middle-ear infection that is caused by a virus or bacteria. Damage or dysplasia may occur in the middle ear. The final damage is irreparable. Besides these sorts of acquired problems, there are also clearly visible signs of damage that can come about as a result of serious accidents or as the result of war where an organic damage has arisen, or even if one of the body

parts has been lost. Even if the psychological impact of this damage has improved, the missing body part will never grow back! Unfortunately, if Bad Clusters are activated over a long period of time, the body can develop irreversible damage. For instance, activated Bad Clusters can cause high blood pressure. After several years this can cause a heart attack. As a result, the damage in the heart tissue will be irreversible. Keep in mind that the heart attack was not the direct result of Bad Clusters, but the result of Bad Clusters that stayed activated over a long period of time, piling up the intoxication of an incorrect and imbalanced Bad Cluster physiology.

2. Genetically determined symptoms. We all have strong and weak organs. We receive these from our ancestors because they are determined by genetic factors. Also, the tendency for a particular illness or health problem can be genetically determined. That does not necessarily mean it has to manifest itself. If we make sure that we have enough energy reserves built up and keep alert that these don't ever get completely depleted, then there may never be a problem. This is due to the fact that exhaustion is namely the first step of activating genetically determined illnesses. Active Bad Clusters consume lots of energy! Just imagine how much more you are capable of if you eliminate your Bad Clusters and this energy becomes available for positive use!

Our conscious and the physiology

Our physiological processes are always working. If they were to cease, we would die! They enable us to move, breathe, widen or constrict blood vessels, flex or relax our muscles, cause digestion to slow or speed up, and allow the heart to beat faster or slower. Although all these physiological processes are of vital importance, it appears that they are not consciously controlled! Our conscious brain, has for the most part, absolutely no control over these processes. Then, what does control these processes? Why is it so important to concern ourselves with this now? Well, without an understanding of the control over physiological processes, we will never get a good understanding about the development of psychosomatic illnesses. Therefore, it is very important that we understand which mechanism is responsible for controlling the physiological processes. As we already know, our Proto-physioclusters (on/of switch) controls the life-support mechanisms and will always maintain the highest possible level of physiological balance. On the other hand we have the subconscious program that creates our emotions, totally controlled by incoming sensory signals who activate previously stored data including their attached Physio-clusters. Their physiological source is responsible for many of our imbalances and physiological instabilities.

Your mind directs your body

The effect that your brain's sensory perceptions has on your body is clear when, for example, you consider the activation of your salivary glands when you see something that looks delicious, or the production of tears when you feel sad, or the activating of your laughter muscles when you are happy. Consider also your physical reactions to fear, or turning white when you are angry, flushing when embarrassed, or yawning as a reaction to seeing someone else yawn! You sense something that is happening externally, your brain processes this and reacts by altering your physiological state. You immediately feel these alterations in your body. If your brain were to remain limited to reacting to these harmless stimuli, then there would be no problem. Unfortunately, the influence of the subconscious brain on your body reaches much farther than that. Studies with mice show that the T-lymphocyte levels in their blood decreases when under prolonged stress. The T-lymphocyte is a determining factor in the immune system. If the level of this sinks too low, then so does one's resistance to sickness. The decrease in the levels of these T-cells can be as much as 80% in cases of prolonged stress. Stress is clearly the result of activated Bad Clusters and their negative physiological effects on the body. The fact that the incoming sensory signals can have such a strong effect on our physiological reactions is clear and undisputed by any who is aware of the facts and know the workings of the PMA method and has experienced its effects. Insight in this process will give us a better understanding what role Bad Clusters play in this process! In order to understand and gain more insight, it is necessary to consider some facts from scientific experiments. The well known phenomena known as *Pavlov's conditioning*, named after its discoverer and Nobel price winner, Ivan Pavlov (1879-1966), is what comes up during these types of experiments. An interesting example of this phenomenon can be seen in the following example:

> ***Pavlov's experiment*:**
> Measure the blood glucose levels of several test animals. Then, give them an injection of sugar. But before the injection, make a certain noise (for example, a bell, a flute, a clang). Repeat the process numerous times. After some time, make the noise, but do not give the sugar injection. The level of the blood glucose in the animals will immediately sink as soon as they hear the noise, and the animals will then eat. This is because the sugar injections activated the pancreas to produce more insulin. After some repetition, the pancreas started to do this whenever the animals heard the sound without even receiving the sugar injection. The result was

that the glucose (sugar) levels dropped and the animals started to eat.

The executed Physio-cluster

Why did the glucose levels in the blood of these animals sink? It happened because they heard the same noise that would sound before given the injection! This shows us that physiological reactions to incoming sensory signals can be learned through training! In the usual scenario, the noise will have nothing to do with the food or the blood glucose level. And yet, the body responds to it! Why is that? Because the noise was heard every single time before the sugar injection. The rise in the blood glucose levels is a natural physiological reaction to the injection. The different receptors inside the body sense this and respond as a reflex or send their signals to the various sensory centers in the brain. These signals are combined with all other incoming sensory signals, like the sound. After analysis, everything is stored away in a Cluster. Connected to that Cluster we find the Physio-cluster that contains the codes that activate the production of insulin in the pancreas and the other glucose burning processes. As the process of hearing the noise and receiving the injection is repeated over and over, each time the response is the same: an increase in the blood glucose levels (by the sugar injection). Each time this process is repeated, the external stimuli (the noise) is connected to the internal response (raise in insulin). These two sets of data are connected and stored as one Cluster, with a Physio-cluster containing all the physiological data attached to it. So now we make the noise without a sugar injection. Immediately the subconscious calls up all the Clusters that were made recently. They all contain the data about the noise. However, the Physio-clusters that are connected to these Clusters contain information and instructions to try to reduce the blood sugar by producing more insulin. Now we have a problem because the appropriate receptors sense that there is no increase in the blood glucose levels in the body! In the meantime, of course, the Physio-clusters attached to the noise instructing more insulin to be produced have already been executed, or carried out. So what happens now? The usual blood glucose levels will quickly decrease because of all the insulin that was released. So, to amend the situation, the body is signaled to get something to eat! What can we learn from this? We can learn how the mechanism works that calls up Clusters and the Physio-clusters that are attached to them, are stored away together, and are called up together as well!

Let us now connect this information with the physiological aspects of a Bad Cluster. The most powerful ingredients of Bad Cluster is pain and fear. Pain and fear consume large amounts of energy. How do we mainly produce that energy? Mainly by burning glucose. Consequently, activated Bad Clusters will raise the insulin production. This can lead to hypoglycemia as well as overeating or even eating disorders.

Your conscious does not control the physiology

Could the conscious part of the brain be responsible for the physiological processes in your body? Let us assume for a moment that you see something that interests you very much. On an extremely hot day you see someone eating an ice cream. Wouldn't it be great to eat such a cold ice cream? You want one, too! Which mechanism made that decision? The only one that can make that decision is your conscious brain because this is where the free will is located and the only place we register feelings like desire. By means of the free will, and driven by desire, it makes the decision to go eat the ice cream. As a result, you order an ice cream, pay for it and bring it to your lips. All these behaviors are conscious, not subconscious. Does that also mean that the conscious brain is in control of the physiological processes? Absolutely not! True, the conscious made all the judicial decisions, but the actual carrying out of the decision has to be analyzed. This analysis cannot take place without the appropriate subconscious comparison material. If the conscious were to make such decisions and carry them out without analysis, then we wouldn't even know what we were doing, where we were walking, and what we were eating.

So this means the subconscious must also be in the picture. The evaluation of the subconscious is based on the existing comparison material. The conscious brain can make the decision and carry this out by setting the voluntary muscles in motion to do what it has decided. In order to accomplish this simple action, all sorts of physiological processes must be set into motion. However, just because we have stated that the conscious has control over moving the voluntary muscles, it does not mean that the will to carry out a certain movement is the same as controlling the physiological processes involved in that motion! Nor does it prove that the conscious controls the physiological processes. If the conscious had some influence on this process, then it could only be in regards to the voluntary muscles. The involuntary muscles and the many other physiological processes are not under its control. They operate independently or automatically. Our will has no control over them. In spite of the fact that the conscious is not in control of the physiological processes, it is the only one that can feel the effects of them, since instigating movement and sensing are both conscious processes. But for example, the fact that it can feel that something is too warm does not mean that it has the capability of turning the inner thermostat down.

Physiology and Bad Clusters

What kind of physiology will we store during a Bad Cluster event? The brain will store the highest level of pain and fear that we could ever reach. An emotion that is so intense that we feel we lose control. It is the physiology that causes the feelings of panic. Our system is not made to cope with this kind of physiology. In case of a one-time activation of a Bad Cluster its physiology will only be active for a short while. Our body is able to tolerate and compensate that. But our body is definitely not made to experience that kind of physiology for a prolonged period of time! However, this is exactly what happens if a Bad Cluster is activated over a longer period of time. But how can a Bad Cluster be activated over a longer period of time? Do you remember Janine who lived for 5 years in a constant fear of being HIV positive, activated by the smallest physical problem or reading or hearing about aids? Or the 44 year old lady from our previous chapter constantly activated by the memory moments of her office and her computer? To illustrate this even more, let's suppose that you experience a recent activation of a Bad Cluster that was stored in your subconscious a long time ago. How does it get activated? What is the nature of the relationship between the activation moment and the Bad Cluster? To better understand this, let's look at the following example:

> ***Example*:**
> There was a 36-year-old manager of a large toy factory who had a promising career for he was a great leader and team builder. He was in very good health, was happily married, and had two children. But abruptly a dramatic change took place. From one day to another he did not feel well and could not understanding why. He felt depressed and he lost his drive and proactivity. His

department did okay, but the spirit, growth and enthusiasm was gone. His relationship with his wife became more and more difficult. Driven by his feelings, he often responded aggressively to both his wife and his employees, and of course, they responded in a similar way. This created the ideal foundation for some powerful belief systems. These belief systems gave him the "answers" as to why he had begun to feel so awful. It was because of the unreasonable behavior of his wife and the fact that his employees had lost their enthusiasm and motivation. This was simply too much stress to handle! Whenever they responded in an aggravated way, or did something he disagreed with, he experienced this as a confirmation of his belief systems. After trying several therapies and medication, he participated in the PMA program by attending a seminar. Already during the seminar, he made a discovery through the PMA method: With the PMA technique it was easy for him to trace the exact moment when these changes of feelings took place:

- His negative feelings all started in his company after an argument with a young and insistent supervisor. The young man had blue eyes and was wearing a green shirt.
- This memory (Cluster) lead him to the next memory in which he saw the interior of the office building he worked in. He realized that the building was redecorated and painted during the same period he had the discussion with this young supervisor. He sees the newly painted green walls, white doors, and gray tables and desks.

- While connecting all that information, another memory popped up that also happened during that same period. He was in a hurry walking out of his office when he ran into his secretary. He is about five inches taller then she is. Her forehead hit his nose. The severe pain he felt brought tears to his eyes. He thought his nose was bleeding and he felt dizzy. Simultaneously, he briefly glanced at her blue eyes and red blouse. He went back to his office and sat down for a moment at his grey desk, while watching the white door and green wall. Instantly, he felt drained, knocked-out, and depressed, and had a hard time resisting to cry.
- Using the PMA technique, he now focused on the detail of the last picture and on his feelings. The was the red blouse of his secretary. There, he got stuck for a moment because focusing on the red blouse intensified the negative feelings he experienced. He new that this happened because he came closer to the content of the Bad Cluster, therefore he allowed himself, without resistance, to accept whatever picture his subconscious would 'spontaneously' give him.
- In a flash he saw an event at school that occurred when he was only ten years old. He used to be very popular among his classmates until a new guy enrolled in the school. This newcomer was very insistent in challenging him over and over again. In one of the disputes our boy courageously looked straight at this guy's blue eyes and tried to argue with him. Suddenly and unexpectedly, the young man punched him

hard on his nose. It started to bleed profusely, spreading blood all over his hands. Shocked, he looked at all the blood and then towards the green doors of the school building for help. A very concerned teacher in a gray suit came towards him and handed him a white towel. As he cleaned himself off, he felt dizzy, drained, knocked-out and depressed. He was sobbing and thinking that no one would ever respect him after they seeing this humiliating fight.

- When he saw this last picture during the PMA session, he realized that he had not thought of this event in many years. But more than that, he realized the similarity of feelings and data to his present situation and environment. There were details that he couldn't remember, such as:

Recent event	**Bad Cluster**
Aggressive supervisor	*Aggressive look of a child*
Blue eyes	*Blue eyes*
Hit his nose	*Punch to his nose*
Unexpected	*Unexpected*
Red blouse	*Red color of blood*
Green shirt, green walls	*Green doors of school*
White doors	*White towel*
Grey tables and desks	*Grey suit of teacher*
Tears of pain	*Tears of pain and sadness*
Drained feeling	*Drained feeling*
Knocked-out	*Knocked-out*
Dizzy	*Dizzy*
Depressed	*Depressed*

- Once the content of the Bad Cluster popped up and the Bad Cluster changed into a normal encoded Cluster, he instantly felt a tremendous relief and a lot of energy. His wife, as well as his employees and coworkers, immediately noticed his positive change. He understood that they actually never acted in a manner that was unreasonable or not motivated. It was all due to his Bad Clusters driven belief systems that made him think that they were acting in such a manner.

As you may notice, there was no similarity between the several events that activated the Bad Cluster and the content of the Bad Cluster event itself. The only similarities are isolated details, such as colors, eyes, tears, dizziness, etc. Each of these separate "Fragments" are in connection with the Limbic System. You could say that they have a horizontal connection in the Cortex along with the other fragments that together form a Sub-cluster and/or Clusters (or Bad Clusters) to create the absolute code or value. And they have a vertical connection down to the Limbic System that determines the relative code or value in order to decide what each piece of data means to you. How does this connection work? Through the two, already discussed, communication routes: the hard-wiring (dendrites), and ligand flow through the body fluid (directly from cell to cell), which is the larger of the communication systems. The cells that contain the activated Fragment will send out a ligand configuration to the connected cells in the Limbic System. These cells respond by sending out their electrical impulse or their Ligand configurations to the several parts of the body. The approached body segments, or organs, respond and their activity create the symptoms that our conscious brain interprets as emotions.

The past controls our behavior

It is clear that our feelings originate from these physiological processes caused by the activation of previously stored events. The activated physiology creates our feelings and this results in belief systems that control our decisions and behavior. Therefore, our behavior is controlled by our past. We often hear remarks like: *"He did not experience love in his childhood"*, or *"She had a very domineering father"*, or *"There was a lot of rivalry between him and his brother"*. Although this sounds logical, and of course these situations definitely have an impact on our behavior and our views on life, it is not the main reason for reactive behavior, emotional problems, or relationship issues. The subconscious, which controls and dominates physiology, has its own language and rules. Think of one of its basic rules: stimulus/response. A stimulus – or signal – is always specific. Consequently, it will always activate a specific piece of data from a specific event of our past. So, it will not activate overall patterns (such as a bad childhood or a dominant father), but very specific data from a specific event! Therefore, in order to reach the material we are looking for, we have to follow the language of the subconscious, not reason or conclude, but simply follow the stimulus/response rule. This is why in PMA we don't use the question "WHY?", but always "When?". To illustrate this, we'll look at one of the many cases in PMA.

Continue on medication

Let us return to our example of the toy factory manager. What if he had not used PMA to locate the related Bad Cluster that caused his problems? Would his activation have automatically come to an end? Not very likely. Remember, his office and the people that work there are constant activators. The sensory information from the very first day that the Bad Cluster was activated is stored in a Cluster, therefore, approachable for the conscious and the subconscious. As long as he works there, this Cluster will be activated and, in turn, activate the Bad Cluster over and over again, creating a long chain of Clusters with negative physiology attached to it. Of course many wouldn't want to quit their job because of how they feel. What they usually do is start taking medication to suppress their negative feelings in order to continue their job. However, the use of medicine will not change the fact that they are activated. It may consciously not feel so strongly anymore because of the medication, but the physiology is subconsciously still carried out in the same way.

You may wonder what are the long term consequences of not getting rid of the Bad Clusters? It is essential to understand that the human body is not made to experience this kind of constant and prolonged physiology. This will wear you down and constantly rob you of vital energy. If you do not notice this anymore in your body, then you've probably gotten used to it. If you're wondering why you are always so tired, you probably think it's because you're getting older (belief system)! But actually, the activation of a Bad Cluster on a continuous basis is more likely the real cause for negative influence on your functioning, thinking, decisions, actions, relationships and health. Normal Cluster physiology will never harm us. But the Bad Cluster physiology does. Let us take a closer look at the relationship between psychosomatic health problems and Bad Clusters.

What does psychosomatic mean?

What do doctors exactly mean when they say a disease is psychosomatic? Actually, this is where the problem starts because doctors don't really know exactly what psychosomatic is! They mostly refer to this by telling you that *your brain makes your body sick*. They don't know the real answer to these two basic questions:

- *Why* would my brain make me sick?
- *How* does my brain make me sick?

This leaves us with a huge gap in our understanding. Just think of it: it is assumed that at least 75% of all illnesses and complaints are based on the idea that our brain makes us sick, and yet the medical profession has no answer to what really causes it! Just realize this! PMA may just be the first serious explanation ever about psychosomatic illnesses! And PMA supports that statement with practical results. We probably all know how it feels to be ill, even if it is just a cold or the flu. Do you have a high level of performance when you're ill? Usually not, right? You would normally stay at home and in bed! But if you would go to your office anyway, how successful would you be on a day like that? The same applies in the case of psychosomatic illnesses. Of course we would create some belief systems to explain our feelings, such as: *"I ate something that didn't agree with me"*, or *"Lately, there is too much stress at my job",* or in the case of a woman, *"I have my period"* or *"It's the menopause"... "This is why I have these symptoms, but they will soon disappear."* Even if we try to ignore our physical symptoms, our ligand configuration is still out of balance and it will affect our thinking, decisions, behavior and actions! We also have to realize that physical and/or emotional health problems do not just happen all of a sudden. The development of chronic health complaints usually have a long history behind it. Due to our innate compensation mechanism we usually do not notice, or refuse to notice, little changes in our physical and/or emotional state. This compensation mechanism makes it possible to have high blood pressure but not feel it. We may even have a tumor the size of a tennis ball, but we don't notice it. A part of our compensation mechanism is based on the activity of Proto-physioclusters. Another big part is based on lying to ourselves!

We are masters in deceiving ourselves!

Why do we do this? Because we are so afraid of pain, and even more, of losing control and because we are driven by that enormous power *away from pain*! We tell ourselves that everything is fine, all because we don't want to face the pain or the loss of control! We will convince ourselves with a million belief systems that what we feel is normal. In the case of a dangerous disease like cancer, it can even go as far as oncologists (the doctors that treat cancer) immediately recognizing cancer in their patients, even if these only show a few classical symptoms, but some oncologists won't recognize their own cancer, in the event they have it although they are showing all the classical symptoms. This lying mechanism, or this "blind spot", is so strong that sometimes they do not even believe the opinion of a colleague doctor or even X-rays and blood results that prove that they really do have cancer. Once again, we consequently go away from pain, even if that means lying to ourselves, and these lies turning into strong belief systems. Over the years this can convert into all sorts of psychosomatic health problems.

The development of psychosomatic symptoms

Psychosomatic symptoms are always caused by physiological changes. These physiological changes are always provoked by external stimuli. They activate previously stored data and their connected Physio-clusters. Everything that we perceive enters our system through our sensory organs. There are absolutely no emotional factors involved in the analyzing process of the sensory data in order to assign the absolute code to the data. The emotional value will be determined after selecting the comparison material (Clusters and Bad Clusters). The relative code of that material determines what kind of physiology will become active. And ultimately, the result of that activation determines how we feel about the new incoming data.

No emotion without physiological information

Emotions are therefore felt or strengthened by the execution of the Physio-clusters that are attached to the activated Clusters or Bad Clusters. So, first, sensory data comes in from external sources, and then there are physiological reactions to that data. However, someone might say, *"That doesn't make sense. Because if I am sitting, content, with nothing going on around me, all I do is just think about a touching event, and as a result I will feel emotions. That's when I'll really feel the physiological reactions."* The latter part is correct, but the former is not! People don't "just happen" to think about things. There are always external signals coming in that set one's thoughts in motion. Even when you are lying in the dark on your bed, there is external data present. There is the smell of the bed sheets, the fact that you are lying in a soft warm bed, the creaks and groans of the house, whatever you heard or saw before you went to bed and many other perceptions. Let's assume for a moment that a thought did just pop up spontaneously into your head or that you were intentionally thinking about something that would evoke an emotion. Even in such cases, the emotion can only be felt after the physiological changes have taken place in your body. Keep in mind that all memories that you call up are stored in Clusters, not in Physio-clusters! There are no physiological codes, that cause our emotions, stored in Clusters. Emotions are only felt after the Physio-cluster has been executed. It will not be executed unless its ever-present companion, the Cluster, or Bad Cluster, has been activated first. So, first a Cluster or Bad Cluster is activated, then, and only then, are the physiological reactions executed, and as a result the emotions are felt. If these are originating from Clusters, then we are fine. The actual problems begin when the physiology comes from Bad Clusters, and especially if this happens on a continuous basis.

The chain breaks at the weakest link

The existence of Bad Clusters strongly influence our decisions, behavior and actions. Moreover, they actually define our health, and our mental and physical energy! Medical scientists tell us that 75% of all existing physical and emotional illnesses are psychosomatic. This is reason enough to take it seriously. Of course, you could now argue that you cannot develop an illness for which you have no genetic predisposition to. A chain will not break at its weakest link if there are no weaker links in it. This seems logical. But you may also imagine that if you are aware that a chain has several weak links, then you will take extra precautions to see that you never overload the chain. You know that you can do all kinds of things without ever encountering a problem, as long as you do not overload it. However, as soon as you use the chain to hang unusually heavy items, then you know for sure it will break at one of these weaker links. The same rule applies to your body. Once you are aware of the fact that you have certain genetic weaknesses in your body, then it would serve you to make sure your body does not suffer from exhaustion. Every human on the face of the Earth has these genetically predetermined weak links! So does that mean we can never again give all our perseverance on a particular big project? Of course not! Exhaustion is something completely different than being tired from activity. Exhaustion exists when we are under pressure for an extended period of time, months or even years. That can certainly be due to physical pressure, but usually it's because of psychological pressure. If this lasts too long or if the pressure is too high, then our reserves are depleted. The consequence of this is illness. The majority of all exhaustion comes from active Bad Clusters. We know now that genetic predisposition to certain diseases does not automatically mean that you will ever get that disease. Some ninety-year-olds have genes for a disease they never got. Exhaustion, combined with an overload of certain signals from outside or inside the body (ligands), will determine if the genetic disposition will become active or not.

Change or die

Although our genes determine the strength and weakness of our organs, the genes are not self-activating. They always need an activation from outside the nucleus of the cell. However, if Bad Clusters are active over a long period of time, the cells are forced into protection mode instead of being in the healthy nurturing mode. What is the danger of this? If they are in protection mode for an extended period, their defense system weakens and they become more susceptible to negative signals. Many diseases are so called auto-immune mechanisms. This means that the immune system turns against its own body cells and starts to fight them as if they were the enemy! In the case of pathological intruders, this is a natural reaction of the body in order to protect us. However, in the case of an auto-immune disease, the immune system no longer recognizes its own cells as a part of the body! This is because the cells slightly mutated due to continuous incoming and disturbing signals. Why would the cells do that? Simply to survive! A cell cannot continuously stay in the defense mode. Other than being in a neutral mode or being dead, cells can only be in two active states:

- *Protection or defense mode*
- *Nurture or growth mode*

As long as a cell is not in danger, under attack, or poisoned, it will stay in nurture mode. A cell that is in nurture mode does not defend or protect. On the other hand, a cell in protection mode does not nurture or grow. So it can only be in one of these states at a time! Every cell in our body is specific and has its own unique shape and task. If its unique shape or task is constantly under pressure because of disturbing incoming signals, it will at first go into the protection or defense mode. After being in the defense mode for quite a while, the cell starts to weaken because it will not be nurtured in the defense mode. At a certain level of weakness, the cell will be forced to change or die! At that point it will do whatever it takes to survive. Therefore it will develop another genetic pattern that is not so susceptible to the constantly incoming disturbing signals. So it will slightly change its shape and task. This means that at a cellular level, auto-immune diseases are not an actual illness, but a survival mechanism of the cell. Unfortunately, because of their adjustment, those cells are now no longer recognized by the defense mechanism as belonging to the body. The signals that caused the cell to change can come from the outside. They can be chemicals, radiation or all kinds of disturbing substances. However, the majority of those signals are not coming from the outside, but from inside the body, by means of unhealthy ligand combinations. They are produced by the Physio-clusters of prolonged activated Bad Clusters.

A long-lasting, undesirable physiological state

In some cases, there is a Bad Cluster that is nearly always active. Consequently, the negative physiological reactions are constantly barging in on the appropriate physiological state. If these changes in the physiology continue without letting up, then this can lead to damage to the organism. How does such a thing occur? Here's another example:

***Example*:**
A tense situation comes about at work. Carl had a rather intense disagreement with one of his coworkers. He accuses Carl of stealing an idea that he developed for the company. This resulted in a heated discussion with his boss. His boss stood behind the coworker 100% and threatened to fire Carl if he wouldn't drop the matter. The threat was so intense for Carl that he felt horrible. After that confrontation was over, his horrible feeling continued. It was obvious that the confrontation activated a Bad Cluster. If he would have left the company and never come back, then this Bad Cluster most likely would have not been activated on a daily basis, posing no threat to his health. But Carl stayed and his boss and coworker were still ever-present in his surroundings resulting in constantly activating memory moments. Because of this, the Bad Cluster will be continuously active. What did he feel during the confrontation with his boss and his coworker? What does anyone feel if he/she is threatened? What physiological changes take place? The blood pressure elevates, the heart beats faster, breathing intensifies, adrenaline levels increase, blood flow to certain areas of the brain and muscles maximizes, muscle tension is greater, and numerous other reactions take place. Nevertheless if a baby would have heard the same words and accusations as Carl, would she have experienced the same physiological reactions? Not likely, because she has no comparison material for that! So where did Carl's physiological reaction come from? From his activated comparison material. Because of the negative nature of his physiological reaction and the fact that it did not go

away after the confrontation, we can be sure it came from a Bad Cluster. The data of that activated moment he now stored in a Cluster.

What are some of the pieces of data that he created during that unpleasant confrontation and will be stored in the Cluster? He stored all the data about his boss and coworker, but also the surrounding area where he works, the furniture in the office where the big argument occurred, the sounds of the office and all the little details that he took in. Because at work he is constantly surrounded with memory moments, it is only logical that this specific Cluster of the confrontation with its high relative codes will also be constantly active. As soon as his boss or his coworker comes too close to him, he will start to feel the same physiological reactions as he did during the argument. Making use of his natural defense mechanism, he suppresses the emotions that come up by use of rationalization, by creating belief systems. Those belief systems, however, do not eliminate the Bad Cluster, and its Physio-cluster will not cease being active, either! So what is the result? For all outward appearances, he has the situation under control. Using his defense mechanism he has done some positive rationalization and created wonderful belief systems. Yet, in the meantime, his blood pressure is rising, his heart starts beating faster, the adrenaline level is on the high side, the muscle tension and the blood flow to his brain and muscles continue to increase, and he gets a pain in his neck and back, which causes a headache on a regular basis. His joints are pressed together by the constant muscle tension, causing his arthritis to act up, too.

It is much deeper

After a few months, Carl began to notice that his final symptoms no longer resemble the original feelings that he had during that conflict. That is because a prolonged change in the physiological state has a different effect on the body than a quick, temporary change in the physiological state. This results in physiological components piling up and affecting other organs and mechanisms in the body. After a while these organs get disturbed in their normal functions. Then they start to cause totally different physical symptoms and complaints as the ones felt during the original activation. We can all run into this sort of experience in the workplace but also in any other situation, relationship or location. But if this does happen without the activation of a Bad Cluster, then we have only a limited problem to deal with. However, it becomes much more complicated when we are dealing with the activation of a Bad Cluster. If such an activation takes place with our boss, co-worker, relative, family member, or friend, that's exactly where the real problem begins. Usually we will stay in regular contact with these people. In that case, there are so many memory moments that it makes it unavoidable activating a Bad Cluster. The physiological load attached to the Bad Cluster is then executed and felt on a regular basis. Therefore, we start to feel the negative physiology! An additional example will clarify this a bit more:

> ***Example*:**
> Once, as a child, Carl was accused of stealing money. He was not guilty of this and the accusation really offended him. To make matters worse, his father believed the accuser and was irate with Carl! He grabbed Carl by the neck and started cursing, swearing and hitting him (driven by his own Bad Clusters, no doubt). Carl had never been so afraid of his father in all his life! He is

literally in fear of his life. *"He's really going to kill me,"* he thinks at that moment. Obviously, a Bad Cluster is formed at this point.

Sick from long lasting memory moments

The disagreement that Carl had with his coworker was about stealing. He accused Carl of having stolen from the company an idea that he created. Carl is truly not guilty! This is the first similarity, the first memory moment: to be unfairly accused of theft! He goes to Carl's boss, someone in a position of authority, just like Carl's father. The boss believes his coworker. This is the second memory moment. His boss reacts very strongly and uses a number of the same words that his father used back then. Here's the third memory moment! When his father was hitting him and he created a Bad Cluster, he focused on the gray carpet on the floor. In this case his boss was wearing a gray suit. The fourth memory moment. This is already enough. Now the Bad Cluster is activated. All the physiological reactions attached to it are executed in his body. Every time that Carl sees his boss or his coworker in the same office, the Cluster of that conflict will be activated. This Cluster contains all the details enough to activate the Bad Cluster over and over again. At the same time, he has to keep working in order to take care of his family. So what will he do? Rationalize and create acceptable, although destructive, belief systems! *"Oh, it's not all that bad. There are problems at every job all over the world; no place is perfect. It won't kill me; look at all the people who are desperately seeking jobs; at least I am employed. Besides, I'm out of here by five, and I go home and forget all about it!"*

Nevertheless, the Bad Cluster is still active and its Physio-cluster is continuously being carried out in his body. At first, these symptoms will resemble what he felt when the Bad Cluster was activated for the first time. After some time, he begins to repress his emotions by hiding them under his belief systems, but the physiological reactions that cause these feelings are still active. The end result is that the physiological aspects pile up and affect several organs. After a while his final symptoms no longer resemble his original feelings at the time of the activation of the Bad Cluster. As a result of that, Carl ultimately suffered from burn-out syndrome, arthritis and migraines. None of his physical symptoms equal the original symptoms during the point of activation. Nevertheless, they are all caused by the physiology of the Bad Cluster that was activated at that moment. Not because of that brief moment of activation, but because its physiology stayed activated during several months.

A temporary problem

Psychosomatic symptoms come about by long-term physiological changes that are the result of a Physio-cluster that was connected to a Bad Cluster that stayed activated during a prolonged period. When a Bad Cluster is continuously activated for a longer period of time, then most likely the emotions associated with it will be rationalized away by creating a whole set of belief systems that might explain the feelings and complaints, or maybe we may even decide to take medication in order to suppress those symptoms. However, the altered physiological state will remain because of constant activation. This will undoubtedly lead to health complaints or symptoms because our body is not designed to handle the intense physiological state appropriate for fear or pain during a prolonged time period. It consumes energy! Some examples will help us to distinguish between a temporary situation and a chronic, recurring problem. Let's first take a look at a situation that is temporary in nature:

***Example*:**
You are seated at a table, drinking a glass of wine. You just had a huge dinner but had engaged in a heated debate with someone. You can feel your heart beating in your throat due to the unreasonableness of the other person. The huge meal in which you just overindulged yourself is causing a feeling of fullness in your stomach. As you are still not feeling so well, unexpectedly, someone walks into the room, grabs you by the shoulder and tells you that your brother had a fatal accident. A Bad Cluster is created at that very moment. So what will be stored in that Bad Cluster? Correct! All the data from that incident including your surroundings as they were perceived by all your sensory organs. What was the physiological state of your body at that moment? Your digestive system was in full swing, your heart was beating in your throat, your adrenaline levels were higher, and when you heard the news of your brother's death, you had the feeling as if all the blood drained from your head.

It could be the wine

Of course, the full content of the Bad Cluster doesn't have to be activated ever again. But it is possible that after a few years, you are once again seated at the table, ready to enjoy a lovely dinner. While the food is being served, a heated discussion develops over the same topic as before. Irritated, you take a sip of wine. You just don't understand how the others can be so unreasonable! Your host comes and stands behind you and slaps you on the shoulder and tells you that he is so happy that you were able to come, despite your heavy work load. The decisive memory moment is when he slaps you on the shoulder. Now the scene is similar enough to activate the Bad Cluster. All the physiological data is executed in your body. Some of the data you can directly sense, such as feeling warm and your increased heart rate. After a moment, you feel slightly faint in your stomach and you feel as if the blood has drained out of your head, creating a feeling of panic. This painful feeling is created by the digestive system that is in full force even though there is still no food in your stomach for you have not begun to eat. In a panic, you seek an explanation for your feelings. You can't find a reasonable explanation because the explanation is tied up in the Bad Cluster which cannot be read or interpreted! So you keep searching for a rational explanation in your surroundings. What is the most logical thing that you can find? The wine, of course! You still haven't eaten, and everyone knows that wine on an empty stomach can make you sick. So now the belief system about the wine will be stored in a Cluster and be given a very high relative code. However, this high relative code is created because of the physiology of the activated Bad Cluster and not because of the objective situation of that present moment!

It must be the wine

If this set of circumstances is never repeated, then most likely the Bad Cluster will never be activated again. Why do we say "most likely"? Well, the likelihood of you ever being at a fancy dinner, drinking a glass of wine and engaging in a heated discussion over that same topic is very small. However, to activate the total content of a Bad Cluster there needs more than just one or two similarities like wine and grabbing of the shoulder.

Imagine that on another occasion, you are visiting the same friend where you heard the tragic news of your brother's death. You will be surrounded with all those same memory moments because you are sitting in the same room where the news first came to you. Imagine that your friend relates an incident where he had an accident that could have been very serious, but fortunately ended up being just a minor one. As he is telling the story, you take a sip of the wine that he served you. Again, you get that uncomfortable feeling. You know this feeling, you had it last time, too, when you were here for dinner. You immediately realize, "*Hey wait a minute! I'm drinking wine on an empty stomach again*" (belief system). Once more, the wine is assigned a high relative value. The next time you are at a nice dinner, you won't drink any wine before you eat; or perhaps you never drink wine ever again! This would be a limiting belief system that is based on incorrect assumptions. We all have many of these unrealistic inhibiting belief systems originating from long-term activated Bad Clusters. This belief system is an innocent one, but other belief systems determine our whole life and some of them originate form Bad Clusters.

I can't fall asleep

Another example will show clearly how an activated Bad Cluster can plague our lives:

> ***Example*:**
> A middle-aged man suffers from insomnia. He usually lies awake in bed for hours before being able to fall asleep. He doesn't really worry or brood over anything, but no matter what he does, he just can't fall asleep. His heart rate is rapid, he sweats and becomes afraid.
>
> ***Session*:**
> He does not like to do PMA on himself, so he decides to visit a PMA Coach. The PMA Coach asks him to describe the situation of the previous evening when he again could not fall asleep. He tells the story, and

describes his symptoms. After doing this several times, he is asked at what exact moment did the fear set in, and his heart rate began to increase and he began to sweat. After going over the story several more times, it becomes clear that as soon as he lies on his back and puts his arms at his sides, these feelings began. He simply cannot relax. The PMA Coach asks him to keep the situation in mind and to try to feel the same way he did the night before as well as at the present moment. The PMA Coach asks, *"What comes up in your mind?"* Suddenly he recalls a problem that he had several years ago. His first reaction is to think, *"This has nothing to do with that"*. The PMA Coach urges him to just go ahead and tell the story anyway. It seems that several years back he awoke suddenly in the night and felt absolutely horrible. He woke up his wife to let her know that he was going to vomit. She ran back into the bedroom with a bucket just in time. The vomit was mostly blood. He went stiff with fear. At that moment, the normal processing of the subconscious was blocked. His wife immediately called the family doctor and he arrived very quickly. The doctor confirmed that there was bleeding in the stomach and wanted him to go to the hospital immediately. But the man was completely opposed to the idea. The doctor explained that a another loss of blood could possibly be fatal because so much had already been lost. He continued to refuse to go to the hospital and asked the doctor what he could do to avoid a repeat of the incident. The doctor advised the patient to lie quietly on his back and to especially not move. After the doctor left, he became very frightened. His heart went crazy and he started to sweat. He lay down on his back and laid his arms straight next to his body. He thought, *"I better not fall asleep because I just might move while I'm asleep and start to bleed again."* He could not sleep from 2:00 A.M. until 5:30 A.M. He lay flat on his back with his arms and hands stiffly at his sides until he finally fell asleep in utter exhaustion.

The contents of a Bad Cluster are not logical

So what were the contents of the Bad Cluster? Blood in the bucket = a stay in the hospital = do not move = bed = lie on your back = keep your hands stiffly by your side = stay awake = all the physiological data including the true fear of dying! After he sees for himself during the session the similarity with the experience he had with the stomach bleeding, his Bad Cluster was eliminated. Although he is not clear why this Bad Cluster was ever activated in the first place, the insomnia disappeared as if by magic. Many times these sorts of Bad Clusters are activated by something that happened or was said before going to bed. While you are in bed you lie thinking over and over what was said in the day. In his case it could have been a discussion about stomach bleeding or it could have even been a TV program that involved stomach bleeding. Once the Bad Cluster has been activated, then it can be reactivated in the same situation over and over again.

This is how someone can go on for months or even years suffering from insomnia. In most cases, it can be traced back to something the client would never imagine had anything to do with the original Bad Cluster. Why not? Because he cannot see a logical connection between what happened then and the present insomnia. The contents of a Bad Cluster are never logical and will never reveal themselves spontaneously by just reasoning or thinking! This cannot be repeated too often!

The power to compensate

Illness doesn't just fall out of the sky; it always has a prehistory! But before a pattern of illness makes itself known, all sorts of developments unfold within the body. The body has the wonderful ability to compensate. If an inherited weak organ upsets the balance, then other organs in the body will take up the slack. Once we reach the point of exhaustion, then we have to face the music and pay the bills. Perhaps you have gone for months with minor symptoms that were nagging at you. These warning signals were not strong enough to knock you out of commission. Then suddenly, from one day to the next, you collapse or get sick. Does it really happen so suddenly? No, definitely not. Sometimes it has been building up for years. So why didn't you get sick sooner? We have the compensation power of our bodies to thank for this. How does this compensation power work? The determining factor is: energy reserves. The more reserves we have, the greater and stronger the compensation power is. Some see this reserve as the result of their overall genetic constitution, others call it *life force* or *Chi.*

The energy drainer

You might compare this life force to a bank account that serves ten different businesses. Imagine that nine of the businesses faithfully deposit and withdraw in a balanced way. The tenth business only makes withdrawals, but never makes any deposits. After a few years, the account has dwindled down to the point of being overdrawn. Why does it take several years? Because the constant draw of the tenth is continually made up by the other nine. That's the way it is with our bodies. The life force of energy, or Chi, that we get at birth can be compared to the bank account. The energy that we are talking about here is not the energy we receive when we burn energy from the food we eat. We are talking about life-energy, the life force of a person. The definition of this term has been in dispute for centuries. The most familiar with this energy are the Chinese. By means of their experience with acupuncture and the associated ways of thinking, they view all disturbances in the body as disturbances in the life force. In the previous illustration of the ten businesses with one bank account, we can imagine our organs and organ systems as the ten businesses and our energy as the bank account. In this example, which organ system uses the most energy and is the most likely to deplete the funds? If we suffer under a great deal of stress, then this energy is being drained and all the results will become apparent. One of our organs can be under constant attack by an unhealthy, unbalanced combination of ligands that originate from the physiological commands of an activated Bad Cluster. By eliminating the negative effects of the Bad Cluster, this unhealthy flow will instantly stop and the attacked organ will regain its balance. It will now come out of its 'protection mode' and switch to 'nurture mode' and will heal rapidly.

With clenched fists

Stress can come from time constraints or by biting off more that you can chew. Stress can also come about by circumstances outside your control and which you cannot change. Think about the illness or death of someone you love. This can put a great burden on your shoulders with so much grief. This kind of stress can happen to any of us from time to time. In reality, however, these actually form the smallest percentage of stress problems. The greatest percentage of what we call stress is caused by activated Bad Clusters! During prolonged stress, more and more Bad Clusters are activated. A complete change in your physiology can come about as a result of this constant activation. Muscle tension increases. And sometimes this muscle tension is so great that some have been awakened in the middle of the night with clenched fists. Or think of the many neck and shoulder muscle cramps, and not to mention the weekend headache, as well as your blood pressure, heart rate, intestinal function and a whole list of reactions and changes that are influenced by stress. The greatest problem about this is that it goes on, day and night, twenty four hours a day! So, how does it get this far?

Take a vacation every day

Why do people sometimes ignore all the signals from their bodies and all the good advice that friends and helpers give them and just push forward like a blind horse? The answer is that people don't know themselves well enough and they overextend themselves and go too far for their reserves and deplete their life force. Then they are no longer able to relax. They "always have to do something," they are always busy, yes, and they even feel guilty if they aren't doing something. *"That's the way I learned to be,"* is a common belief system. That's right, you have learned to be that way, and you will have to unlearn that. You will have to relearn how to relax yourself. A good beginning to that is this: make time to relax. In these free hours you deserve to have the feeling that you are "on vacation" and realize you don't have to worry about your work or anything else . During these "vacation" hours you could start to discover the root-cause of your behavior, starting with questioning some of your belief systems about work and being busy all the time. In the chapter where we discuss the belief systems you will find powerful tools that help you to do so. You will highly enjoy this process and it will give you more energy than any vacation ever could.

Chapter 8 – The power of our Friend Mechanism

Our protection mechanism

The brain is a complex and sophisticated equipment. To understand its functions, sometimes it is necessary to subdivide the brain by modules. This is very helpful for educational purposes. However, neuroscience demonstrates shows that the brain and body are one! So, if we subdivide them by modules this is purely for educational reasons. When we discuss our innate protection mechanism, called your Friend Mechanism in PMA, it is important to understand that this is not a secluded system, but one of the many parts that makes us what we are. More directly: you don't *have* a Friend Mechanism, instead, you *are* your Friend Mechanism.

The Friend Mechanism

Your Friend Mechanism is your protection mechanism. This mechanism follows the strict rules of the language of the subconscious and is driven by the force "*away from pain*". It will always push you as far as away as possible from pain, fear and danger. Not only from pain and fear in the present, but also from pain and fear in the past. For instance, when you try to make Bad Cluster events visible, you will discover a force inside yourself that will want to take you away from there. That is your Friend Mechanism at work. The more fear that is involved, which is at the bio-chemical level (the presence of certain peptides [ligands] on fitting receptors), the more the Friend Mechanism is signaled to produce "counter" peptides to take your brain processes away from that fearful moment. This is an autonomous process that always happens based on stimulus/response and on the selection of data with the highest relative code! Now we will further elaborate on this absolutely important and intriguing Friend Mechanism.

The Warning Friend Mechanism

The Friend Mechanism is a very powerful system. Under normal circumstances it is responsible for preventing us from burning ourselves in the fire while camping, and from not falling off a cliff during a mountain walk, or it helps us choose our words carefully to avoid unnecessary commotion, and so forth. These are all very helpful and welcoming actions. To discern it from another form of Friend Mechanism that we will discuss later on, we call this original one our *Warning Friend Mechanism.*

Your Warning Friend Mechanism

- it's a mechanism not a person
- it warns you against pain, damage or suffering
- it's always there for you
- it helps you to ease existing pain
- it helps you to survive
- **it has your best interests at heart!**

When we get engaged in the more extreme Bad Cluster circumstances that we are not equipped to handle, the Warning Friend Mechanism will still do whatever it can to take us away from the pain. It's just a stimulus/response mechanism (reading codes) that can only do what it's genetically programmed to do.

The loss of control is unacceptable

If we get into Bad Cluster circumstances, where pain and fear can no longer be avoided, and we cannot control our surroundings or our response to it, we will experience a feeling of panic. Others might prefer to describe this as a feeling of drowning without anybody around who can save you, or others would refer to it as "going crazy". It has also been described as a feeling that you're falling into a bottomless pit without anything to hold on to, or a feeling that the world around you stops and you are all alone, unable to react. Regardless of how you describe it, the bottom-line is, you experience a total loss of control! This is an unbearable feeling. Just imagine what total loss of control could mean. You would have no control over your speaking abilities, your saliva, bladder, urine, bowel movement, muscles or anything in your surroundings, you would not be able to respond in any way, and yet, you're fully aware of the state you're in. We are stimulus/response machines who have consciousness, a conscience, and the ability to communicate with our surroundings, but at that moment it feels we are losing all of that. If we lose our possibility to interact with our environment, we will feel totally isolated. It therefore feels like getting disconnected from life, from letting the environment know that we exist. We will do whatever is necessary to regain that control. The fact that we all do this in the same way, led to the assumption that this is an innate mechanism that we all have. So, how do we regain control in a situation that was so threatening or painful that we felt we lost complete control? By restricting the amount of consciously perceived sensory data. How? We narrow down our perception of the scary reality by focusing on one single element that is less threatening. Or, in other words, we narrow down our conscious world to a level we *can* control! That is what our Friend Mechanism automatically does, just as water will automatically flow towards the lowest part of the surface.

Focusing

Focusing on a non-threatening element in the direct environment turns out to be an effective means to reach that goal. By total concentration on a single element, our consciousness gets narrowed down to a tiny part of reality, a part which we manage to maintain a level of control, a small safe place in our mind. The Friend Mechanism carries all of this out automatically, just by following its one simple rule. As a result, the painful details of the moment are not fully experienced by our consciousness and are not correctly analyzed by our subconscious modules. Regardless of how sturdy we focus and concentrate, it will not stop the technical functions of our ears, nose, eyes, touch and taste. Focusing will block these incoming pieces of data only from our awareness, from the conscious brain.

In what state is our physiology at such a moment? Total panic, and that's exactly why the conscious brain forces itself into a safety mode, blocking everything we don't want and need, especially if it intensifies that feeling of panic. This is the state of the highest relative code possible! "Code red"! The consequence of that is, that all the incoming sensory data that does not reach the processing of the conscious brain, will be stored without the proper encoding. All incoming pieces of data will have assigned the highest relative code. The subconscious just follows its rules and, therefore, it will analyze and encode every single piece of incoming sensory data before storing it. Every piece of data needs an absolute and a relative code. Only then will the subconscious be able to store the data. To complete this task, the subconscious is in a constant high-speed interaction with the conscious part of the brain. It is a constant back and forth activity. Incoming new information will activate only a limited amount of comparison material, enough to analyze (absolute code) the new data.

However, every piece of data also needs a relative code. That process is more complicated than the assignment of the absolute code. At a tremendous speed, the process goes in stages. During the first stage, the conscious experiences the feelings of the physiology of the selected comparison material. Based on those feelings, the conscious will then focus on specific details of the incoming sensory picture. This focusing will order the subconscious to activate the next group of comparison material, based on the details that the conscious is focusing on. This group of comparison material has its own Physio-clusters. The effect of that will be registered by the conscious brain. It will focus on the details of that incoming mental picture, etc. Again, all of this occurs at a tremendous speed, but the outcome of this process is that every piece of data has its correct relative position in the contexts of the overall picture. This relative position of each piece of data is essential in giving meaning to what we perceive through our senses. Even every word in a sentence has its own relative value. As an example, just look at the following sentence and ask yourself if every word has the same emotional meaning to you:

- *This is a great day, for I have great news for you: You won the lottery, and now you are a millionaire!*

If this message would truly apply to you, and if you would have to highlight the words that stand out, do you agree that each word has a different value? Most likely you would first highlight the words, "*won*", "*lottery*" and "*millionaire*", but even of the remaining words, the words "*you*", "*are*" and "*now*" will have a higher value than the rest of the words that are left over.

The specific parts of the information that the conscious will focus on, will determine what kind of comparison material it will activate in the subconscious. So, what happens if the conscious narrowed down its world to a very small size by means of extreme focusing during a Bad Cluster event? This would mean that the same detail is sent to the subconscious over and over again. Then the usually large comprehensive process of comparing would be limited to that specific detail. Remember, the subconscious is a stimulus/response machine, and can only start its comparison and encoding process based on incoming data. Although limited by the focusing of the conscious, the data has an absolute code and has a relative code, although every piece has the same extremely high relative code, and all because of the lack of processing, for the conscious continued to send the same message over and over again as long as it stays in the extreme "fight or flight" mode. But the senses are working normally. This means that all other incoming data is not properly processed because the focusing of the conscious brain blocked this process.

Just imagine! Regardless if it's a smell, an object, a color, a taste, a scent, a word, and so forth, they now all have exactly the same high relative code! This means that every single piece has the same physiology of "fight or flight" panic attached to it. According to the subconscious rules, the material gets stored because everything is fine; every piece of detail had both codes assigned. It's not the task of the subconscious to discuss or doubt the correctness of the codes. That's the department of the conscious! As a result, a Bad Cluster is born. Now we see why we call it a 'wrongly stored' memory, because during a Bad Cluster only a part of the usual comprehensive process takes place.

What we do register

So, what happens when a Bad Cluster is about to be created? No matter how fast it may happen, there is always a build-up of fear before we consciously start to block the awareness of incoming data. If the trauma doesn't end in death, which can of course be the outcome in case of a road accident or falling down the Grand Canyon, then, step by step, the individual will regain normal consciousness after the worst is over. Consequently, the Friend Mechanism stops blocking and reality comes back to its full capacity. The small world the individual focused on becomes gradually larger. And because the strong emotions are still present, the Friend Mechanism will keep on performing soothing rituals to ease the pain. But, even though the immediate danger has gone, the feeling is still there! Now, because the communication between the subconscious and the conscious is reestablished, we store all incoming data from that point on in Clusters.

> ***Example*:**
> You are on the road and have experienced a near fatal accident. A truck missed you by just a few inches! Even though the danger has totally passed, you still have to park your car at the roadside and your body starts to shiver all over in sheer nervousness. This is no longer a Bad Cluster situation, since you're not in immediate danger anymore, but it is a definite example of the continuation of strong emotion after the threat has subsided.

These Clusters that are produced just before and right after a Bad Cluster is created, carry important information that will come into play when a Bad Cluster gets activated. The Cluster that is produced immediately after the Bad Cluster contains the same coding of tremendous fear that was overwhelming the individual just before that moment. It also has all the 'rituals' that the Friend Mechanism produced to protect the individual against fear and pain. So what is created here is a normal encoded Cluster with soothing and comforting 'rituals' with the purpose of denying and ignoring the fear and pain created during its preceding Bad Cluster. As we will see, this turns out to be a very dangerous combination at the moment the original Bad Cluster gets activated.

The rituals of our Friend Mechanism

What do we mean by the "rituals of the Friend Mechanism"? Our Friend rituals are behavioral patterns that we developed during a Bad Cluster event. The purpose of these 'rituals' is to provide a specific, controlled and limited behavior, a conscious focal point to concentrate on. Through focusing and extreme concentrating, we manage to narrow down our world to these specific focal points. The focal points, or rituals, differ from person to person. Each person will use whatever works best for to avoid the awareness of fear and pain. A few common rituals are: clenching fists, holding breath, focusing on a specific spot, staring, telling yourself that "*everything will be okay.*", or "*this is not true*". There are hundreds of different rituals we use during a Bad Cluster event to create our own "controlled" little world to concentrate on in order to block our awareness of fear and pain. Later on in life, these rituals become soothing behavioral patterns during other unpleasant events. But how is it possible that we are able to remember these rituals that comfort us, when the subconscious can't read the content of the Bad Clusters they are stored in? First, we do not consciously "remember" them, and secondly, the subconscious does not select these rituals from Bad Clusters. After we experience a Bad Cluster event, we will gradually regain full control over all our incoming sensory data. But it is still scary, so we continue our rituals. The moment that the creation of a Bad Cluster ends, we store every incoming sensory data in Clusters. This means that we stored our rituals in Bad Clusters, as well as in Clusters. In both cases, the rituals gave us comfort and easing the pain and fear. The rituals stored in these normal encoded Clusters are approachable for the subconscious processes. We hold on to these rituals because we feel that this comforts us during unpleasant moments. Also, these feelings lead to behavioral patterns, resulting in the creation of strong belief systems about why these behavioral patterns are correct and legitimate.

It feels so right

This new mechanism of belief systems and behavioral patterns, that originate from Bad Cluster events, can grow extremely strong over time by being copied into more and more Clusters (just like a computer virus). In extreme cases this may even drive the individual involved to choose death instead of facing the Bad Cluster. Unfortunately, this is not just theory, it happens in many people's lives. Because of its destructive end results, we call this new mechanism the *'Inhibiting'* Friend. It is a projection of the activities of the original Warning Friend Mechanism. During a Bad Cluster event, this Inhibiting Friend is born out of a short-circuiting and starts a life of its own, and from then on, inhibits us through its physiological effects. We even consciously call upon its rituals because of their comforting nature, without being aware of their real danger. The Inhibiting Friend follows exactly the same protective program and genetic rules as the Warning Friend Mechanism. In a matter of speaking, we can say it is an image of the Warning Friend. We always have to realize that we create our own rituals and habits of the Friend Mechanism, regardless if it concerns the Warning or the Inhibiting Friend! Its program is genetically determined, but its Database is created by what we experience and will increase the older we become. The creation of this "image" of the Warning Friend has a lot to do with the Database.

The main distinction between the Warning and the Inhibiting Friend is their Database. The Warning Friend Mechanism is based on the content of our total Database, but the Inhibiting Friend has its own, very limited, Database. How come? During a Bad Cluster event, the conscious brain stays focused and rejects the majority of the new incoming sensory data. Every single piece of this data, as we already know, will have the same relative value. Although the subconscious mechanisms were satisfied because all the data had an absolute and a relative code (making it acceptable for storage), the data is still in conflict with the subconscious language rule that it will always base its selection on the highest relative code. In order to read it and select data from it, the subconscious tries to select the pieces of data with the highest relative code. However, every piece of data in this "weird Cluster" has the same high relative data. This makes it unreadable and unusable as comparison material.

Why it is so difficult to change people

Throughout life, we are constantly learning, and this often leads to a change in our opinions, or belief systems. Whenever powerful information is delivered to us of which we were unaware of before, we connect this new information with previously stored data. This creates new neurophysiological connections, which in turn, leads to new belief systems. This process is healthy and we call it personal growth. The more reasonable and open minded we are, the less active Bad Clusters are involved. Does this mean that being unreasonable is purely a matter of Bad Clusters? No, it is mainly a matter of choice, but it is well possible that Bad Clusters play an important role! Usually, people find it difficult to change and they often resist to it. However, in most cases it is not so difficult to change people if their behavior only stems from Clusters. Clusters are correctly encoded and, therefore, 100% approachable, and as such, easy to incorporate in our feelings of logic. The difficulty starts when Bad Clusters are involved because its physiology created in that person powerful belief systems which, in turn, created habits, rituals and behavioral patterns. These rituals and habits feel so right to us, that as a result, it feels so wrong to change them because of their powerful Bad Cluster physiology.

> ***Example***:
> Maria was a beautiful 6-year-old child. She always played at her neighbor's house with a friend her own age. One day, her friend's older brother, who was 16 years old, was babysitting them. The girls wanted to play and they discovered those really 'nice' colored cards that were on his desk and used them to draw on, not realizing that they were his valuable collection of baseball cards! The moment he became aware of what they were doing, he got furious! He hit and kicked both girls. Maria was not used to this kind of violence and was terrified. He

> then yelled at his sister: *"You ugly fat pig! I hate you! Nobody loves you!"* Maria felt horrible, lonely, rejected and guilty. She created a Bad Cluster because of this. During this event she was too afraid to look at him, so she focused on the dark green chair in the room. And once in a while she looked at his white shirt while she was clenching her fists and holding her breath, terrified. After a short period, Maria gained back her full awareness. He was now in the other room, still yelling at his sister and using the same words.

Maria's Bad Cluster got activated shortly after. Keep in mind, that the words he used were stored in the Bad Clusters as well as in the Cluster that was created immediately after the Bad Cluster. The words were not even spoken to her, but to her friend! However, the content of a Bad Cluster is not properly encoded and therefore, contains no logic. And the activation of the Bad Cluster always takes place based on basic similarities. Later on, this Bad Cluster became the drive that led to the belief systems Maria developed. Let's see how the Bad Cluster became active:

> A few years later, when Maria was nine years old, she was watching an exiting adventure on T.V. of Miss Piggy on the *Muppet Show*. She felt the thrill of the movie, and when the movie reached the most exiting moment, she was clenching her fists and holding her breath. At that very instant, her mother entered the room and was a little upset. Maria looked at her white dress with dark green flowers. *"Look at this,"* her mother said to her husband, *"I planned to wear this dress tonight*

> *when we visit your boss, but it doesn't fit anymore! I am so fat, I look so ugly in this dress!"* Her husband responded: *"But honey, you are beautiful! Nobody thinks your fat, and besides, I hate that dress, anyway... But I love you!"* The amount of similarities reached a level that Maria's subconscious, based on the stimulus/response rule, activated the Bad Cluster. Just look at the amount of similarities: Clenching fist, holding breath, pig (Miss Piggy), the colors white and dark green, the words "*fat*", "*ugly*", "*hate*" and "*love you*". Maria instantly felt horrible, and without any understanding why. She felt lonely, rejected and guilty. It was the similarities that activated the Bad Cluster and the Cluster that was created immediately after that. The words in that specific Cluster, combined with the feelings from the activated Bad Cluster physiology, created a belief system that she was fat and ugly, and nobody loved her.

As we already know, the subconscious will always follow the *away from pain* rule. Therefore, it automatically provides the conscious with the most comforting arguments and reasoning to create belief systems that soften negative feelings. These arguments will allow you to keep your dignity and they feel rational enough to satisfy your desire for logic and self-esteem. Based on this process, Maria developed 'shield' belief systems to cover up the deeper belief system that she was ugly and nobody loved her. She developed the following comforting belief systems: *"If you are right in what you do, it's not important if people like you or not"*, *"It's not important what I eat, I'll still be fat because obesity runs in our family"*, *"Being overweight does not make you ugly"*, and *"I need to do things perfect so it won't be my fault if things go wrong"*.

Unfortunately, many other techniques and methods pay attention to our belief systems, and keep in mind that her belief systems, like in most cases, declare the <u>opposite</u> of the feeling (belief system) that is related to a Bad Cluster. Once again, we have to emphasize that during the development of those methods there was no understanding of the existence and power of Bad Clusters. That's the reason that other techniques will only reach the level of your belief systems that are found in Clusters. The majority of those belief systems are 'cover ups' for the real destructive belief systems we have that originate in Bad Clusters. Therefore, don't be surprised if those deeper hidden belief systems pop up and they turn out to be the exact opposite of the original belief systems that you had always told yourself and others, and to discover your real belief systems. This process will give you an enormous relief, for it will free you from so many inhibiting behaviors and decisions! Enjoy the process!

Let's return to Maria and see how her belief systems shaped her behavior, decisions, relationships, and yes, her entire life! We have to realize the enormous power of the *away from pain* drive behind the Friend Mechanism:

> Maria created her belief systems as a protection against the deeper, and so very negative belief system (feeling) that she was ugly and nobody liked her. This kind of belief system does not support a healthy and happy life.

> And if there is only the slightest amount of data in your Database that can be used to suppress that negative feeling, your Friend Mechanism will deliver it as input for new and more 'pleasurable' belief systems!

Now try to understand what happens if someone tries to change these protecting belief systems. Whenever somebody tried to convince Maria that her "comforting" belief systems were incorrect, she felt attacked! Even thinking that the person could be right, activated her Friend Mechanism incredibly! Why? Well, if these comforting belief systems are wrong, what does that mean? It means that her protective shield would be pulled away. What is behind that shield, what did it cover? Exactly! The deeper belief system that she was ugly and that nobody loved her. As soon as that feeling (belief system) comes up, the related Bad Cluster becomes active. As a result, her Inhibiting Friend will do whatever possible to prevent her from focusing on that activating opinion of the other. Even seriously considering that the other might be right will instantly activate the Bad Cluster.

> Attacking her belief systems, that's not what Maria is looking for! What she really needs is the constant conformation of her embraced belief systems. So she worked hard and became more of a perfectionist. Whenever she started a discussion or a new task, she was prepared and knew exactly what she was talking about. She had to *be right* all of the time! And whenever she felt frustrated, she started to eat. Anyway, that didn't matter because "*obesity runs in her family, and being a*

little overweight doesn't make you ugly". So why suffer if you can enjoy! Whenever she "won" a discussion or got a complement because of her perfect work, or when she enjoyed junk food, she somehow experienced a good feeling because it confirmed her "comforting" belief systems. Whenever someone accused her of making mistakes, she would do whatever it took to prove the other person wrong, or even worked harder to make up for the mistake, because "*you have to be right in what you do, so it's not important what others think about you.*" She always lived under extreme tension. No mistake was allowed! We all need other people, but these kinds of belief systems have detrimental results because they will force us to constantly please them, seeking their approval and respect, and trying to win their love. This opens the door to all kinds of people with a parasite mentality: *"Maria is so good at what she does, I will ask her if she can help me with this."*

Just realize how one single Bad Cluster shaped the life and behavior of Maria! Did people like her? Most people did because she was trying so hard to please them, but there were others who thought she was an arrogant, unpleasant and stubborn person. Their attitude towards her confirmed Maria's belief systems over and over again, which led to more extreme behavioral patterns. When she saw people whispering to each other she thought: *"They're talking about me. I know they can't stand that I am well educated, and that I am always right and good at what I do."* The sad thing about this very common behavior, like Maria's, is that every time they seek for confirmation of their belief systems, they also activate the reason why they have those comforting belief systems: to cover up the Bad Cluster! Based on the stimulus/response rule and the connections that are made in the past with the original negative feelings that caused the creation of these "comforting" belief systems, the subconscious has no other choice than to activate the connected negative material.

Maria made it very hard on herself by being a perfectionist who always had to win, and at the same time, always trying to please everyone. Simultaneously, she became increasingly frustrated and exhausted because of her way of living, and her negative physiology of the constantly activated Bad Cluster. Although her total behavioral pattern came from her Inhibiting Friend Mechanism and was driven by the *away from pain* rule, it harmed her more than it really helped her! The reason for that is that her Inhibiting Friend is based on the power of Bad Cluster physiology. The effect of this physiology empowered and confirmed the "comforting" belief systems. Whenever someone tries to convince her that these belief systems are wrong, the powerful physiology of the activated Bad Cluster physiology lets her clearly feel that the other person is incorrect. It feels so wrong to change! Let us examine this a little further.

We always search for ways to feel better

If somebody hurts us, but not enough to create a Bad Cluster, we will store that event in connection to negative feelings. We don't like feeling that way, and therefore, we will do whatever it takes to get rid of those negative feelings. Some of it will go away simply by a good night's sleep. This is so because we dream. The main purpose of our dreams is to make connections between previously stored data with the data that entered our brain the day(s) before. Dreams are a tool of the subconscious to perform the huge task of connecting the new data in the short term memory with older data in the long term memory. This is mainly to make more comforting connections with similar comparison material with a lower relative code in order to feel better. This process is always based on its most dominant 'language' rule: *away from pain*!

Nevertheless, if the results of a good night's sleep isn't satisfying us and we still experience these negative feelings, we start to search for other ways of getting rid of those negative feelings. We usually manage this by making comforting connections. One way is by means of thinking and finding reasons and arguments we had overlooked in order to explain the behavior of the person who hurt us. Another way to make comforting connections is to come up with a rational answer to how we can change our opinion about the event in order to get rid of those negative feelings. The subconscious is of great help in this matter, because this is what it does automatically, always following the *away from pain* rule. It will therefore deliver the data with the most positive physiology possible. In the case of connecting Cluster data (even when it was an unpleasant experience) with previously stored Cluster data, there is no problem managing this. We will easily be able to change our belief systems as the following example will show you:

> ***Example***:
> Ann just heard that her friend Cathy, who she hasn't seen or spoken to for a few months, moved to her

> neighborhood. She wanted to invite her to meet at the nearby mall and have a good time together. Ann telephoned, and her friend picked up the phone. The tone of her voice was everything but friendly, *"Oh, its you...No thanks, the last thing I have on my mind right now is going out with you to have a good time!"* Before she could say anything else, her friend hung up the phone. Ann was totally upset about her friend's rude behavior. Was this the same Cathy that she trusted for years, the one she called her friend? That night she could not sleep, thinking, *"What did I do to her?"* She couldn't find a reasonable answer. To comfort herself she created a belief system: *"I don't need her", and "She will have to apologize before I ever speak to her again!"*

In her case, this belief system is based on hurt feelings derived from Clusters and not from Bad Clusters. This belief system could easily destroy a good friendship, or if these kinds of things would occur in a company, it would shatter the team spirit! Let us now see how easy it was for her to change her belief system:

> A few days later, she runs into another friend. They have lunch together and she tells her about the experience with Cathy, without mentioning her name. Her friend asks: *"You're not talking about Cathy, are you?"* Ann looks surprised! *"Yes, I didn't mention her name because I know that she is also your friend."* Ann continues, *"Did she ever treat you in the same way?"* Her friend looks at her and says: *"You don't know, do*

> *you?"* Ann is startled, *"I don't know what?"* Her friend now clarifies, *"You obviously don't know that she lost her husband. He died in a car accident two weeks ago, around the same time you must have called her."* This hits Ann like a sledgehammer, *"Now I understand why she was not interested in having a good time with me!"* In a split of a second her belief system about Cathy changed. So she decided to visit her and offer help.

This shows how easily one piece of information can change a belief system and influence behavior instantly! However, if belief systems are not based on Clusters but on Bad Clusters, we have a completely different scenario. If our belief systems are created to cover up the negative feelings and deeper belief systems that originate from Bad Clusters, your Inhibiting Friend will deliver all kinds of arguments and reasoning to keep your "comforting" belief systems upright and legitimate. Keep in mind that these kinds of belief systems protect you from searching for the content of the Bad Cluster because it is loaded with pain and fear. Whenever someone tries to convince you to change your belief systems, you feel the activated physiology of the related Bad Cluster. This physiology is so powerful that it will overrule every other Cluster physiology, regardless of how reasonable and correct the arguments of the persuader are. You simply feel that your belief systems are correct!
In review:

- Activated Bad Clusters lead to the formation of the inhibiting Friend Mechanism.

Your Inhibiting Friend Mechanism

Source:	The warning friend mechanism
Roots:	Genetic drive + limited resource of comparison material
Origin:	Created under pressure during trauma and loss of control
Force/Drive:	Away from pain - if necessary in the direction of death
Purpose:	Preventing total loss of control and managing the pain

- Bad Clusters are the power behind our "comforting" belief systems.
- The "comforting" belief systems of the Inhibiting Friend are a cover up for the real powerful and deeper hidden belief systems.
- The deeper hidden belief systems often display themselves only as a feeling.
- Many times this feeling contains a belief system that is a total antagonist of the "comforting" belief systems created by the Inhibiting Friend.
- The "comforting" belief systems control large portions of our decisions and behavior and they stop us from being proactive and successful.
- The Bad Cluster physiology gives power to the Inhibiting Friend and strengthens our conviction that

these belief systems are totally correct and we refuse to change them. Now let's take a closer look at the Inhibiting Friend Mechanism.

Recognize your Inhibiting Friend

It is imperative that we learn to recognize the Inhibiting Friend Mechanism. It is a projection of the Warning Friend with a very limited Database consisting of very powerful belief systems that will works against our interest because of the underlying Bad Cluster that it unwillingly protects. This is the 'bug' born from the originally correct principle of '*away from pain*' that ultimately makes us suffer even more pain, violating its own initial purpose. This makes the activities of the Inhibiting Friend Mechanism a harmful extension of the original Warning Friend Mechanism, in spite of the fact that it also follows the *away from pain* rule. Through PMA we have come to identify the Inhibiting Friend. We know its ways and purposes. The only thing is, it can manifest itself in many different disguises, in different individuals, and in different circumstances. PMA will teach you to become aware of your Inhibiting Friend and how to change its behavioral patterns, and sabotaging belief systems, so that they will no longer harm you, but only protect and benefit you in certain circumstances, and reach your Bad Clusters in order to do away with them. Once the source of the Bad Cluster's existence is eradicated, the inhibiting belief systems of the Inhibiting Friend will automatically change and it will not harm you anymore. So all we have to do with our Inhibiting Friend is recognize it, know when it's active, give it access to the full Database, and then turn it into our helper in tracing our underlying Bad Clusters. Remember, the Inhibiting Friend holds a huge amount of power and because it follows the rules of the subconscious language, it is programmed to help us live our lives as pleasantly as possible. Just imagine how this will increase your *desirable power* after your Inhibiting Friend gets "educated" and receives access to the total Database!

Related to many Bad Clusters

The Bad Clusters that empower the Inhibiting Friend are usually part of Bad Clusters that were made very early in our lives. It is not unusual to learn that Bad Clusters formed in the first three years of our life. Keep in mind that an experience that is very painful in the eyes of a child, might strike you as a minor thing, something that you, as an adult, don't even consider a painful event, but just a normal occurrence in the life of a child. But you stored it back then, based on your perception and feelings as a child! Some of our childhood experiences are definitely stored as Bad Clusters, and until you reveal the content of those Bad Clusters, their content will stay unchanged, loaded with its full power of negative physiology and accompanied by a loyal Inhibiting Friend imprint! However, we may also form the Inhibiting Friend later on in life. If an individual has a relatively protected childhood, and later in life is confronted with extreme fear and/or pain, then it is possible that the Inhibiting Friend imprints were formed later on in the individual's life. So we need to understand that each individual is different.

Each Inhibiting Friend Mechanism is different

What ingredients does the Inhibiting Friend Mechanism use to create our rituals and "comforting" belief systems? It all depends on the kind of incoming data and limited amount of activated comparison material the individual had available to use during the moment of distress. At such moments our Friend Mechanism might come up with the strangest, weirdest things to focus on in order to lessen the conscious awareness of pain and fear. Whatever pops up in our mind depends entirely on whatever memory moments are present from our previous experiences. Because the normal processing is blocked during a Bad Cluster event, our conscious has no other choice than to accept and use the first, and seemingly most appropriate, piece of comparison material that the subconscious comes up with. Our comparison material will then determine the feelings and physical behaviors that will make up the rituals of the Inhibiting Friend Mechanism.

> ***Example*:**
> A small boy gets a beating in his bedroom as he lies in his bed. He clenches his fists and holds his breath to suppress his pain and grief. On the wall, there is a poster of a landscape with children playing. Because of the extreme fear and pain he is feeling at that moment, the boy narrows his world down by focusing on the poster. In his thoughts, he is there with the children, playing. By doing this he is able to block the awareness of all his other senses and not feel the fear and pain.

His Friend Mechanism forces him do this automatically, for it has to drive him away from the pain. As a result, the Inhibiting Friend data created at the moment of being beaten up, will include all the ingredients of the poster as well as all the feelings and physical behaviors he utilized to achieve the ultimate goal of not feeling anything. This is merely an example of all the existing possibilities so that we may understand that we never know in advance what kinds of rituals will make up our Inhibiting Friend Mechanism. Remember how Clusters get activated in three different stages? Fragments, Sub-clusters and finally, the whole Cluster? So, when the Friend Mechanism has to protect the individual later on when the Bad Cluster gets activated, it will make clever use of this phenomenon, as we may expect. Whenever, in the future, the Bad Cluster is again activated by random memory moments, the existing similarity in data in addition to the emotional symptoms will not only activate the Bad Cluster, but also the Cluster that was created immediately after the Bad Cluster. This Cluster contains all the comforting rituals initiated by the Friend Mechanism during the Bad Cluster. The fragments and Sub-clusters that contain the rituals are then activated to display the same effective soothing behavior.

Our mediator between the conscious and the subconscious

We can see the Friend Mechanism as an interface between our conscious awareness and our subconscious processes. The Friend is the mechanism that works both ways. It can control subconscious processes and it can also hand the conscious brain a set of conscious acts and little rituals that make him or her feel more comfortable and even suppress the pain of activated Bad Clusters. Because it always serves its guiding principle of *away from pain*, it also plays a filtering role in its intermediary position between the conscious and subconscious. If, for instance, the Clusters that have developed immediately after the formation of a Bad Cluster get activated along with the Bad Cluster itself, the Friend Mechanism will pass Sub-clusters that contain the comforting rituals to our consciousness. Concentrating on these rituals help us to block the awareness of the fear and pain of that moment. The subconscious will not pass on the memories of the pain and fear that is also stored in the Cluster that was made immediately after the Bad Cluster. This would go against its most basic rule, *away from pain.* It will only pass on the comforting rituals, for they already proved to be effective. The other painful memories that are stored in that Cluster can technically be retrieved, however, at the time we stored that Cluster we explicitly added a special warning code to it that states we don't want to remember it anymore. This will also prevent the Friend Mechanism from delivering this data to our consciousness. Nevertheless, these specific Clusters are the ones that play an important role in discovering the content of the Bad Clusters, and although they will not reveal themselves just like that, they can easily be retrieved through PMA sessions (whether you practice PMA by yourself or with the support of a professional PMA Coach).

Clusters before and after a Bad Cluster

In a PMA session we activate a chain of Clusters that lead to the ones that were formed just around the Bad Cluster. Once these Clusters are fully back in focus they activate so much of the Bad Cluster that the event and the missing details actually pop back into our conscious mind. This time it enters our conscious willingly and in a safe environment, so the brain will not go into protective mode again. In reliving a Bad Cluster event during a session, things differ considerably from the real experience during which the Bad Cluster was created:

- We know that the danger in the Bad Cluster isn't really present at the moment of reliving.
- This time we want to experience it, while originally, we wanted to escape from it.
- Now we want to experience it in order to make the proper neurophysiological connections so that we get rid of the negative physiology of the Bad Cluster.

- We are now in control of the process because we can stop the reliving and take a brake at any moment we want to.
- Due to the high speed of the subconscious, in just a few seconds, we are able to relive minutes and even hours.

Our conscious awareness of these facts make the Friend act differently during a session and creates enough leverage that we allow ourselves to finally see the contents of the Bad Cluster. This demonstrates how the Friend Mechanism interacts both with our conscious mind and our subconscious processes. It is truly a universal principle that helps us get away from the pain. And it takes instructions from the conscious brain because we created its rituals and belief systems, using that part of the brain, by ourselves! Remember, your Friend is not another person, it is you! Here lies the next trap that we must learn not to fall into.

Belief systems and the Inhibiting Friend Mechanism

Our Friend Mechanism will protect us at all times! The fundamental force, *away from pain*, drives it. In obedience to that rule, it will try to stop painful memories from popping up. To achieve that goal, it creates a fundamental system that will dictate the conscious mind to follow a pattern of "comforting" behavior in order to avoid pain. Based on previous experiences, the Friend Mechanism will dictate a large amount of our belief systems! How does that process work? First of all, two things have to be clear to us:

- *Our belief systems dictate every decision we make*
- *We are not born with belief systems, we create them out of our own experiences*

Whenever we make a decision, regardless of how important or insignificant it may seem, every single one is dictated by our belief systems.

> ***Examples***:
> You wake up in the morning and you look at the clock. It is a belief system that tells you that it is, or is not okay to stay in bed for another 30 minutes, and based on that belief system you will determine what you will do. You may think, *"My first business appointment is close to my home so I have some time on my hands,"* or *"I have to get up immediately because I have to prepare myself for my business meeting this morning."* It's the same situation, but a totally different outcome based on different belief systems. Or, you may be faced with a more important decision: You are engaged with someone you love and you have to decide, *"Will I marry him/her, or not?"*; *"Marriage will inhibit my career,. and therefore, make my unhappy"*, or *"To share my life with a soul mate like this is the fulfillment and purpose of my life!"* Two completely different outcomes based on different belief systems.

Try to discover one single decision you have made that was not based on a belief system. You will not find any! We cannot make decisions unless we have a drive or reason to make this decision. These drives or reasons are our belief systems. Later on we will go deeper into this subject. All of our belief systems are based on what we previously experienced and stored in our subconscious Database. If these belief systems originate from Clusters, then everything is fine. Unfortunately, you will discover that the majority of your belief systems are based on Bad Clusters, instead of Clusters! The emotional (physiology) power of Bad Clusters behind belief systems is much stronger than the emotions that originate from Clusters. This enormously negative power leads to a mechanism of decisions and behavioral patterns that are illogical and do not serve you at all. Overall, we constantly have to be aware of the fact that the Friend is a mechanism that follows the rules of a program.

Creating the Inhibiting Friend Mechanism

Once again, our Friend Mechanism cannot reason or feel! It is just like a computer program that follows the fundamental principle of stimulus/response. It is an innate program to protect us. It always follows the powerful principle:

AWAY FROM PAIN

As soon as we are confronted with complete loss of control, and there's nothing we can do about the extreme level of fear and pain that is reached, our system goes into overload. Consequently, our protector, the Friend Mechanism, will develop into a different profile. The original fundamental profile of the Warning Friend will always continue, but because our system is in overload caused by extreme fear and pain, it will activate the profile of the Friend Mechanism that in the past already proved to be qualified for these specific overload situations. Whenever a Bad Cluster is activated, this force takes over immediately. Doing what? Rerouting our thinking, decisions, actions and whatever it takes to direct us *away from pain.* So, can it feel, and therefore, recognize the fear and pain? No, it cannot feel, but it is able to read the physiological (relative) code of the activated data. Although the subconscious cannot process the content of a Bad Cluster (due to the fact that every piece of data has the same relative value), the subconscious can read that relative code even if it is the same code for all the data! Because the subconscious is a stimulus/response mechanism, it cannot just ignore or reject this high relative code. Therefore, the activated Bad Cluster stays active.

Now there is a conflict! The subconscious cannot reject the Bad Cluster, but its high relative code activates the Friend Mechanism, the most powerful force in our body, *away from pain*! The activated physiology of the Bad Cluster creates a number of symptoms in the body. The subconscious instantly recognizes the codes of these symptoms. What activated the Bad Cluster? Similarities at a basic level, like scent, movement, taste, words, colors, etc. So now the subconscious has the symptoms of the activated physiology, plus, several pieces of data that together activate and intensify the Bad Cluster. How will the subconscious now follow the *away from pain* rule? Since the subconscious cannot read the content of the Bad Cluster, it is unable to subtract the *away from pain* rituals, but it can read the data in the Cluster that was created immediately after the Bad Cluster. Remember that this specific Cluster also contains many of the present symptoms and similarities that activated the Bad Cluster.

A belief system develops

Based on the combination of the three most powerful rules of the subconscious, it will automatically select the Cluster made immediately after the Bad Cluster, as the most dominant one. The rules are:

1. *Stimulus response*
2. *Away from pain*
3. *Selecting the highest relative code*

No matter what are the rituals of the Friend Mechanism that were stored in that Cluster, they will be passed on to the conscious brain as the most comforting rituals and behavioral patterns. Once you experienced the comforting effects of these Friend rituals, you will keep using them in many unpleasant situations, even when there is no Bad Cluster activation involved. Why would you do that? Because it clearly 'proved' that whenever you are stressed, or experience negative feelings, it served you well enough to suppress those emotions. At any given moment, in the present or future, when those unpleasant physical symptoms become similar to the content of that specific Cluster that was formed after the Bad Cluster event, we will use the rituals that are stored there! The pattern helped us in the past to cope with fear and pain; it will help us in the present, too! We develop strong belief systems based on our Friend rituals. An example will help us to understand how that works:

> ***Example*:**
> Jack was 7 years old and was raised with his cousin who lived next door. They were more than cousins, they were close friends. One day, Jack got into a fight with another kid at school. Jack was stronger and won the fight. The next day, he walked to school together with his cousin and there was the same kid again. However, this time the kid was not alone. He brought two friends along with him. It was obvious what they wanted: revenge! Jack did not worry because he knew he was stronger and so was his cousin, his best friend. When the boys came closer and threatened to hit him, Jack still wasn't impressed. Suddenly, he felt that his cousin grabbed him from behind and shouted to the other boys, "*Hit him!*". It was like his world collapsed! His best friend betrayed him! They really hit him hard. Jack created a Bad Cluster

> from this experience. One of the Friend rituals he used was to repeat in his head: *"Never trust a friend"*. After they were gone, and Jack gradually came out of the Bad Cluster status, he still repeated this phrase: *"Never trust a friend."*

This Friend ritual, this phrase, was now stored in a Cluster. As time passed, whenever Jack experienced problems that concerned friends, relatives, or coworkers, the Cluster created immediately after the Bad Cluster got activated, and with that, the related Bad Cluster became active. The feelings caused by its powerful and negative physiology, empowered Jack's belief system and even created other belief systems based on the first one. Of course, prior to practicing PMA, he was unable to trace the origin of these negative feelings, but he was sure of one thing: *"If you want to have things done the right way, you better do it yourself and don't trust anyone else."* This became a very powerful belief system that controlled many decisions and actions in Jack's life.

He consciously never connected that to the feeling of betrayal he experienced from his cousin. But his original Friend ritual are the words, *"never trust a friend"*. How can that lead to the belief system he developed later on in life? What was the feeling Jack had immediately before the Bad Cluster? He felt confident because, together with his cousin, they could handle that situation, they were strong. Because the subconscious is driven by the *away from pain* rule, it will not only activate the Cluster immediately after the Bad Cluster, but also the one just before. Why? Well, this Cluster contains major similarities with the one after the Bad Cluster as far as location, involvement of people, colors, movements, and so forth. Since this Cluster has so much similarity, but also a much more positive relative code (*away from pain*), the subconscious will also activate this one as comparison material. Remember, the subconscious processes a million times more data than what will ever reach our awareness. It also makes selections based on the highest relative code, the codes that create emotions, feelings.

We always look for confirmation of our belief systems

What are the feelings in Jack's Clusters right before and immediately after the Bad Cluster? For one, there is clearly the trust in a friend, then the disappointment, followed by a strong feeling that you cannot trust other people, especially those that are close to you. This created the 'feeling' that Jack translated into the words: *"If you want to have things done the right way, you better do it yourself and don't trust anyone else."* Can you imagine how this belief system can create major problems in a relationship or a career? If these belief systems would originate from normal encoded Clusters, we would learn fast and easily that they do not serve us and we would automatically change them. But this does not happen automatically when they originate from Bad Clusters. Changing such belief systems will only occur if you change their roots, the data where they come from. But this data is stored in Bad Clusters, and we cannot remember the content of Bad Clusters. If you try to remember, you will activate them and their relative codes will immediately activate your *away from pain*, your Friend Mechanism. Then the Inhibiting Friend will instantly deliver its rituals and belief systems to keep you away from the painful content of the Bad Cluster. In this way, we end up storing the inhibiting belief systems in more and more Clusters. As a result, they become the foundation of our entire perception of life. Based on the powerful physiology behind them, we are totally convinced that these belief systems are correct and serve us, regardless of what other people think! But at some subconscious level, we 'know' that they are connected to major pain and they are not correct! To overcome that uncertain 'gut feeling', we will automatically look for the conformation of our 'comforting' belief systems. So, whenever Jack experienced that he was right and that he couldn't trust others because the outcome proved once again to him that it was better to do things himself, he confirmed his belief system. This way he stored it in hundreds of Clusters and his belief system became increasingly powerful over the years. It became "the story of his life".

The Friend Mechanisms and the sessions

What role will the Inhibiting Friend play if you start doing PMA sessions, regardless if you use the self-help method or use the support of a professional PMA Coach? Just remember that the Friend Mechanism has always helped us to survive distressing circumstances. The mechanism has become our reliable means of survival. In deep pain and sorrow, it often seemed to be the only mechanism that was always faithful to us. The Friend Mechanism never abandoned us. It are the rituals and belief systems of the Inhibiting Friend that enables us to act as if nothing happened and to just continue with life, perhaps concentrating on work after such an extremely traumatic experience. It is the force of this mechanism that works in an inhibiting way during a session. After all, the Inhibiting Friend Mechanism has a closed loop perception of a very small world; this will block us from going into the real pain. Its limited access to the Database is based on this 'small world' that it created during the Bad Cluster event. Unfortunately, with its limited tools from the past, it tries to control our lives in the present.

As we've learned, the Inhibiting Friend Mechanism is not inborn, but was created from extreme fear and pain, and continued to serve us afterwards, every time the Bad Cluster it is linked to got activated. In practice, we can feel no distinct difference between the original inborn Warning Friend and its projection, the Inhibiting one. After all, the latter is in fact the first, only loaded with an isolated and limited set of effective rituals for the occasion. To make the right connections in the brain during a session, we have to go back and relive something we have denied and suppressed our entire life. This means we would need to acknowledge that something happened in our past that hurts us tremendously. This acknowledgement will feel as if we would have to give up our Friend Mechanism and all its rituals and belief systems that helped us to survive traumas. Yet you should never have to be afraid of that. You will never loose your Friend Mechanisms or the little habits that you use to calm yourself down. On the contrary! For the first time in your life, you will be in control of how and when to use these habits and rituals, as opposed to being subjected to unexpected takeovers of the Inhibiting Friend Mechanism. Sometimes you want to use a habit from this mechanism. After you practice PMA, you will recognize the signals that activate these habits and why. This will help you to find and recognize the specific moments that you get activated! It becomes one of the many tools in locating your Bad Clusters. It also serves you on your exiting journey to understanding the processing mechanisms of your own brain. It will be a revelation to see and feel how your subconscious made nightmare type of connections in order to lower the negative relative codes of activated Bad Clusters, and also to experience how your possibilities, insight and understanding will grow exponentially.

The purpose of our dreams

The conclusion of scientists, after years of experiments and research about the mechanisms of our dreams, shed an interesting light on this subject. Although there are different types of dreams, the main significance of dreams is to process information during a state that the conscious brain is resting. That way, the conscious will not interfere with the processing. Especially when all kinds of new incoming data that activated negative feelings need to be, based on the *away from pain* rule, processed and connected to Clusters that have less negative relative codes. Unfortunately, new incoming sensory data during the day also activates several Bad Cluster Fragments, or even whole Sub-clusters. Again, based on *away from pain,* the subconscious will automatically look for Clusters with similar content, but with a lower and/or more positive relative value to it. This also clarifies why we feel better about a pondering problem after a good night's rest. When you wake up the next morning, the problem suddenly seems to be a lot smaller and more insignificant than the day before. Keep in mind that the mechanism of the subconscious is always based on the rules of its language! It does not feel, reason, argue or conclude. It just follows the rules. This means that, to the subconscious, it is totally irrelevant how and to what it connects the data to, as long as it serves the purpose of its basic rules. This is why dreams are mostly unrealistic. Although they never happened in real life, all the separate ingredients (Fragments) of our dreams originate from our own Database. Put those Fragments in a random order and combination and you will come up with quite a number of weird mental pictures, especially if you use bits and pieces of data coming from totally unrelated events. As long as this whole process takes place at a Cluster level, we are fine, because these 'weird' connections are always based on the *away from pain* rule and serve the continuity of our existence.

Decisions controlled by nightmares

Yet, our dreams are not always pleasant. Sometimes we experience the strong anxiety of a nightmare. Why do we have nightmares? This was not meant to be. They only occur if parts of a Bad Cluster are activated during the day before. Based on its rules, the subconscious will try to process the data that activated the Bad Cluster. In doing that, the Bad Cluster automatically becomes activated again during the dream-process. The inevitable result of that is, that its attached physiology gets executed in our body. This creates strong physical symptoms. These symptoms can become so strong that the conscious brain, who should be resting during sleep, gets overloaded by physical symptoms, and we wake up. Did you ever try to analyze and make sense of your nightmares? Are the nightmares realistic and true? No, of course not! What about their feelings, the physical symptoms, like heart pounding, heavy breathing, sweating, etc.? Are they real? They are, but our subconscious cannot feel. It will proceed and connect the new incoming sensory data, that activated the Bad Cluster the day before, to whatever Cluster with less negative relative codes the Database can provide.

This is the reason that you see people in your nightmares who absolutely never have been on that specific location, or you see people together that never met each other, or they were already dead when the other person in your dream was not even born. As long as there is enough similarity on a basic level between the newly perceived data and older data, the subconscious will connect the new data to data with the lowest negative relative code as possible. However, this new data already activated Fragments of a Bad Cluster, and the activated physiology already created negative physical symptoms. And the subconscious will process these symptoms, too. It has to, because the subconscious will always follow its rule to select the data based on its available relative value. It will always select the most possibly adequate data. Because the subconscious does not think, reason, conclude or feel, it doesn't matter to the subconscious if the connections are 'logical' or historically correct! All that matters is that it serves the most basic rule – *away from pain*! Once again, keep in mind that the subconscious processes a million times more data than what is sent to your conscious brain. Even at night it does not rest! Among this huge amount of data are the Fragments that create our nightmares. Are they of any importance in our process of making decisions and creating reality? And do they have powerful relative codes? Based on the rule of the highest relative value, your subconscious cannot reject or ignore them. How do you like the idea that a large portion of your decisions and actions originate from the same feelings caused by nightmares? Don't worry, there is a solution. Now to change that…

Learn to trust your subconscious

It is very important to realize the things we just discussed, because your Friend Mechanism will definitely use the content of your nightmares to stop you from unraveling the content of your Bad Clusters. So, don't be surprised during your session if you see quite a number of pictures with a very weird content before reaching the contents of a Bad Cluster. You have to develop a great deal of trust in your own subconscious brain to overcome your inhibiting belief systems, and the fear of "letting go", and to discover the contents of your Bad Clusters and the roots of your rituals. This insightful information is necessary in order to know when, and in what way, we installed our rituals and belief systems. The reliving during a session will help us understand and relive everything in its original perception.

> ***Illustration of trust***
>
> In order to get an idea of the level of fear you might feel during a session, you could imagine that you are hanging

> high from the edge of a cliff. You fell over the edge of that cliff, and after about 20 feet, you managed to grab onto a piece of rock that was sticking out. Below, you see the depths that await your fall.
> Now, an experienced climber begins to scale his way down to rescue you. The climber will get as close as possible to you, but he is not quite able to reach you. You are gripping fearfully onto the rock with both hands. The climber then asks you to let go of the rock with one hand in order to grab his. You can't let go because you believe that it would be impossible for you to support yourself with only one hand. Not to mention that his hand appears to be too far of a reach for you. You are totally convinced (belief system) that if you let go of that rock, you will fall down and die. Meanwhile, the rescuer is asking you to let go of the only thing that feels as a real lifesaver to you! Remember it is your belief systems he is asking you to go against, something you really <u>believe</u> to be right!

This is a mere shadow of what you might actually feel. The feeling that you have to give up (belief system) your only real trustworthy security, your Friend Mechanism, your embraced belief systems, feels like an outright betrayal. You used the Friend rituals and the belief systems it created for so many years in order to survive, and now you want to go against a real piece of you, against your protection mechanism!

Distinguishing characteristic of the Inhibiting Friend

How can we imagine the actions of the Inhibiting Friend in a concrete way? This is hard to predict because the only constant characteristic quality is always *away from pain* and this can be expressed in many forms. However, PMA provides the tools to trace the actions of your Inhibiting Friend. To discover the first layer of its belief systems and rituals, you can ask yourself the following questions:

- What do you do when you feel pain or when you are afraid?
- What is it that you usually do to lessen the pain or fear or, if at all possible, to keep from feeling anything at all? (Building up tension in your muscles, clenching your fists, holding your breath, staring, playing with your fingers, grinding your teeth, etc., etc.)
- What do you tell yourself? Do you say things like:
    - *"I don't feel anything",*
    - *"I don't know",*
    - *"Just keep going on, like nothing happened",*
    - *"Don't worry about it",*
    - *"It really isn't as bad as it seems",*
    - *"I am not really here",*
    - *"This is not real, I am dreaming."*

These, and many other possible statements, can be a part of your personal ritual designed to keep you from feeling fear and pain. Let's go to the next set of questions:

- How do you behave when you are afraid or want to avoid pain?
- Do you withdraw and get quiet or do you get very busy?
- Would you stay seated or would you stand up; would you crawl away or hide?
- How would you move your body?
- Would you alter your position?

- What would you do with your hands, feet, facial expressions, breathing, or voice?

All these forms of expressions are characteristics of the Inhibiting Friend Mechanism!

Identifying the Friend Mechanism

How can this help you to identify the Friend Mechanism? You will have to trust your intuition, or even better, your subconscious. It does not make mistakes! The Inhibiting Friend Mechanism will use many forms of expressions. The simplest way to start is by asking yourself what you do during situations that are irritating; or when you do not want to show your emotions or pain, especially when you are in the company of other people and something is said that would evoke intense emotions. How would you repress such emotions? Usually, you don't give it one thought, you just do it. In some cases, however, you are able to perceive some indications of what you do. It's very important to recognize and/or write down this information. You will need it later as a reference to recognize when the Inhibiting Friend becomes active. By asking these questions in advance, you will get to know some of the characteristics of your Inhibiting Friend. Usually, you don't pay attention to how you do this. It doesn't seem that you're doing anything out of the ordinary. You are so familiar with the automatic switching of the Friend Mechanism that you really don't notice anything wrong with it. The goal is to identify what is really going on inside your mind that assists you in not feeling. What will you start doing when you begin to feel fear and/or pain? All of these patterns are a part of the Inhibiting Friend. The Friend is a master in self-deceit, because he is so smart, and because you are that Friend!

Self-deceit to confirm your belief systems

We all have our own specific configuration of Inhibiting Friend rituals, belief systems and behavioral patterns. Some people have developed a very dangerous one. This specific Inhibiting Friend behavioral pattern makes these groups of people very difficult to approach. Let's look and see if you recognize this pattern in some of the people surrounding you. It's not very likely that you are one of them. Why not? Because if you were, you would not have bought or read this book to educate yourself and find answers. This specific group of people never look for real solutions, it is not a part of their behavior! We talk about a form of self-deceit that frequently occurs and strongly inhibits growth and development. People with this specific behavioral pattern are always in search of affirmations to support their belief system that growth, and especially change, is wrong and unnecessary. Their conclusions are seemingly based on facts. You could totally agree with someone on the facts of a case, and at the same time, each of you has a totally different mindset about its significance and meaning (different relative codes). Everything that is not relevant to such a person's presumption will be set aside, and everything that confirms their ideas they will seize. Their attention is rigidly aimed at selective pieces of evidence from which they can draw their own conclusions that support their already existing opinions. This is why these 'suspicious individuals' can be totally correct in their own perception and at the same time, be totally wrong in their judgment. Their way of reasoning can be found in the form of a political, social, or economical opinion that they defend extensively with all kinds of arguments, religious dogmas, or even conspiracy theories. It occurs even more frequently in everyday thoughts, like: *"Everyone is against me"* (belief system). Their specific view of the world is often based on an unbalanced interpretation of facts. In their thinking, they barely make a true distinction between what they perceive in reality and what they actually have in mind. Snapshots and vague memories become facts, and facts that have nothing to do with each other are put together. An unstoppable development is being set to go from their imagination to suppositions, to fearful presumptions. And as a result, a system of invalid and immovable belief systems will develop over time. It is extremely frustrating to dissuade someone like that from his/her belief systems. Rational arguments carry no weight whatsoever. This person will single out one detail (often even an insignificant one) to prove his/her own vision without any effort. Even a simple attempt on your behalf to try and convince that person can become the object of his/her suspicion towards you.

Blind and deaf for reasonable arguments

When these kinds of people have investigated everything in detail and their conviction isn't confirmed, they will continue to find it unnecessary to adjust their supposition. Their sustained convictions, despite the inability to confirm fearful suspicions, demonstrate how cunning people can be in deceiving themselves. It does not trouble them to set aside the contradiction of facts and keep hold of trivial and irrelevant data if it suits their game. Their sometimes fancy vision of reality and maneuvers they make to confirm their convictions are the signals of hidden Inhibiting Friend Mechanisms. These characteristics point to a specific form of self-deceit, a complex pattern of belief systems and behavior created to suppress their deepest fears. There are some distinct characteristic features of their Inhibiting Friend Mechanisms:

- *The denial of their own weakness and refusal to contemplate/consider the worth of warnings and signals of others regarding their behavior and way of thinking.*

- *The projection of their own weaknesses on others.*

- *A continuing effort and struggle to confirm the justness of their projections by seeking 'revealing' indications and arguments.*

The denial/projection combination is extremely strong; they do not only deny their own inability and anger, but also renounce it by accusing others. They themselves are not false, wrathful or jealous; no, the other people are the ones that cherish these feelings about them! By turning around the facts, they justify their own touchiness and wash their hands off. 'Projection' makes people 'difficult' to deal with. To them, they're surrounded by dishonest and unscrupulous people. Also, dealing with people in a position of authority is often difficult for them, especially when they feel their autonomy is at stake. The same goes for their relationship with loved ones, spouses, and family; they feel limited in their freedom. The isolation that this person lives in only makes his/her problems bigger. This is due to the fact they aren't willing to trust others and speak about their doubts and insecurities. They deny themselves the company of people who are willing to listen, who could give them insight that better fits reality. And not willing to see reality can let suspicions develop boundlessly, and they'll even use the most absurd theories to support this, if necessary. Consequently, they run the risk of losing sight of reality and suffering a lot of damage.

They are not looking for <u>the</u> truth, but for <u>their</u> truth

Why do we pay so much attention to this specific Inhibiting Friend pattern? For protection! The reason is this: you will become very enthused after eliminating some of your Bad Clusters. This gives you an enormous drive to share these powerful tools with others. In doing so, you will run into people with exactly the same kind of behavioral pattern we just described. Here is the warning: Don't invest time in people like that! They will rob you from your energy and kick you in the back afterwards. Are they that Bad? No, it has nothing to do with good or bad. It is all about decisions, and they've already made the decision that they won't change! They're not looking for the truth, other than their own truth. You can give them useful information, but don't start a discussion. If they are ready for it (and some will never go that far), they will contact you. Then, and not a second sooner, you will experience the excitement and joy of freeing them of their powerful and so very negative belief systems!

The Friend Mechanism interacts with the conscious brain

We must realize that the Inhibiting Friend Mechanism is much more than just an actor on Bad Cluster material. It is completely interwoven with our feelings of protection and becomes part of our personality. Remember, it was created at a very emotional and threatening moments in our life. On those occasions, you gave the Friend Mechanism this clear assignment:

I Don't Want to Feel! (*Away from pain*)

The Mechanism will now execute this assignment consistently, using the behavioral patterns and rituals that you selected during a Bad Cluster event! Do not underestimate this. We are not speaking about a rational thing, but about a drive that originates from extreme emotions and the strongest driving force in a human being: *away from pain*. This powerful mechanism became the instigator of a large portion of our belief systems. The ever present tools of the Inhibiting Friend Mechanism are:

- *Denial*
- *Feelings of guilt*
- *Shame*
- *Blackout*
- *Reasoning*
- *Doubt*

The Friend Mechanism is there to prevent you from feeling pain and it especially makes sure that activated Bad Cluster data do not get to the conscious. Let's take a closer look at its frequently used tools:

Denial

Fear is the most important emotion in a Bad Cluster. It's because of this emotion that the Friend Mechanism will come up with all kinds of behavioral patterns and belief systems to prevent you from going towards the pain. You installed these behavioral patterns yourself during a Bad Cluster event. That's why these patterns are different from person to person. Some of the belief systems that originate from denial are:

- *The PMA method doesn't work for me.*
- *I just can't imagine that experiences from my past would have anything to do with my present problems.*
- *I think I am just making this up.*
- *I am convinced that my symptoms are purely physical and/or genetic, and not psychological.*

The Inhibiting Friend causes these and other kinds of denial statements. In order not to feel the pain from the past again, the installed program (not wanting to feel) of the Friend Mechanism will literally try to do anything possible to prevent you from having to relive the past. Let us, before we move on to the next tool of the Inhibiting Friend, go a little deeper into the subject of guilt.

Feelings of guilt

If denial doesn't seem to work, then the Friend Mechanism will use the feelings of guilt as another tool. It will use it at the moment that the first 'hidden' mental pictures reveal themselves. Some of its belief systems that try to stop you are:

- *I don't have the right or the money to spend that much time on myself.*
- *This simply cannot be true.*
- *I should have done something about it.*

Animals follow their instinct without being bothered by the conscience. As humans, we have a conscience and sometimes it bothers us. More importantly, our Friend Mechanism will use it to block us from getting to the Bad Cluster content. How can the Inhibiting Friend do that? By using a powerful tool of the conscience: Guilt! Mostly everyone knows how uncomfortable it is to feel guilty. How do feelings of guilt come about? It is not a tangible phenomenon, but a feeling. One person may feel exceedingly guilty about something, whereas another has no idea there is anything wrong. Feelings of guilt are not objective, but subjective perceptions. They are feelings that arise from physiological changes in the body, just like all other feelings do.

What is guilt based on?

There are several aspects that play a role in regards to feelings of guilt. For instance, they exist when something we do is not compatible with our primary attributes: love, justice, power and wisdom. Another aspect is the culture we are raised in. Something can be out of line with our moral values because of the way we were raised in our culture, religion, family or social environment. These are all normal feelings of guilt that come from Clusters.

It is important to understand that guilt feelings go hand in hand with fear; fear of being condemned, fear of being rejected, fear of not being liked or not being valued, fear of responsibility for the results of our wrong conduct. Fear is also the most common element in a Bad Cluster! Therefore, if feelings of guilt are combined with extreme fear, then this may indicate an active Bad Cluster, instead of a violation of our conscience. Bad Clusters have no analyzed, meaningful data that could be passed on to the conscience. So in this case, the feeling of guilt that bothers our conscience may not have anything to do with something we did wrong! So what is the real meaning and benefit of feelings of guilt? Guilt should warn and protect us from making mistakes that harm us or others! If it does more than that, like making you constantly worry or even making you emotionally or physically sick, or it blocks your effectiveness, then the guilt feelings are out of proportion! They should just help you to not make mistakes or repeat the same mistake twice, and they should never hinder you in normal life. Therefore, it is quite possible that we will rightfully feel guilty about something. If the feelings of guilt get to the point where they do hinder you in your normal functioning, then it can almost always be assumed that in addition to the normal guilt feelings, there are Bad Clusters active. This becomes quite obvious when you discover that the feelings of guilt are out of proportion, and reasonable arguments cannot reduce these feelings.

***Example*:**
Christine was a very successful sales person. Yet, she was not happy in her profession. Frequently, she felt guilty that she did not sell enough for the company, and at other times, she suffered from guilt feelings that drove her to almost forcing people to buy stuff they did not really need. She even had a hard time asking her employer for a raise, although she deserved it! In her first PMA session, Christine revealed several moments of her childhood when somebody gave her the feeling that she was guilty and had failed. Passing through several of these events, she arrives at the moment when she was 9 years old and her mother died of cancer. Her mother had often accused her of being a liar, and when something went wrong in or around the house, it was always her fault. She was not there at the time her mother died because she was visiting her friend to help her with a garage sale. She felt great when she came home because she had sold

> a lot, and was exited to tell her mom about her success. It was a complete shock for her when she came home and was told that her mother had died. *"She died and I was having fun and was not even here!"* Christine felt so guilty! In her session it became clear to her that whenever she was successful in selling something, she would first have a great feeling, followed by an unidentifiable negative feeling about herself. She realized that both feelings where present in the Cluster just before and immediately after the Bad Cluster, and that both of them were connected to the related Bad Cluster. The moment she came home with that wonderful feeling, she was confronted with the death of her mother, which created a horrible feeling! After she brought up all the details of the Bad Cluster in her session, she felt and acted totally different. In the following 3 months, her effectiveness in sales went up steadily, and she finally asked for a pay raise, and got it!

Guilt feelings can also block you from being as successful as you could by feeling guilty about taking time to do PMA sessions on yourself. All the other things we have to do seem more important than to take time for yourself! We feel guilty if those other things are not done in time while we sit quietly and do a session on ourselves. Keep in mind that doing sessions on yourself will give you more energy and make you more effective afterwards. It is never a waste of time to work on yourself in order to feel better. If you first sharpen the saw, you will finish the job before those who immediately started sawing. This is a mere sampling of the many possibilities of the installed guilt trips the Friend Mechanism can try on you. To get to the truth, you have to be able to dare and surrender to your own brain. You will need to learn to trust your own subconscious brain!

Shame

Sometimes, especially during a session, weird thoughts or mental pictures can pop up in our mind. Some of them might evoke a feeling of shame. Maybe because they contain memories of things we did that we are not so proud of and want to forget, or maybe they are of a sexual nature in a way that makes us blush. It might activate belief systems like: *"I have no right to think this way"*, or *"If I think about these things, I will turn into an immoral person"*. Don't be misled by these belief systems of your Inhibiting Friend! The stronger your aversion is against these mental pictures, the more likely you will stop your efforts in discovering the content of the Bad Cluster. The truth is, the more resistance you feel, the closer you are to the content of the Bad Cluster.

Blackout

In some cases, when you get close to a Bad Cluster, the Inhibiting Friend may use another tool, which we call a blackout. That is the moment when your images can simply 'freeze'. Your last picture is not moving and you do not see anything happening anymore in the pictures during the reliving. Another type of blackout is the total disappearance of the picture. Instead of seeing a new picture, you only see black or any other color. This will give the Friend Mechanism time to gather strength and have the picture and your feelings under control again! Always ask yourself at that moment: What is it that I see in that blackout moment. Your first reaction might be "nothing"! This is not possible! You always see something. The only way you see "nothing" is when you are dead! Even if it is not an image of objects or people you see, you do see something. Where did you see that before? Or, go back to the last picture you did see and focus on the detail that disturbs you the most. This mental "blackout" picture is a part of your Inhibiting Friend Mechanism and originates directly from Bad Cluster experiences.

Reasoning

The worst of all this is reasoning. It leads to all kinds of arguments that are totally unimportant for that moment. Keep in mind that all the reasoning is done in the Frontal Lobe of the Cortex where the conscious is considered to be located. However, Bad Clusters are not stored in the conscious part of the brain! If reasoning would solve the problem and would reveal the contents of the Bad Cluster, you would not need PMA. You would have solved the problem a long time ago by simply reasoning. Reasoning is not something that you are born with. To reason you need language, which you don't have knowledge of at the time you are born. Reasoning is a module you develop later in life. But if you reason during a session, it will only block you from finding your Bad Clusters. To reveal your Bad Clusters, you have to learn and accept the language of the subconscious and its rules. Only then you will get the answers you are searching for.

Doubt

This is the final goal of the Inhibiting Friend. If it can bring you to the point of doubt, you will stop the continuation of your search for the content of the Bad Clusters. When would you most likely start to doubt? The most common reasons for doubt during a session are:

- *The pictures can't be true because of their illogical or unrealistic content;*
- *When something pops up as a picture from your subconscious that you don't want to accept.*

The last one is especially the most powerful one. Imagine if a picture spontaneously pops up in your mind that someone you dearly love did something horrible to you in your childhood. You don't want this picture to be true! This is impossible! But, do you still consider the power of nightmares and their weird content and connections? Do you really understand that the Inhibiting Friend will absolutely use any kind of mental picture to stop you from finding the Bad Cluster? Please realize, your Inhibiting Friend means well, but it is just a mechanism and not a person with feelings. Once again, this is a reminder that the following cannot be emphasized enough:

In a PMA session you do <u>not</u> look for <u>the objective truth</u>, but for your mental <u>pictures</u> that are loaded <u>with negative physiology</u>, regardless of what the content is, and regardless if they are objectively true or not!

The ultimate form of not feeling

The Inhibiting Friend has been instructed 'not to feel'. The most optimal form of not feeling is death! Therefore, we are not talking about something small and limited here, but about the strongest force in a human being, *away from pain*, that could actually lead you to death, even though it should keep you alive! By using the tools of denial, guilt, shame, blackout, reasoning and doubt, the Friend Mechanism tries to prevent you from unintentionally reaching the deepest source of your fear: the Bad Clusters. Why unintentionally? Because the Friend Mechanism will act upon the genetic program of taking you away from immediate pain. You have no option but to first allow the pain in order to root it out completely. The result is, that this mechanism will work in an inhibiting way. Often, it will affect your energy levels making it difficult for you to enjoy life to its fullest. This road could steadily lead you down the path of 'not feeling' at all. This often goes by way of self-destructive behavior, self-sabotage, or psychosomatic illnesses. Perhaps in the future it may be discovered that all the so-called autoimmune illnesses can be cured by the dismantling of the Bad Clusters and their attached physiology that's kept alive by the Friend Mechanism. Please be always aware of the fact that it was you who created the Inhibiting Friend. So, it is within your realm and possibilities to change the inhibiting power into an energy source of *desirable power*.

Cooperate with your Friend

Once we know that we all have an Inhibiting Friend and we know how to discover its behavioral patterns and rituals, we can start to practice this. To show you that your brain always follows the rule "*away from pain*", let us do a couple of exercises. Just let go and have fun! This is an exercise in steps. We'll start easy.

Exercise one:

This is just a test to see some mental pictures: Look at an object. Take any object in your surroundings. Now, close your eyes. Can you still 'see' this object with your mind's eye? Can you see another 'spontaneous' occurrence connected to the same object?

Exercise two:

If I say "vacation", what is the first picture that pops up in you mind? What did you like the most? In other words, what is mostly dominant in that picture? Focus on that. Now, look and feel, and enjoy that vacation feeling until a new picture pops up spontaneously. The new picture may seem unrelated, but is the feeling similar?

Exercise three:

Go to a recent moment when you felt irritated, aggressive, depressed, afraid, or any other negative emotion. Relive that moment. Be there! Look at the picture and feel the emotion. What moment affected you the most? Relive that moment repeatedly until you feel what is the exact detail in that moment that really irritates or affects you. Focus on that detail and allow the attached feelings to come over you. Keep looking and feeling until a new picture pops up!

Did you find such an irritating situation or a negative emotion? Normally, it is not difficult to find this starting moment. Was it difficult finding the most dominant moment followed by the detail in that situation? Usually this is the farthest most people can go without any resistance from their Inhibiting Friend. After this point, some (about 30-40%) will have a hard time to continue (this usually occurs when you are just starting out with PMA sessions). It seems as if they cannot see the next level of pictures! If this applies to you, why do you think you did not see the next picture? Did that also happen in step two when you were thinking about the word *vacation* and its related pictures that popped up? What do you think is the reason that in that particular exercise you easily went from one picture to the other, but now, apparently nothing happened in your brain? If you belong to this 30-40%, then what you just experienced is the power of your Friend Mechanism! It protects you from seeing the pictures you need to see. Once again, not because this mechanism is bad! On the contrary! It protects you. Keep in mind it is a mechanism and not a person or an individual that can feel, reason, argue or think! It just follows the simple rules of stimulus/response! The stimuli are the symptoms of danger, fear and pain; the response is to block (blackout) and distract you, leading you in another direction! Don't worry! In fact, this is a positive circumstance. The fact that you got blocked, clearly shows that you were definitely heading towards a Bad Cluster. Just continue reading and do the exercises and you will experience how easy this process is, once you understand the whole picture.

Do not lie to yourself

In a session you will be confronted with your Bad Clusters. The content is unknown to your conscious brain, but your body will clearly feel its attached physiology. The closer you get to the content of the Bad Cluster, the stronger you will feel its activated physiological load. Your Friend Mechanism will do everything to push you away from those nasty physiological effects. This is the classical moment when we all start to lie to ourselves and bring our inhibiting belief systems into play. We don't want to feel what we feel! Therefore, our Friend Mechanism will activate rational arguments and distracting pictures. Eventually, the picture will freeze or disappear to make place for another picture or just a color, like when we are looking at a screen of a movie and the film brakes. That moment will prove how much leverage you have in order to be in charge of your subconscious processes. How strong is your desire for more energy, better health, more stamina, more success, and happiness? Remember what you have learned by now: suffering from the negative physiology of your Bad Clusters is a choice, just like being happy and successful is a choice. It is your choice! So give yourself permission to accept all the pictures that your subconscious delivers. This is also the moment when pictures can pop up that obviously - in your opinion - have nothing to do with the previous pictures. Pay attention to those pictures, they are important.

Keep in mind that the subconscious is a sophisticated computer, therefore, the subconscious does not make any mistake in this process! Your Friend Mechanism will try to stop you from following the pictures that take you in the direction of the Bad Cluster. As soon as you choose to accept the doubt, your Inhibiting Friend will win. Why would you doubt? Again, the most common reason for doubt is that we don't *want* to believe what we see. We say to ourselves: *"I have to be sure that it is real!"* Why? Why do you so desperately have to be sure that all the pictures are real? What if you read a science fiction book, or you thought about your nightmares? Do you also hold on so rigidly to this belief system that they *have* to be true? Holding on to that belief system already should tell you that there is something wrong, for we already agreed that we do not search for the truth, but for wrongly stored pictures with a powerful negative physiology connected to them! The resistance you feel to look at these unrealistic "nightmare" kind of pictures, should make you aware of the fact that your Inhibiting Friend Mechanism is already working at full force! Now, it is totally in your hands what you are going do with this. Do you want to grow to your full hidden potential or do you want to be controlled by those who caused your Bad Clusters and empowered your Inhibiting Friend Mechanism?

Go to the final room

This simple picture shows many rooms. They each represent one of the events that pop up spontaneously while you are collecting data to analyze the content of the activated Bad Cluster.

GO TO THE FINAL ROOM

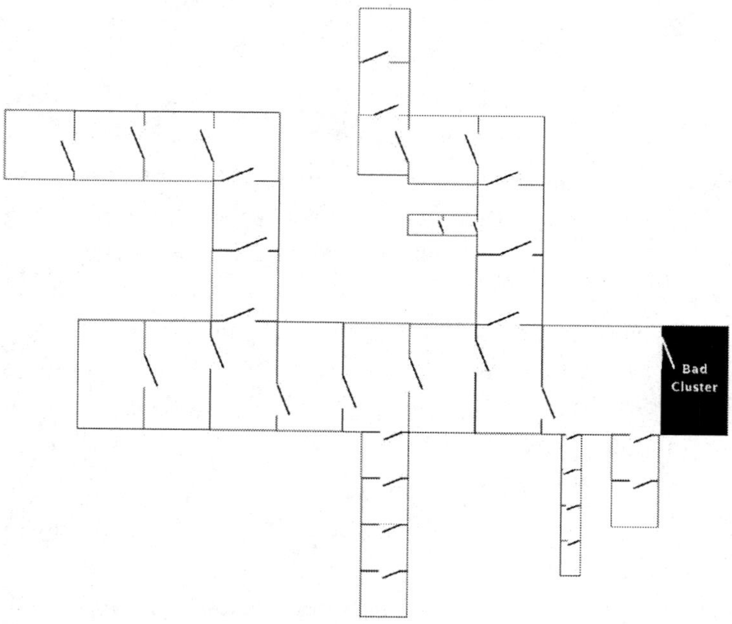

As you can see, there is more than one way to get to the content of your Bad Cluster. Actually, it is of minor importance where you start. The rules of the subconscious, in this case, the rule that the data with the highest relative code will be selected, will always lead you to the Bad Cluster because it was already active before you started the session.

The closer you get to the Bad Cluster, the more powerful your Inhibiting Friend will become. So enjoy the process if some 'weird' pictures and thoughts pop up, and experience the amazement and excitement to discover what your subconscious has created over the years without you ever having conscious awareness of it. The only thing that is important, and real enough, is if there is strong physiology attached to those pictures. If this leads you to other pictures with an even stronger physiology, and you arrive at the last room, you will instantly eliminate the negative physiology of the Bad Cluster once and for all. After that happens, you can ask yourself if what you saw was true or not! Even then, it is not important. The only thing that is important is that obviously there is a picture with a strong physiological load that bothers you and restrains the great opportunities for success, happiness and health you have inside of you.

Usually, the content of a Bad Cluster is true and realistic. However, if you created a Bad Cluster while you were using drugs, you could see some weird pictures during the reliving in a session! It is not important how weird, illogical or unrealistic they are! The only thing that counts is the amount of negative physiology that is attached to that picture. It will never bother you anymore after you've revealed the content of the Bad Cluster. That is the thing that really counts in your session!

Don't be misled

Let's look at this example to give you an impression of what to expect during a session. Let's assume this is a picture that you see in your session.

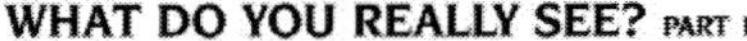
WHAT DO YOU REALLY SEE? PART I

It is not 100% clear, but you know one thing's for sure: This picture is impossible! Now you think for certain that your brain is misleading you! You see yourself, at about 9 years old, while your father hits you. Your younger sister is sitting on the couch with one of her friends. However, in this picture, she looks at least ten years older than you! And grandpa is there, too, but he died when you where only four years old! So, you will stop this right now! This is pure nonsense! But, actually, it is not! The only thing that happened is that your Friend Mechanism is very active at this point. This mechanism is genetically programmed to do everything possible to avoid pain. But it cannot think, reason or feel. It just reads the data of the physical symptoms that are known and registered in your brain as symptoms of pain and fear. It is a mechanism and not a thinking person. It cannot make things up. It can only use what is already stored there. That's exactly what it does. So then why would the Friend Mechanism do that? My father's beating was the Bad Cluster, right? No…wrong! This was just another picture that you need as comparison material in order to enable you to analyze the content of the Bad Cluster.

Just continue and everything will fall into place

Where you really needed to go was the death of your grandfather. He died in that same room when you and the whole family were there. The moment your grandfather suddenly fell on the floor and died, everyone panicked. You loved your grandfather dearly. To you, it felt like your world had stopped there. As a four year old, you did not understand what happened, but you did see and experience the panic, and you also saw your grandfather on the floor and you knew that this was not good!

How did your Inhibiting Friend try to mislead you here? Your Inhibiting Friend can only activate data that is already present in your Database. However, he can activate whatever is available in the Database that can be delivered by the subconscious to support his inhibiting belief systems, even unrealistic pictures that the subconscious in the past already combined in your dreams and nightmares. Because you are persistent in going towards fear and pain, so you can find your Bad Cluster, the subconscious will also deliver pictures that are pain and fear related. That's why it came up with the picture that your father hits you. Based on *away from pain*, the subconscious immediately added three pictures with less negative physiology to that picture and combined it to an unrealistic, "dream like" picture that confused you and stopped you from pursuing the Bad Cluster.

WHAT DO YOU REALLY SEE? PART 2

According to the rules of the language of the subconscious, it showed you the less painful picture of the beating first, before it came up with the true content of the Bad Cluster. The pictures you will see, before you reach the content of the Bad Cluster might sometimes be a little confusing to you, but what counts is the end of the process. The resistance you feel is not coming from those pictures that you see before the Bad Cluster. Each of those pictures has some data in it that will also be found in the Bad Cluster. Every new picture in the process brings you a little closer to the content of the Bad Cluster. The consequence of that is, that each new picture will intensify the Bad Cluster "fight or flight" physiology. As soon as you reached the content of the Bad Cluster, the process goes very fast, and in a matter of seconds, your brain will make the proper connections, and you will feel the release immediately. No difficult or endless constructions to learn. Just allow yourself to let go, and see and feel your own pictures. You will be amazed how powerful this process works and how rewarding it is!

Looking for the unknown

What are we looking for? What makes PMA so different? It is the connection of factual data with the attached physiology and the fact that there are two distinct types of subconscious material, Clusters and Bad Clusters. PMA is different and reaches deeper levels than any other method because it recognizes and respects all the rules of subconscious language. PMA provides you with a technique that is 100% based on the knowledge of that language! The knowledge and the fact that we know how to get around the innate protection mechanism to reveal the Bad Clusters and eliminate their physiology, makes PMA a next generation method. PMA is structured to go directly to the Bad Clusters and eliminate their physiology, changing them into a normal encoded Cluster that is approachable for the conscious brain. More than half a century ago, Luft an Ingham developed the so called Johari diagram. Today, it is still used and explained in many ways, and is still a useful model of the human brain functions, although at that time Bad Clusters were an unknown phenomenon. Let's take a look at the four quadrants.

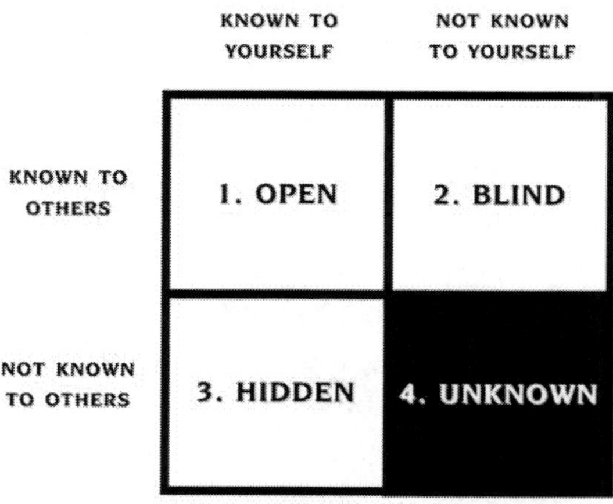

THE JOHARI-DIAGRAM, DEVELOPED BY LUFT AND INGHAM (1955)

Quadrant 1 - Open

This is how we present ourselves and want to be known to others. We know this part of ourselves, we don't hide it and everybody around us may know it, too.

Quadrant 2 – Blind

People around us know this about us, but we don't see it. For instance, others can notice that we always cough when talking about a certain subject. It is seemingly unknown to us. Why "seemingly"? Because deep down, we do know! But our Friend Mechanism blinds us from it, and it is our choice to stay blind. Why? Because the awareness of it will activate negative feelings like pain and fear! Mental blindness is based on Bad Clusters. It is, or was, at one point our choice to hide certain feelings by denying them and develop behavioral patterns and belief systems that are effective enough to suppress the negative feelings.

Quadrant 3 – Hidden

This is something we consciously hide. These are the things that we know very well about ourselves, but we would love to forget them forever. We are not proud of these memories, for they contain the memories of the bad things we did, and the things we are ashamed of. We stored those memories in normal Clusters.

Quadrant 4 – Unknown

This is the area of our brain where first generation methods, like NLP, NAC, RET, Gestalt, EMDR, PRI, tapping techniques, Homeopathy, Acupuncture, and so forth, do not enter. This is the area of the Bad Clusters and where PMA is active! And this is also the area of unclassified material that PMA will change into classified Clusters with normal physiology. First generation methods only work with quadrants 1, 2 and 3. But, they do not work on "Quadrant 4 - Unknown", for three reasons:

- *They are not aware of Bad Clusters, nor their impact and characteristics;*
- *The technique of these methods are not structured to approach this material;*
- *They do not understand and speak the subconscious language to a full 100%.*

This does not mean that first generation methods are not good. They are often very powerful and achieve a lot. But they will always stay in the realm of the Clusters. The consequence of that is, that if you don't eliminate the Bad Cluster, then, after a while, you will fall back into your old habits and belief systems because the real drive behind them is still there. Although the Clusters fill up 99.9% or more of our Database, they only control less than 25% of our negative emotions. The practice of PMA proved that more than 75% of all our belief systems are controlled by Bad Clusters. This is why people find it so difficult to change. They have never reached the root-cause of their inhibiting belief systems at a Bad Cluster level. PMA is focused on this "unknown" material because it has the strongest physiological load known to man, and therefore, it determines our strongest belief systems that control such a large part of our behavioral patterns and decisions.

The point is, that you are not even aware of the existence of these Bad Clusters, although during activation you feel their negative physiology in your body. They are, by far, the most important part of our comparison material that we need to know to be healthy and successful in life! No one wants to be controlled by unknown data in their system! It is a part of our nature to always be in control. It is just because of the physiological load of wrongly stored data during an emotional overload that our protection mechanism stepped in to save us at that time, but left us with a nasty residue. We have to correct that, and we can do it in a simple and permanent way! Let us now discover how our Friend Mechanism, our protector, creates and uses belief systems to inhibit us.

Chapter 9 – Our belief systems

For everything there is a cause

There is a cause for everything we do, say, think, feel, decide, conclude and even how we move, sit, dress, etc. We are born with a lot of possibilities and promising potentials, but none of us is conceived with existing belief systems. We develop them during the experiences of our life. Like our belief systems, all our thoughts, decisions, behavior and actions never emerge just out of the blue. They are all controlled by our comparison material. We have to realize that when we are born we do not speak a language, we do not know how to walk, talk, reason, dress ourselves, etc. We have to learn all these things and store these 'exercises' in our Database as comparison material for later use. Just compare it to the skills and behavior of a newborn baby. Whatever you can feel, say, do, decide, conclude, think, etc. at this point that differs from what a newborn baby can do, is based on something you have learned in the past. Usually we call this: experience. The reverse is also true! Whatever you experienced has shaped the individual you are now. Therefore the way you behave, think, feel, move, decide, sit, walk, etc., is based on your comparison material. As we already know, this stored comparison material consists of two components:

- Factual data
- Physiological data (emotions)
-

All our behavioral patterns are determined by these two factors. There truly is *nothing* that we do without a cause – everything we do has a cause and these two aspects direct it.

EVERYTHING HAS A CAUSE

every decision you make
everything you do
everything you say
every move you make
every choice you make
every word you choose
everything you think
everything you feel

HAS A CAUSE!!!!!

That cause is your

COMPARISON MATERIAL

If this would be solely based on normal comparison material (Clusters), this would be fine. However, a large part of our decisions are colored by Bad Clusters and not by Clusters! Be aware that the main part of this process goes on in our subconscious! The process of what and how our subconscious is really comparing and analyzing does not reach our conscious perception. Present input is always compared to past data. The connected pain/pleasure feelings (physiology) that are attached to that past data (comparison material) will be executed in our body as soon as the subconscious starts the comparison process.

> ***Example*:**
> You experience sudden mood swings or a sudden stomach ache or heartburn during work. You think this is only because of the junk food you ate (belief system). But you will be surprised! It is more likely the effect of activated Bad Cluster material.

We cannot consciously remember the content of an activated Bad Cluster but our body feels its physiological load. Now we have a problem. We feel all kinds of negative feelings but we don't know where they come from. We don't like this kind of uncertainty. Therefore we will start to reason with ourselves and we develop belief systems that explain our feelings. That's why you might blame it on the junk food, or maybe the alcohol you had yesterday, or too many cups of coffee today, or maybe you're catching the flu, or, or, or... This is how we develop belief systems. They are always based on our comparison material and the feelings that are created by their connected Physio-cluster. Albert Einstein once said:

> *"The difference between past, present and future is an illusion, but a very persistent one." In other words, every decision you make now, is based on your comparison material from the past and your decisions based on that will determine your future."*

Whatever you decide today will always be based on your comparison material that you gathered in the past. Just imagine that the subconscious will always select the comparison material with the highest relative code. Although our Database is only occupied by a tiny amount of Bad Clusters, their physiological power will override any Cluster physiology. You will be surprised to find out that at least 75% of all your belief systems are strongly influenced, if not totally controlled by your Bad Clusters. Just imagine what that means for your future! What do you have to do with your inhibiting belief systems?

1. *Change your old belief system into a new one.*

2. *Make the decision that you will apply this new belief system.*

3. *Repeat this new belief system whenever the old belief system pops up.*

4. *Force yourself to apply it when you would normally apply your old belief system.*

Bad Clusters are the source of all inhibiting belief systems. You are now able to change all that. To do so you always have to focus on the solution and not the problem and get rid of the material that disrupts your health, performance and happiness!

The foundation of our behavior lies in our belief systems

To become more energetic, creative and effective we have to find the hidden force behind our belief systems. We have to find the inhibiting ones that stop us from being successful and being the person we feel we can be. To do so we have to change the belief systems that are originating from Bad Clusters into belief systems that serve us. Keep in mind that these belief systems are the product of your Inhibiting Friend Mechanism!

You will feel a lot of resistance from your Friend Mechanism if the belief system originates from a Bad Cluster. Create new positive belief systems and force yourself to follow these new ones. The resistance will gradually become stronger. It is this feeling of resistance that will help us find the Bad Cluster. As soon as the old belief system pops up and tries to force you to override your new belief system, you have to condition yourself to stick to your new belief system. But, the resistance will grow. Now focus on that feeling. Try to find the exact moment that brought up your old belief system, the moment you felt the resistance.

The origin of our belief systems

Our belief systems always originate from our emotions. Because of our own protection mechanism we will think and feel that our belief systems are totally correct, serve us, and are the best for us. However, a large amount of our belief systems originate from Bad Clusters. The emotions attached to these convictions are extremely strong. These beliefs may have served to protect us during a Bad Cluster situation and probably helped us to survive the event. In most cases, these belief systems do not really serve us in our present life, but on the contrary, they limit and harm us. They are often the reason why we sabotage ourselves and make the wrong decisions.

Challenge your belief systems

Our experiences and how we interpret them will create our belief systems. As we already know, our interpretation is our reality and the interpretation is always based on our existing comparison material. So, some of your belief systems originate from material of which you do not know exists. The content of that material is loaded with negative physiology. How will this influence your belief systems? What kind of belief systems will you get from that?

What really shapes your world and abilities?

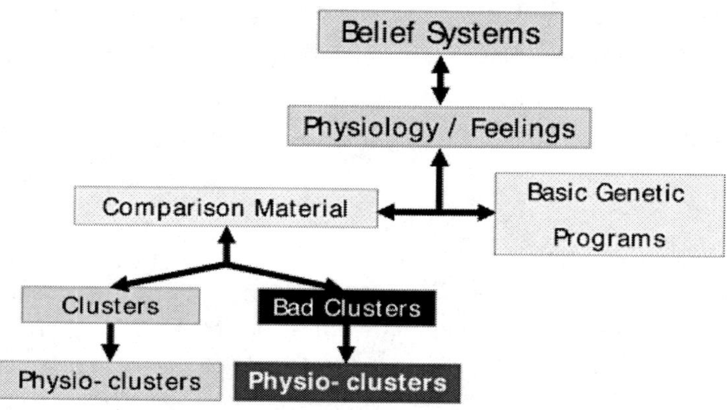

Would you agree that you would need to get rid of this material and change those negatively inspired belief systems? Because this material is so powerful, it will overrule any kind of conditioning you will attempt! You will never be able to change your belief systems with just "positive thinking" or the notion that you have to change them. The harmful effects of the Bad Clusters are too strong for that! They will overrule any change you try to accomplish. The only way to change those belief systems that originate in Bad Clusters is to get to the root cause and get rid of the Bad Clusters. After that happens, you can make the proper decisions and, as a result, the belief systems will automatically change.

Why find our belief systems?

Is it really important to find our belief systems? Absolutely! If our belief systems are driving all our thinking, decisions, and behavior, it would seem logical that we find out what really shapes and determines our life. What is the benefit of knowing our belief systems? A tremendous one! The good thing about our belief systems is that we can change them! By changing our belief systems we will definitely change our whole life for the better! How can we find our own belief systems? Keep in mind that they are the driving force behind all our thoughts, decisions and actions. The first step to finding our belief systems would be to ask the following questions:

- Why did I choose what I do in life?
- What are my most important convictions and rules in life, and why?
- Would I like to change those convictions and rules?
- If the answer is no, why not?
- If the answer is yes, what stops me from making the necessary changes?

We need to try to follow our feelings about these questions and not just think rationally. Our belief systems are not created by rational thinking, but mainly by our emotions! Some of the most powerful belief systems are usually the early ones in life, and don't even have words assigned to them. They exist only as a feeling.

A great tool to discover our personal belief systems

Some people find it hard to discover or recognize their own belief systems. The following tool will help you to find your belief systems. Actually, we recommend using this tool even if you don't find it difficult. The next exercise shows 17 major areas or important topics in our lives. Please read the instructions carefully. Don't think too long about the answer, just mark the number based on your feelings.

A tool to find and change belief systems

Willingness to change is at the core of growth. Our thoughts, behavior and decisions will not change as long as our belief systems remain the same. Therefore, we are strongly encouraged to examine our belief systems. Do our belief systems really benefit our life? How can you make the necessary changes to improve the quality of your life? Using the list below, let's start by determining to what degree you feel you are at the present in each area of your life. How satisfied and successful are you in the following areas? Indicate each of the areas on a scale of 1-10, with "1" being very bad and "10" being excellent.

Some of the areas of the following exercise might need a little explanation of what exactly is meant by the brief statement you find there. For instance, number 5: Intellectual development. Are you satisfied with your education and the areas you have studied so far, or do you want more? The figure should represent how satisfied or unsatisfied you are. Number 6: This includes your total status of spiritual development. It can refer to religion, but if you are not religious, it refers to what level you are satisfied with your choices in regards to spiritual issues. Number 12 refers to your ability in accepting changes. Are you flexible, easy to approach, open minded, or the contrary? Number 15 helps you to find out to what level you are satisfied with the relationship you have with your family and friends. Finally, number 17 refers to the level you are capable of making decisions that serve you and not always putting others first. Do you love yourself enough to say "no" if someone interferes with your plans to do something that you like?

You will benefit the most from this very important exercise if you first fill it in spontaneously, continue reading the text after this exercise, and then look back again at the scores you filled in and check if they are still correct in your opinion.

1. Emotional health

1❑ 2❑ 3❑ 4❑ 5❑ 6❑ 7❑ 8❑ 9❑ 10❑

2. Physical health

1❑ 2❑ 3❑ 4❑ 5❑ 6❑ 7❑ 8❑ 9❑ 10❑

3. Freedom

1❑ 2❑ 3❑ 4❑ 5❑ 6❑ 7❑ 8❑ 9❑ 10❑

4. Inner peace and balance

1❑ 2❑ 3❑ 4❑ 5❑ 6❑ 7❑ 8❑ 9❑ 10❑

5. Intellectual development

1❑ 2❑ 3❑ 4❑ 5❑ 6❑ 7❑ 8❑ 9❑ 10❑

6. Spiritual development (religion)

1❑ 2❑ 3❑ 4❑ 5❑ 6❑ 7❑ 8❑ 9❑ 10❑

7. Energy

1❑ 2❑ 3❑ 4❑ 5❑ 6❑ 7❑ 8❑ 9❑ 10❑

8. Relationship with your partner

1❑ 2❑ 3❑ 4❑ 5❑ 6❑ 7❑ 8❑ 9❑ 10❑

9. Work (joy, enthusiasm)

1❑ 2❑ 3❑ 4❑ 5❑ 6❑ 7❑ 8❑ 9❑ 10❑

10. Enjoyment of life

1❑ 2❑ 3❑ 4❑ 5❑ 6❑ 7❑ 8❑ 9❑ 10❑

11. Measure of happiness

1❑ 2❑ 3❑ 4❑ 5❑ 6❑ 7❑ 8❑ 9❑ 10❑

12. Mental flexibility

1❑ 2❑ 3❑ 4❑ 5❑ 6❑ 7❑ 8❑ 9❑ 10❑

13. Decision-making

1❑ 2❑ 3❑ 4❑ 5❑ 6❑ 7❑ 8❑ 9❑ 10❑

14. Interests (work, hobbies, people)

1❑ 2❑ 3❑ 4❑ 5❑ 6❑ 7❑ 8❑ 9❑ 10❑

15. Association/relationships/family

1❑ 2❑ 3❑ 4❑ 5❑ 6❑ 7❑ 8❑ 9❑ 10❑

16. Personal progress/growth

1❑ 2❑ 3❑ 4❑ 5❑ 6❑ 7❑ 8❑ 9❑ 10❑

17. Measure of self-love

1❑ 2❑ 3❑ 4❑ 5❑ 6❑ 7❑ 8❑ 9❑ 10❑

Because of the importance of this exercise, we have collected a number of questions and belief systems for each of the 17 areas you just filled in. Before going through them, first ask yourself the following questions in order to find some of your present belief systems:

- Are all my answers realistic?
- Why do I believe that my answers are realistic?
- Why do I believe that I am at these levels?
- Are these the desirable levels where I want to be?
- If not, what are my belief systems that stop me from getting where I want to be?
- What is my personal belief system that formed the basis of my answers?
- Am I satisfied with my scores in all of these areas?

Once you discover in which areas you are not functioning to your satisfaction, then ask yourself the following questions:

- What prevents me from achieving the progress or success in the areas that I want to change or grow in?

- What will I need to do to make the necessary changes from this moment on?
- What could prevent me from making such changes?

We recommend that you take time to write down your findings. To your amazement, what you write are usually your belief systems. With your personal notes, walk through the examples in the following pages.

Let us consider our belief systems

In order to give you some suggestions about belief systems, we will show you some samples for each one of the 17 topics. Please note: These are just examples and do not necessarily reflect your personal belief systems. They are just examples to help and encourage you.

Emotional health

Ask yourself:

Am I in balance?
Do I take medication for any emotional problems?
Are my emotions in balance with others around me?
Are my emotions overwhelming me or others around me?

The belief system could be:

- I have a weak nervous system
- I live under too much stress
- People do not understand me
- I don't show my emotions because it will make me vulnerable
- Others can achieve it, but I can't
- I don’t allow myself to feel

- I'm neurotic
- I have a chemical imbalance
- My life is not going right
- Everyone else is important, but me

Physical health

Ask yourself:

Do I take medication for physical problems?
Am I in a good physical condition?
Do I have pain, blood pressure complications, intestinal problems, etc.?
Do I usually wake up with the feeling that I will enjoy the day?

The belief system could be:

- I don't have time to pay too much attention to my health
- I have a genetically weak body
- If I am spiritually healthy, my body will automatically be healthy, too
- I come from a strong healthy family
- I'm fat and ugly
- If I'm fat, people won't look at me in a sexual way
- My parents made me this way; they were bad, and that's why I am bad, too
- I need coffee in the morning before I can do anything else
- My body has a sugar/carbohydrate need, so I eat chocolate

Freedom

Ask yourself:

Do I really feel free?

Am I really free to think and say what I want?
Do I truly feel free in my community, club, relationship, etc., to say what I feel and think?
Can I be what I am?
Do I usually feel relaxed around other people?
Do I feel enough freedom to express myself among others at work or school?
Do I wear the clothes I want to, or am I afraid of what people think?

The belief system could be:

- In this society it is impossible to be free
- Real freedom does not exist
- I will have a lot of problems if I say what I believe
- Freedom is for people who need it, not me
- If I keep my mouth shut, I won't get hurt
- I can't trust myself
- I can't trust others
- I have to be in control
- Freedom comes with a price

Inner peace and balance

Ask yourself:

Do I have a good overview of the possibilities in my life?
Is it easy for me to make decisions?
Can I enjoy doing nothing and being alone with my own thoughts?
Do I experience inner peace?
Am I balanced in solving all kinds of problems?
Do I believe that I can live by myself, without a co-dependency on someone else?

The belief system could be:

- Inner peace and balance is boring
- I function well under stress
- Having inner peace would take away my drive and motivation
- If I do things only for myself, I am a bad person
- I can only relax if and when the house is proper and perfectly clean
- I don't care what other people think!

Mental development

Ask yourself:

Do I have strong opinions on most issues concerning life?
Am I satisfied with my position on how I understand things?
Do I believe I am smart enough?
Do I comprehend easily?

The belief system could be:

- I'm not smart enough
- I don't think that other people are interested in what I think
- No one takes me serious
- I'm afraid I'll hurt someone's feelings if I say something wrong
- I'm really stupid, I can't learn
- I have to do what I am told
- I will turn out just like my father/mother
- I don't believe things will ever change
- Everything will be okay if I make a joke

Spiritual development (religion)

Ask yourself:

Am I happy with my relationship with God?
Am I still searching for the correct religion?
Do I have peace of mind in regards to my spiritual future?

The belief system could be:

- I don't believe that God exists
- I think God is inside of each person
- I don't think God is interested in me
- Religion is opium for the people
- God is dead
- I can't live without my God
- God sees it all
- I'm not naturally a spiritual person
- I hate religion

Energy

Ask yourself:

Do I wake up with lots of energy every morning?
What could be the reason that I may or may not have enough energy?
Am I often tired?

The belief system could be:

- My health is weak
- I will never have enough energy to do what I want
- I'm tired all of the time
- I conserve energy
- I can only do one thing at a time

Relationship with your partner

Ask yourself:

Is my partner the one that I want to grow old with?
Is he/she the best partner for me?
Do we understand each other a full 100 percent?
Is it impossible for me to live without my partner?
Would/should I leave my partner if I could?

The belief system could be:

- My partner doesn't understand me
- I'm too difficult to live with
- Without my partner, my life has no value
- I can't leave my partner because of my/our family, culture, religion, finance, etc.
- If my partner would leave me or die, I would have no reason to live, either
- Love hurts
- I'll be alone forever
- I can't make it alone

Work (joy, enthusiasm)

Ask yourself:

Do I enjoy my work?
Is this the type of work I would like to do for the rest of my life?
Do I look forward to going to work every day?

The belief system could be:

- This is all I know
- I can't find another job
- A job is just something I have to do in order to make money

- The only reason why I work is to support my family
- I don't have to like my work
- I'm not a team worker
- I am too old to work

Enjoying life

Ask yourself:

Am I aware of the little things in life that give me joy?
Do I consider life a gift?
Do I realize that I own my life and that I can do what I want with it?

The belief system could be:

- I did not ask for this life
- Life is difficult!
- Life is a gift from God
- I don't want to live
- I don't deserve to have fun
- I enjoy life when I'm alone
- My life is garbage
- First, everything has to be clean and in order, before I can enjoy life

Measure of being happy

Ask yourself:

Do I experience happiness on a regular basis?
Do I live my life with passion?
How many things can I name that give me happiness in life?

The belief system could be:

- In this society it is impossible to be happy

- If I have to work as hard as I do, I will never be happy
- I see too much misery to be happy
- You can't buy happiness
- Life is not about happiness, but about duties and responsibilities
- I have to buy things to be happy

Mental flexibility

Ask yourself:

Is it easy for me to change plans?
Do I accept facts that attack my belief systems?
Am I judgmental?
Do I usually think logically?

The belief system could be:

- I am too disorganized
- It is difficult to make decisions
- You'll never know what you lose if you change
- If I am flexible, people will think I am weak
- Changing is not always an improvement
- I am conservative and old fashion
- I like to keep what I have

Decision-making

Ask yourself:

Can I make a decision easily?
Do I need a lot of proof and convincing arguments before I make my decisions?
Do I postpone things?

The belief system could be:

- If I make the wrong decision, I may not be able to undo it afterwards
- I'm afraid to make a mistake
- My decisions don't matter
- I always make the wrong decision
- I have no choice
- There are too many consequences in making decision

Interests (work, hobbies, people)

Ask yourself:

Am I really interested in how others are doing?
Do I pay attention to others when they talk?
Do I stop and listen to someone's reply when I greet him or her?
Do I always try to learn new things about my job?
Can I afford to have a hobby?
Do I deserve to have a hobby?
Do I spend a lot of time finding things out about my hobbies, work, people, etc.?

The belief system could be:

- I have no time to have a hobby
- I have no ambition to get a promotion at work
- Most people are selfish
- I have more interests in certain things than the time to really do them
- I don't really care about anything
- My job does not depend on me and/or someone's appreciation of what I do because it's not that important
- I don't understand technical things; it's too complicated for me

Association/relationships/family

Ask yourself:

Do I have a great family life?
Do I have fun with my relationships?
Is it easy for me to make new acquaintances?
Do I spend a lot of my time with family, friends and others?
Do I want to spend as much time as possible with my family, friends and/or others?
Do I feel obligated to spend time and money on my family?
Do I put my family first before myself?
Do I put my family ahead of having fun?

The belief system could be:

- My family is everything to me
- I don't need anyone
- I could never leave my family
- I am an outsider
- People don't like me
- I don't trust people
- It's impossible for me to measure up to others
- I can't meet people half way
- I have enough problems of my own
- I can't do something for myself
- My family has the right to expect things from me

Personal progress/growth

Ask yourself:

Do I feel that I grow in all aspects of life?
Do I have the feeling that my life is stagnant and lacks growth?

Do I have strong goals?
Do I make progress in reaching my goals?
Do I really believe in myself?
Do I set achievable goals, or do I set myself up to fail?

The belief system could be:

- I can't change anything!
- It is hard to change myself
- My opinion is not important
- I accept life as it is
- I go with the flow
- I take one step forward and two steps back, and can't get ahead
- I will never reach my full potential
- I am too old
- Success could make me selfish or prideful, it could be dangerous

Measure of self-love (selfness)

Ask yourself:

Do I have things I dislike about myself?
Do I have characteristics that I like most about myself?
Do I take time out just for myself?
Can I look at myself in the mirror?
Do I like what I see in the mirror?
Do I often choose for myself?
Do I always think of others before myself?
Do I consider life a gift?
Do I have self-worth?
Do I value myself?

The belief system could be:

- I'm not worth loving
- It's selfish to love oneself
- God will punish me for what I am
- I have done too many bad things to truly love myself
- I'm too ugly or too fat to love myself
- I am the best thing in the world!
- No one loves me
- Who would love someone like me?
- Love is pointless
- Love doesn't exist in this world
- Love will make me vulnerable
- Nothing is gained with love, it doesn't do anything
- Love is weakness and I have to be strong
- Love hurts

When you do this exercise thoroughly, you will discover that you have two layers of belief systems: the 'cover-up' type and the deeper ones that really drive you. This is not an exercise that you can complete in just a few minutes. Finding your most powerful belief systems is an ongoing process of growth. You will enjoy this more and more for it will give you a whole new level of insight of your own behavior, as well as that of others. Even after months, you will still discover new belief systems that you were consciously unaware of and you will discover their origin. If they are rooted in a Bad Cluster it will amaze you time and time again to reveal the content of the Bad Cluster, experience relief after discovering it, and feel how this automatically will convert inhibiting belief systems into positive energy, into *desirable power*!

What belief systems did you find?

Try to write down as many of your belief systems as you can. In the coming days and weeks, pay attention to your belief systems and when and how they pop up over and over again. Always ask yourself the question: *"Does this belief system serve me well or does it stop my growth and success?"* After you have written down your belief systems, put them in order of importance according to your feelings. Then ask yourself: *"Are these belief systems serving me so that I can live a better and happier life?"* As you review the order of importance, ask yourself: *"Would this order really benefit my life?"* Where ever it's necessary, create new and improved belief systems. Put them in the order of importance that would benefit you the most. For example, let's say you wrote down security and adventure as part of your belief systems. Let us assume that you put "security" as a number 1 and "adventure" as a number 10 on your list of importance. Now, if you would change number 1 to number 10 and number 10 to number 1, this would drastically change your life! What are some of the belief systems you found out about yourself?

- What was the belief system?
- Why did it or did it not serve you?
- If it serves you, in what kind of way has it served you?
- Did you change your belief system? If yes, what is your new belief system?
- Is it hard to change this specific belief system?
- Do you feel a lot of resistance to change it?
- What part of this belief system gives you the resistance?
- What would happen if you stopped following your belief system?
- What do you feel in your body if you decide to no longer follow that belief system?

- What do you see if you intensify that feeling?
- When did you install this belief system?

Are all belief systems wrong?

Of course not! Normally our belief systems should be based on Clusters and not Bad Clusters. In that case, we should remember where we installed them and why. Sometimes our parents taught us their belief systems, in many cases it is due to the culture we live in, or the education we received. Sometimes religious belief systems formed our moral views on life. If our belief systems serve us well and originate from Clusters, then we don't have to change them. Unfortunately, some of our belief systems do inhibit and harm us, like the one Jack was holding on to, until he practiced PMA.

> ***Example***:
> One of Jack's most important belief systems was: *"If I keep my mouth shut I won't get hurt!"* Unfortunately, his supervisors and managers hardly noticed him and he never made any progress in his career. How come? Although Jack was very skilled and saw things better than some of his superiors on how to improve things in the company, he never spoke up and never told his superiors that he disagreed with certain things. But he was held back by the belief system that it was better to keep his mouth shut, driven by the fear of getting hurt. He could not remember when, where or why he installed such a belief system. He experienced strong resistance as soon as he tried to change this belief system by trying to speak up and show his superiors that he disagreed with them on certain issues. He felt the physical reactions of fear and anxiety when he tried this! His belief system definitely originated from a Bad Cluster.

As a child he adored his father. His mother and father were always fighting with each other. When he was only 10 years old his father threatened to leave his mother. He was terrified with idea that his father would leave. He tried to help them so that they would stay together. He saw that his mother was very unreasonable and always created a fight by telling his father what to do and what he did wrong.

He was desperate and tried to explain to his mother that it would be better not to criticize his father all the time. He also told his father that he should try to listen more to her and not to get angry so easily. Little Jack meant well. However, his father took it all wrong and shouted at Jack: *"You little snot! Who do you think you are? Do you think that a ten-year-old can tell me what to do? You are just like your mother, always criticizing me, she never shuts up!"*

He left in anger! And little Jack's world collapsed! This was the moment he installed his belief system! It was his fault that his father, whom he loved so much, finally left. He did not see his father for the next several months. His parents ultimately divorced. From the very moment that his father left he became a silent boy. Later in life and in his career, he would never give his opinion, and especially not to people in positions of authority (like his father). This event shaped his whole life and blocked an otherwise brilliant man in his career.

Jack changed completely after he modified this belief system by eliminating the connecting Bad Cluster. Two years later, he was promoted to a manager's position and no longer hesitates in revealing his opinion.

This is one of many examples of how a belief system that is based on a Bad Cluster can shape our life and inhibit our progress. Can you imagine the tremendous positive impact on his marriage? His wife tried to reach him for so many years, but he just kept silent all the time, never expressing what he really felt. Not that his marriage was bad, on the contrary, he loved his wife and she loved him, and he was always there for her to do whatever she asked of him. And yet, they were not "soul mates"! To become soul mates you have to share your deepest feelings with your partner. Before PMA, this was impossible for Jack. He loves his wife so much, like he loved his father. But the result of being honest and helpful by telling the other what he felt was stored in his Bad Cluster. Can you imagine his Bad Cluster driven by the unrealistic fear of losing her, just like he lost his father, by simply sharing his honest feelings? What is Jack's opinion now? Jack states, *"Even if PMA would not have given me the financial advantage of becoming a manager, it is priceless for both of us to now live with a soul mate instead of just a loving spouse!"*

Change your belief systems

Belief systems that are based on Bad Clusters are always more powerful than the ones that are based on normal Clusters. Why? Because of their high relative value that is based on the strong physiological (emotional) content of the Bad Cluster! How do we know if a belief system originates from a Bad Cluster and needs to be changed? The criteria in identifying this type of belief system is:

- *The belief system does not serve us.*

- *We find it difficult to change the belief system and feel a lot of resistance in doing so.*
- *We cannot recall exactly when, where or why we installed that belief system.*
- *The belief system is based on fear.*

What is the procedure of changing our belief systems?

Step 1
Identify your belief systems. The previous exercise is a great tool for that.

Step 2
Do they originate from Clusters or Bad Clusters? If they come from Clusters, then you know where, when and why you installed them! To find out if they come from Bad Clusters, follow the fourth criteria mentioned above.

Step 3
Change the belief systems that are originating from Bad Clusters into belief systems that actually serve you. Remember, you will feel a lot of resistance in the case of Bad Cluster based belief systems. So, force yourself to follow your new belief system. Expect the resistance to become stronger, and use that feeling to get to the source- the Bad Cluster by practicing the technique you will learn in this book!

Step 4
Are they properly categorized in an order that serves you? If not, change them into a proper order. If you feel a lot of resistance you can almost be sure that this belief

system originates from a Bad Cluster, so it needs to be changed!

How do you change a belief system when you experience a lot of resistance? By provoking the underlying Bad Cluster through conditioning! It will reveal itself and then you can eliminate it. Only then can you really change that belief system permanently. This exercise will give you insight regarding your real drives and their origin. If you want the full advantage of this exercise, then you need to return to these pages after you finished reading this book and you've learned exactly how to perform a PMA session. Then you will benefit even more from the power of this exercise by combining it with the basic PMA session technique.

How do you do that?

After you find a belief system that does not serve you, you change it into a belief system that does serve you. Turn it around, or if necessary, rephrase it completely. This isn't hard to do when this belief system is not active. For instance, in Jack's situation (our example), it was not difficult for him to tell himself that he changed his belief system from: *"If I keep my mouth shut, I won't get hurt!"*, into, *"If I am right, I will tell others my opinion!"*. But at the moment he had to speak up to one of his superiors, or share his deepest feelings with his wife, he felt an enormous resistance and fear.

This is what you have to do in order for this to really work:

- *Change your old inhibiting belief system into a new one that serves you.*
- *Make the decision that you will apply this new belief system.*

- *Repeat this new belief system to yourself whenever the old belief system pops up.*
- *Force yourself to apply it when you would normally apply your old belief system.*

What will happen if you start doing that?

Your old belief systems will not easily be gone if they are based on a Bad Cluster. As soon as a situation arises that you have to apply your new belief system, you will feel the resistance and fear (the main ingredient in a Bad Cluster), and you will have the feeling that you should act according to your old belief system.

Example:
Joanne is a sales person. She has problems terminating a useless conversation with someone who is wasting her time. This would cause her to lose valuable time and affect her sales. Where did this come from? Her mother was a selfish character who was always complaining. She demanded that Joanne listen to her. Whenever Joanne turned her back on her, or started to talk about something else, her mother got very angry.

One night, when Joanne was 12 years old, her mother was complaining again. Joanne did not want to listen to her anymore so she told her mother: *"I understand what you say, but you've told me the same thing many times before. I have a lot of homework and have no time to listen to your silly complaints anymore!"* At that moment her father came into the living room. He was drunk and therefore very unreasonable. He got furious and shouted, *"Who do you think you are talking that way to your mother!"* He beat up Joanne brutally. She

> created a Bad Cluster at that moment. The content of the Bad Cluster is pain and fear caused by an unreasonable punishment for speaking-up for herself! As a matter of fact, she chose for herself! What she did to survive and not feel the pain of an activated Bad Cluster, is a common behavioral pattern. She created a belief system to comfort her and to suppress that negative feeling. Her belief system was: *"When I react nicely and friendly, others won't hurt me!"* This belief system served her during her childhood, but stops her today from expanding her capacities and actions.
>
> The moment she got rid of her Bad Cluster, she was able to interrupt people in a useless, time consuming conversation. Yet, this new behavior changed nothing about her nice and friendly demeanor! In a friendly way, she made it very clear to people that she had other things to do at that moment.

Finding the belief systems that inhibit you, is the first step to an exiting and advantageous process. After practicing the PMA self-help technique, you will experience how easy it is to replace inhibiting, tiresome belief systems into energetic and motivating ones that serve you.

Making changes

Has this book given you any insight and answers so far? If you want to change your life and become more energetic, free, successful and healthy, then it is not just about insight and answers. These are only the beginning! It's all about decisions! Before you can change anything, you have to make decisions first! The first decision you have to make is if you truly desire to make changes in your life! It will only have a positive effect if you really believe in your decision! Let's examine an inhibiting belief system that most of us have. If you are one of them, then we're going to change that instantly. This is a wonderful exercise to share with others, even if they haven't read this book yet.

> ***Exercise***:
> Ask yourself: *"How old am I going to get?"*
>
> If you feel the shape of your body right now and add to that your emotional state, how long do you expect to live? This is not a religious question, but you have to base your answer on your recent emotional and physical health status. How old can you get if you continue as you do now? Write down an age that you are sure you will reach if you did not die in an accident. Why do you believe that you will just live to be that number of years? What in your body or emotions makes you believe that? What do you imagine you will look and feel like when you reach that age? What is your perception of old age and death?

Keep in mind, everyone has their own mental pictures of death! Just tell me, when you think of death, what does that word mean to you? Now imagine that I am an alien who does not know what death is and you can only communicate with me through pictures because I do not speak your language, what picture would you show me? You will see that if you're like one of the many that have a low expectation of how old they will get, you should have very unpleasant images of old age and death. Try to discover your pictures of old age and death. What pops up first? Do these pictures have a good physiological load? Will this physiological load affect your total ligand configuration? How often do you think you activate this belief system ("*I will only live to the age of .... "*)? Paying attention to that from now on will many times lead you to amazement. Just realize, whenever you activate that belief system, you also activate the negative physiology of your pictures of death! How would you like to live to 125 years of age? If you like that idea, your first step is to change your belief system here and now! Biologists and neuroscientists have strong reasons to believe that in the near future it will be possible to live up to the age of 125 years. For now, let's change our belief system to we can live at least 125 years! Just assume that you will live that long. What does that change in your life? Do you have to alter some plans? Do you see new possibilities? You have to believe and want this; otherwise it is not a real belief system, but just empty words. Feel it! You may have to repeat this several times to yourself until it sticks. It will surprise you how often your old belief system will pop up from now on. Whenever you speak about the future, your retirement, your relatives, your health, etc., you have to connect all those expectations to a new age! Let me briefly explain what happens if you do this. First of all, it's important to know we are all born with preprogrammed modules.

Chronological module

We have several biological clocks in our body. You'll notice how strong these are when you travel all over the world and feel the effects of jetlag. We also have a chronological module in our body. This chronological module makes it possible for us to remember that one event took place before or after another event, or gives us the correct feeling of how long we have to wait if we plan something to do tomorrow, in a year, or in 20 years. What will happen if you condition yourself that you will live 125 years? This chronological module will be affected in a positive way. Remember, you connected your pictures of old age and death to the original age of …, but now you connect those pictures to a much older age. It is just like money. If you know that you only need to buy food for two days because you are waiting to receive a new paycheck, you will use your money differently if someone suddenly tells you that the new paycheck will be delayed and it will take a week more before they can give you your paycheck. The message alone instantly gives you a different feeling about how to spend the rest of your money. Therefore, you will notice that if you really start to believe in the fact that you will live to at least the age of 125, your feelings will start to change. Keep in mind that your feelings are caused by physiology connected to Clusters (or Bad Clusters). Your new belief systems will connect total different Clusters. Their attached Physio-clusters will change your physiology. The more positive the physiology, the better you'll function, and the better you'll feel.

Effects on your present and future life

Our health, the way we feel, decide and act, depends on our physiology! Physiology is controlled by the ligands (neuro-peptides). The constant change in our ligand configuration means that we are alive. As soon as there are no more changes in our ligand configurations, we are dead! The ligand configuration changes for several reasons:

- If there is a low or a high of substances such as enzymes, oxygen, water, proteins, sugar, etc. in our body, specific sensors will detect these and create a response. This is based on the genetic programs of the Proto-physioclusters.

- As soon as incoming information enters our brain, through one or more of our five senses, the configuration of this incoming data activates previously stored memories that our subconscious will use as comparison material in order to analyze it. We always store our memories connected to the emotion of that moment. If a memory will be used as comparison material later on, then its attached emotions (physiology) will be carried out and its effects will be felt in the body.

- Thoughts and memories can also cause changes in our ligand configurations. But without sensory input we are unable to think. To do this we first need an impulse from outside to activate the stimulus/response machine.

- Dreams process the information that entered the brain during the day(s) before. In order to go as far *away from pain* as possible, the new data will be connected to low relative Fragments, Sub-clusters and Clusters as it possibly can. The activation of the comparison material that the subconscious will connect the new data to will definitely change the ligand configuration.

As a rule, we can say that Proto-physioclusters are never felt in your body. Proto-physioclusters maintain the balance. A body in balance has no pain or any other bad feeling. As soon as you feel that a part of your body hurts, something is wrong. The only exception to that rule is the feeling of hunger and thirst, although that also could be considered an abnormal situation because if you take care of your body the way you should, and eat and drink on time, you don't need to feel hunger or thirst. As soon as you start to feel anything in your body, the Physio-clusters of activated comparison material have become active and changed the ligand combinations.

Remember Janine

The physiology caused by the Physio-clusters, determine a large portion of our total physiology. If these Physio-clusters are attached to a Bad Cluster, extreme negative physiology will float through the body. This Bad Cluster physiology is so strong that it will overrule any conditioning or balanced situation that is controlled by the Proto-physioclusters. Consequently, the ligand configuration will determine our health, feelings, decisions, conclusions and actions. Therefore, it establishes our present, as well as our future! The physiology that is attached to a Bad Cluster throws our ligand configuration totally out of balance. We will definitely feel that. Remember, we decide and act driven by these feelings.

Of course our ratio also plays its part, but the bottom-line is that we always decide and act based on our feelings. These feelings create our belief systems and our perception of the things we experience. Our belief systems determine the direction of our thoughts, decisions, actions and behavior. Let us now examine how we can use all that we have learned and experienced so far to our benefit by practicing Progressive Mental Alignment.

Do you remember Janine, who we met in chapter one? Just imagine the negative physiological effects that her fear caused on her health and behavior. The constant fear that she was HIV positive controlled her life. For five years she was afraid to start any relationship. This led to a constant controlled behavior in her relationship with men. She was so afraid of falling in love and not being able to have a normal relationship that she constantly rejected all the men that wanted to date her, even when they just want to have lunch! What caused this fearful and unhappy behavior? Belief systems! Was she really HIV positive? No! But her belief systems regarding HIV controlled major parts of her life! None of us wants to be controlled by fear, so let's see what we can do to free ourselves from needless inhibiting fear.

Chapter 10 – How to use Progressive Mental Alignment

Go for it!

We now understand how dangerous Bad Clusters are. We don't need them and we don't want them controlling our belief systems, and thereby, our life! Understanding their existence and power is one thing, but getting rid of their negative influence and freeing their large amounts of positive energy is another. The PMA technique makes it possible to achieve all that, and it is easy to learn. The only difficulty you have is to overcome your own Inhibiting Friend. This *friend* is not some kind of mysterious power outside or inside your body that stops you, but your own inhibiting belief systems. You created them, and you can definitely overcome them! The Inhibiting Friend has no power of its own. Only you can grant it that power! It all comes down to your decisions.

Do you want the rest of your life to be controlled by belief systems that are the result of what others did to you in the past? Or do you go for that *Desirable Power* and take full control over your subconscious comparison material to become everything that you can be? Deep down inside you know that you are capable of achieving much more than what you have achieved so far. Don't let the fear of what might come up from your subconscious stop you. If you really have the desire, there is nothing in your subconscious that you can't handle. It's worth it because its negative physiology controls large portions of your life. Keep in mind, whatever may be the content of your Bad Clusters hidden in your subconscious, you survived it when it was originally stored. And best of all, you will experience an unknown freedom after you have revealed the content of that inhibiting material. PMA not only gives you control over your life, it's also a lot of fun to do. Many people spend a lot of time and money watching exciting movies, even horror movies, or they seek excitement in car racing or Bungee-jumping. Just imagine, you can have all that excitement for free by just watching your own personal movie. Keep in mind that between now and the moment that a Bad Cluster was activated for the first time, your subconscious made quite a number of weird unrealistic "nightmare" kind of connections. Go for it and enjoy the process!

The tension disappears forever

What will happen once a session has eliminated a Bad Cluster? What exactly has been eliminated? The fact is, the contents of the Bad Cluster has not actually been eliminated. The only thing that has been eliminated is the Physio-cluster. Every piece of data of the Bad Cluster is now properly analyzed and encoded. This means that all pieces are connected to data, Fragments and Sub-clusters of normal encoded Clusters. The moment that this happens (in a split of a second), the physiological code that was connected to that Bad Cluster, changes into the physiology that is connected to each of the parts of the Cluster that it is now attached to. This is also the reason that the negative physiology of the Bad Cluster is permanently eliminated and can never return! The moment that the content of a Bad Cluster is analyzed and encoded, you will instantly feel it. The negative physiology will disappear in seconds! You might compare it to watching a horror film. The first time you see it, all the murders and blood shed create fear and tension. When you watch it a second time, it doesn't affect you so much. And if you were to finally watch a documentary of how the film was made, revealing all the tricks and special effects of the tense scenes, then the next time you watch it, you will not be afraid at all.

The effects of the PMA technique

In the PMA technique we want to bring hidden subconscious data to the attention of the conscious. Usually, whatever we use as comparison material remains hidden from our consciousness. During a PMA session we want to analyze and encode the data of a Bad Cluster. Analyzing means comparing, therefore, we need comparison material. Which kind of comparison material are we talking about? Normal encoded Clusters that contain similar basic data that can serve as comparison material to analyze the unanalyzed basic data of the Bad Cluster. Among that comparison material we will also need the Clusters that were created right before and immediately after the Bad Cluster was stored. These Clusters hold valuable data like the location, circumstances, people, objects, colors, sounds, etc. that are similar to a large portion of the data of the Bad Cluster. Once the sum of all the data of the Clusters has been transferred from the long-term memory to the short-term memory, containing enough similar data to make it possible to analyze the majority of the basic data of the Bad Cluster, the subconscious will reveal the content to the conscious brain. Regardless of how long ago the original event occurred that created the Bad Cluster, the analysis of that data will now be done in a split of a second. This means that you do not have to endure the total event and the amount of time that originally created the Bad Cluster. Do you remember the most powerful rule of the subconscious: *away from pain*? It always follows its own rules and therefore, it will lead you *away from pain* as fast as possible! From that moment on, its negative influence will be gone forever and make place for a lot of positive energy. Keep in mind that this is an easy to learn process, but it's only effective if you precisely follow the rules of the subconscious language. The subconscious will not speak to you if you don't respect its rules! You will discover that you have many hidden skills and potentials. PMA will open these for you and also give you the capability to discover the potentials in other people. Just imagine what this can mean for your future, your relationships and career!

Grow to your full potentials

Some might say: *"I have none of the symptoms of active Bad Clusters, I always feel great and energetic, and I am successful in my performance!"* If that's completely true, that's great! Then you can immediately go to a deeper level of PMA! It is like redecorating a home. First you clean and paint it. After you get rid of all the disturbing things, you're going to redecorate it the way you like. In order to "redecorate" your mind, you have to clean it first! But PMA does much more than just "clean your mind". The real power of PMA is to understand the processes of your own brain in order to manage these processes to your full benefit! It helps you to understand yourself and to find and develop your hidden potentials! If you think you don't have active Bad Clusters, then you can start using PMA to discover how you use your comparison material to create your decisions, behavior and belief systems.

An enjoyable process with major benefits

Are you familiar with the feeling that, although someone is very nice, you would still like to know what they really think about you? Did you ever experience a moment in your work that you thought that the customer would buy what you are selling or that you were convinced they would sign an agreement, but for some odd reason, they backed off? Or maybe you had a good relationship with someone and suddenly their behavior towards you changed without any apparent reason? In such a situation did you ever ask yourself: *"What happened? I only wish I knew what they were thinking and the reason that it didn't work out as I planned."* PMA will provide you with the tools to understand the signals of these changes in not only your behavior, but also their behavior, and consequently, you'll have the tools to avoid this. Just imagine the positive effects on all your relationships, regardless if it concerns your spouse, partner, child, parent or a business relationship. By practicing PMA, you will also learn how to "read between the lines". This means to be able to read the signals other people give you, that before you were not aware of. We pass on our knowledge, wishes and belief systems by using language! In other words, we use verbal language to say what we want and think! However, you will get much more information about the real drive of a person from their non-verbal or "body language." It's not only the body language, but also the words and phrases people use and the order they put them in that tells us what people really think and want. Does that mean that we have to pay attention to every single word others speak and to every move they make? No, that is not how it works! To your surprise you will notice that picking up clues will happen automatically after you start to understand and practice the full concept of PMA! Once you understand that everything we do, say, think, feel, decide, etc., has its cause in our comparison material, you will automatically connect their words and behavior to your existing comparison material. Without consciously thinking about it, you will feel and know when they try to tell you something else (or hide something) than what they utter with their words. We are all familiar with this phenomena.

Go the whole nine yards

Did you ever speak to someone and you simply knew that they were not speaking the truth? Women have the reputation to be more developed in this than men. How do you know they are not telling the truth? Do they tell you that? Or do you have to think about it and focus on every word they say? No! You just know! How come? From their entire behavior you can pick up a lot of subtle things that are linked to your own comparison material that, as a result, gets activated. This material has been coded in your subconscious as 'lying' behavior. Did you ever experience that people can seem very nice to you, but you definitely know that they don't mean what they are trying to show with their attitude towards you? Did you ever ask yourself how it's possible that you automatically know this? The more you understand your brain and its functions, and the more you practice PMA, the better you will understand what other people really want and need, and what they are trying to hide. How will this skill affect your professional performance as well as your personal relationships?

But, what may prevent you from acquiring this powerful tool? Fear! You will not be afraid to learn and use the PMA technique as such, but what might really be an obstacle for you is the fear of your own subconscious comparison material! To understand others at a deeper level, you have to first understand yourself at that deeper level. We all want to better understand others and if there is an easy-to-use tool to help us achieve that, we'll want to use that tool. But the effectiveness of this tool is based on the process of mirroring. To understand others, you have to compare their behavior and words to your own stored comparison material. Part of your comparison material is Bad Clusters, loaded with emotions! With other people it isn't any different. To better understand who they are you have to understand their pains and fears. Remember, our strongest belief systems and behaviors are coming directly from the effect of activated Bad Clusters. It is only to the extent that we are willing to see and understand our own Bad Clusters, will we be able to "mirror" ourselves to other people. Therefore, we can only better understand others, if first, we understand ourselves better. There is a true saying: *A five yard rope can never reach nine yards!* If you are willing to only go "five yards" deep within yourself, you will never reach the "nine yards" within others!

Can I practice PMA all by myself?

With the knowledge about your Friend Mechanism in mind, you might think: *"Can I do this all by myself?"* Yes, you can! It just depends on how honest you are with yourself. Basically, it comes down to the question: How much do you respect and love yourself? We do not mean: How selfish are you? Selfishness has very little to do with loving yourself. Selfishness means love for the fulfillment of your own desires, regardless of who and how many have to suffer at that expense. True love for yourself is in balance with justice, power and wisdom. You realize that as a human being you can only be happy if you are in harmony with others around you. People who are unhappy usually live a lie! They condition themselves, with their inhibiting belief systems, thinking that everything is all right and they are happy! As we already know by now, conditioning will never overrule the physiological power of a Bad Cluster. You can lie to yourself as much as you want, but that won't take away the disrupting power of the Bad Cluster physiology! We are all familiar with the phrase: *"Love your neighbor as yourself."* Some people are always very busy caring for the problems and misery of others. And they often lie to themselves by saying that they have so much love for others (inhibiting belief system)! Often, the real reason is that they have a hard time being alone with their own thoughts! They have to be busy all the time so that they have no time left over to realize who they really are. This is a very common tool of the Friend Mechanism. They do not really understand the phrase: *"Love your neighbor as yourself."* They do not love themselves at all. They just run away from who they are and what they really feel!

Allow your subconscious to deliver

Back to the question: *"Can I do this all by myself?"* Absolutely! Once in a while you might need the assistance of an experienced PMA Coach to help you get to another, deeper level. Why? Because our Bad Clusters are stored in levels! Once you are in a certain level, you can work on most of the other Bad Clusters in that same level all by yourself. In order to eliminate the negative physiology of your own Bad Clusters, it is very important that you learn how to allow yourself to look at anything your subconscious brain is showing you during a PMA session. You just look and feel without asking yourself anything else. Don't try to understand or comment in that phase, allow everything that comes up, to come up, without judging or denying it. It is like a movie you look at. As soon as you reach the Bad Cluster, you will understand all the pictures you saw previous to that last one, the Bad Cluster. Your Friend Mechanism will use whatever is in your Database to push you away from the content of the Bad Clusters because it cannot ignore their high relative codes. In the subconscious language, there are no higher codes like the relative codes of a Bad Cluster because the amount of fear and their cause are directly related to survival, and therefore, to the *away from pain* rule. It has to obey this code over any other high relative code because the first priority is to survive. This code is related to the well known *fight or flight* pattern. Nevertheless, during an activation, or an attempt to eliminate a Bad Cluster, there is no real physical danger. The conscious is well aware of that. This means that the subconscious will automatically try to follow its basic rule, *away from pain*, and come up with less painful comparison material to pass on to the conscious brain.

Being aware of the fact that you do PMA sessions in order to find the content of your Bad Clusters, you have to make a conscious decision to let go. Letting go means: to go towards those mental pictures and feelings that you feel the most repelled by. This resistance originates from the reaction between your comparison material and the *away from pain* drive. The resistance shows you, therefore, where to find the content of pain and fear. It is totally within the range of your power to go there, ... or not!

The fear and pain will be there, for just a split second, and then disappear forever. Keep in mind that the Friend is a mechanism. It cannot think, reason, argue or feel! It just follows the rules of stimulus/response. It can only use ingredients that are already located in your brain. As soon as the symptoms that are registered in your body go towards pain or fear, your Friend Mechanism will automatically go in the direction of comparison material with less negative symptoms. The subconscious will always offer comparison material that has codes that bear the most similarity to the new incoming data and also carries the least negative emotional load (relative code). In this way it keeps us as far *away from pain* as possible. At the very moment your brain goes towards a Bad Cluster, several, maybe hundreds, of Clusters are also activated as comparison material. The subconscious will always pick one of these Clusters with less negative data, or material with less 'stop signs' attached to it! The subconscious is just following its program "*away from pain*" without thinking or feeling. Before you begin the exercises that lead to a real PMA session, it is important that you realize that PMA is based on <u>reliving</u> events. You don't want to be disturbed while you are doing that. So, find yourself a spot where you can sit or lay down without being disturbed by others or interrupted by a doorbell or phone. Always remember that during a session your subconscious does not make mistakes! Every mental picture is important and is relevant! We will start with a simple exercise.

Become aware of your senses

To relive an event completely using all of your senses, it is necessary that you first practice the awareness of all these senses during a reliving. This exercise will help you achieve that full awareness of your senses. You will find specific words that will enable you to test your capability in using each of your senses. This is important because, in order to eliminate <u>all</u> the Fragments and Sub-clusters of a Bad Cluster, you have to relive it with all your senses. Read the words in each category. After reading a word, it can be useful if you close your eyes when you experience the things described.

SIGHT

All these words are objects or visible things. The goal is to imagine them as realistically as possible until you can almost 'see' the object with your mind's eye:

tree house chair glasses street

car bed painting cupboard stair

book tower ball lamp light

vase fork porch bucket darkness

table radio knee candlestick piano

COLORS

Sometimes an individual won't see any colors when trying to relive something despite the fact that his sight is functioning well. In order to determine this and improve the situation, do the following exercises. All the objects and colors have to be truly 'seen'. Don't just imagine the color but also the shape of the object. What color is:

grass	pool	silver spoon	crow	gold chain
tar	tomato	autumn leaves	canary	green bean
blood	milk	an orange	cinders	chocolate

MOTION

In the following exercises try to imagine the movement mentioned. It is your goal to have an object in your mind's eye and to see the color of the object moving as well. For example, if you are asked to think of a rabbit, then you need to see the animal hopping, see its shape and its color. This last concept is left up to you, since there are numerous colors for rabbits (white, black, brown, spotted). So imagine the movement of the following things:

goldfish	bird	car	biker	airplane
monkey	waves	dog	walker	ballerina
swimmer	spider	horse	tiger	boxer

SOUND

While we are reliving an event, we should not only see objects, but also hear the sounds they make, if they do. It is especially important to hear the words that are spoken while reliving an event, for they may have an important meaning in a Bad Cluster situation. Also, try to imagine the shape, color and motion along with hearing what sound is made in these following items:

opera singer	motorcycle	whip	barking dog
mosquito	drummer	newscaster	vacuum cleaner
whispering	singing bird	drill	screaming child

SMELL

With each successive exercise we will go one step further. Although the goal of this exercise is to practice recalling smells, it is always the goal to imagine the shape, color and movement of what is asked, when appropriate. Try to imagine the smell of the following items:

oil	leather	alcohol	cooked meat	perfume
roses	garlic	seared skin	coffee	fresh-cut grass
wine	clove	pine needles	baked onion	manure

TASTE

The sense of taste is closely linked to the sense of smell. Try to imagine everything in its entirety in this exercise as well. So as you are recalling the taste, see the color and shape of the dish. Also try to see how people move when they eat the dish and what sounds might be heard. Try to imagine the taste of:

fries	lemon	tomato soup	red wine	potato

milk	vinegar	baked fish	grilled meat	cabbage
bread	orange	cod-liver oil	raw egg	pepper

TOUCH

In this exercise, when we say the word *feel*, we mean the sense of touch. It has many facets. For example, we feel the temperature of something, but we also feel its weight and texture. Again, it is your goal to imagine the items in their entirety. So you must imagine the shape, the color, the smell, the movement, sounds and tastes when applicable. Try to imagine how the following objects feel:

velvet	frog	sandpaper	grass	water
paper	linen	mud	ice cubes	knife
table	cloth	hair	stone	needle

FEEL THE TEMPERATURE

sunlight	warm coffee	cold drink	swimming pool
warm room	tepid water	hot bath	ice cubes

FEEL THE WEIGHT

feather	baby	glass of water	book	chair
1 pound	fork	suitcase	10 pounds	table
handkerchief	bike	wheelbarrow	1 ounce	pen

FEEL THE MOVEMENT

bike	running	caressing hand	train	windmill
car	wheelchair	walking	animal	boat

EMOTIONS

In order to relive an emotion we must relive a situation where we felt it before. Imagine situations that included the following emotions:

aggression	love	fear	guilt	betrayal
repulsion	joy	pain	sorrow	appreciation
happiness	hate	disgust	anger	empathy

TIME

In order to be able to place events in sequence, we need to have a good feeling for time. The events can be placed in chronological order. Imagine a situation, using all of your senses, that occurred at these times:

at sunset	last Friday night
yesterday at 3:00 pm	your last vacation
last December 31st	your first day of school
9:00 am this morning	New Year's Eve, 5 years ago

After you have completed all these exercises successfully, you must still remain alert when reliving events. Even after considerable time, you may notice that during a certain reliving experience, the smell, or color, or another of the perceptions is missing. So be alert to these things during the PMA sessions. In order to eliminate a Bad Cluster, all the senses must be functioning. Keep practicing this with all your senses. There are many opportunities during the day that you can do this. All kinds of objects, drinks, food, and circumstances give you the opportunity to practice these wonderful skills. It is fun and you will train your brain like a body builder trains his muscles. When you exercise your brain, it will become faster, more efficient, and you will store and remember things better. This is not only to your benefit during PMA sessions, but also during your functioning in daily life. Before we continue with the next exercise, let us first discuss some of the basics of the language of the subconscious. Without speaking its language, we will never receive the answers we are looking for. We have to learn to trust our subconscious brain. It is a sophisticated computer, and we know computers do not make mistakes!

Trust your brain

Some people tell us that they find it difficult to trust their subconscious. What these people usually mean is that they have a hard time believing that the pictures they saw are true. Trusting your subconscious means that you believe that the pictures you saw originated from your subconscious and from no other source. *"But how do I know that I did not make this up?"* That is a total irrelevant question! The most important question is: What is the amount of negative physiology that is attached to these pictures? If there is negative physiology and your brain spontaneously produced these pictures, then you have all you need! Another question that comes up a lot is: *"I see so many pictures! Are they all relevant?"* Let's see why all the pictures that come up are relevant.

All the pictures are relevant

The event will activate a large amount of areas in your brain and in each area, a large amount of cells. By focusing on just the dominant moment of the event, the amount of cells that 'fire' (term they use in neurology for an active cell) will drastically decrease. Focusing on the detail will restrict your brain to just one area, one module of the Database.

RELATED COMPARISON MATERIAL

EVENT

MOMENT

DATA

DATA

RELATED COMPARISON MATERIAL

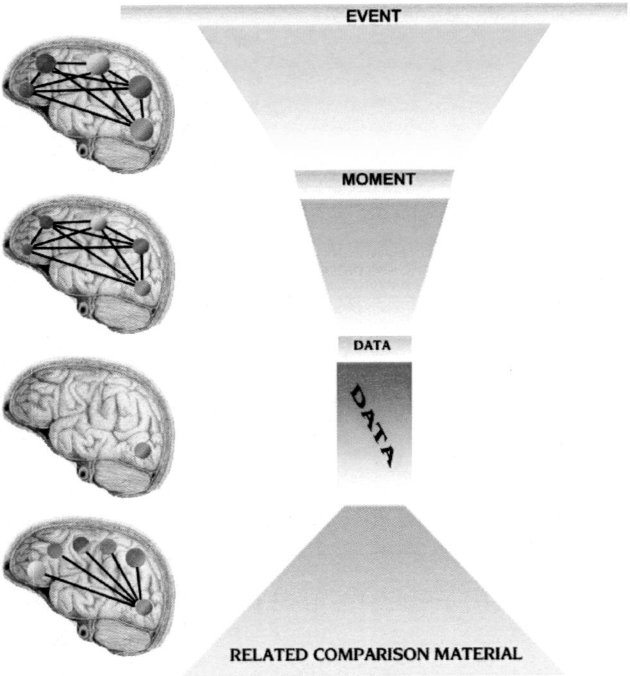

The subconscious can only become active based on stimulus/response. In order to deliver new pictures, the incoming stimulus of the subconscious will only be that one picture you consciously focus on. It has no other possibility than to activate comparison material related to that one picture! All other non-related material cannot be activated because the input goes to a kind of funnel that's focused on just one detail. As long as you keep focusing on one detail and just look and feel, without doing anything else, all the pictures your subconscious will give you are relevant! Please try a session on yourself and trust your subconscious!

Points of origin

How do you do an effective session on yourself? What do you have to do and what do you have to avoid during a session? PMA makes use of the natural processes of the brain. If we experience difficulties in continuing our sessions, or get blocked, it's usually because we are interfering with the natural processes of the brain. If you are in a session you will not direct where you will go or what type of memory has to pop up. You have to give your subconscious *carte blanche*! It can come up with what ever it wants. Don't actively look for pictures, let them come to you. We do not have to control or guide our brain to fulfill its subconscious processes. It is based on a simple rule of stimulus/response.

This simple drawing (next page) shows exactly that to do and what not to do during a session. The point in the middle represents your awareness of a mental picture that popped up. If you consciously try to 'remember' another picture that could be related to the last one that popped up, then your conscious brain is in charge. You are consciously determining the direction your brain will go. If that really worked, you would have discovered the contents of your Bad Clusters a long time ago. However, Bad Clusters are hidden in the subconscious and in the area normally unapproachable by the conscious brain. Therefore, you cannot consciously 'search' which direction to go.

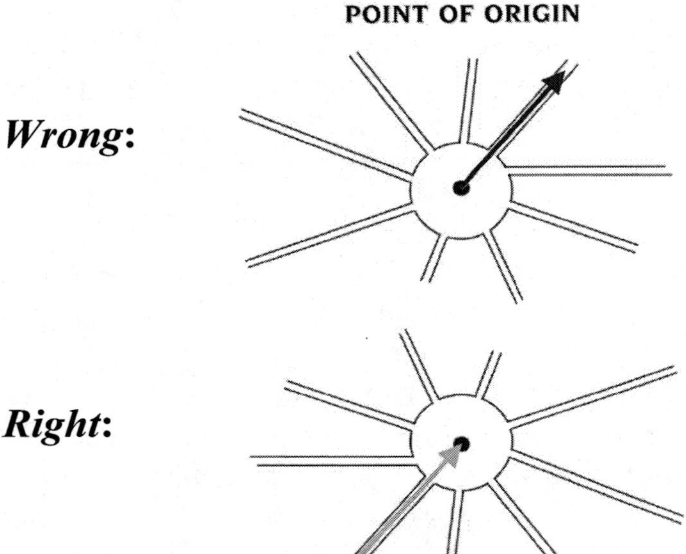

You have to focus on the most powerful detail in the mental picture that already popped up and on the feelings that accompany that detail. Now just wait until your subconscious delivers the next picture. This will usually come from an unexpected direction. That's the right way of doing a PMA session. How do we find the starting point to begin the session? First, find an event in which you felt a negative emotion, like anger, depression, irritation, fear, etc. How do we progress from there? Once you found this 'starting' event, find the most intense moment, and in that moment, the most intense detail. It won't be your brain, but your body, that will tell you what are the moment and detail. So pay attention to how your body responds to the reliving.

Now, just pay attention to two things:

1. *The detail*
2. *The feelings in your body*

Do's and don'ts in your sessions

From this point on you have to let your subconscious do the work and let your brain do what it automatically does, without conscious interference! To put it as simple as possible: After you found the detail, and the feelings are there, you do NOTHING! You just focus on the detail and allow the feelings to come without fighting them. From this point on, what will your brain automatically do? It will process the last incoming data (detail and feelings) and activate similar data as comparison material. If we allow the brain to do this without conscious interference, it will immediately deliver pictures. What do we do after another memory pops up? We do the same thing: Go there and find the moment, and in that moment, find the detail. Focus on the detail and feel. Let your subconscious brain do its work. To avoid disturbing the process during a session you will have to:

Relive

Reliving means that you:

See – Feel – Hear – Taste – Smell

You are at the same location again with all of your senses. Reliving is not the same as just remembering an event. You have to be there again, but this time, only in your mind while your body is now in a safe place. Keep in mind that all the data of a Bad Cluster is stored in your subconscious brain. It cannot be retrieved by your conscious mind. No matter how hard you try, you cannot consciously remember the content of a Bad Cluster! So the answer will not be found in your conscious brain. You can only find it in the subconscious. After you have found it and delivered it to the level of your consciousness, the brain functions will immediately give the data its proper relative code and change the Bad Cluster into a normal Cluster. In order to achieve fast results, the conscious mind will just watch and experience without any interruption! Therefore, during a PMA session you:

- *do not think*
- *do not reason*
- *do not argue*
- *do not summarize*
- *do not describe why*
- *do not control the direction*

All these things are tasks of the conscious brain. The conscious will block you as soon as it gets involved. Why? Because it is the only part of the brain that is aware of feelings! As soon as you activate a Bad Cluster, and if you definitely allow yourself to intensify the feelings of the activated Bad Cluster, your Inhibiting Friend mechanism gets active. You don't want to feel, so you try to follow the impulses of your Friend mechanism and find a reason to block the process.

Example:

> Imagine yourself in a movie theater. You are watching and enjoying an exiting movie. Mentally, you can become a part of the movie, but you have no influence what so ever on the flow and the result of the movie. The only thing that you can do to stop the input of the movie, is to actually leave the theater. However, to enjoy the movie, you just sit there and enjoy the ride.

This is exactly what you should do during a session. You do not interfere or direct! You just enjoy the ride and allow your subconscious to come up with whatever it wants to come up with, including all the emotions (physiology) attached to it! Let us now go to our next exercise. In this exercise we will use everything we've learned so far. The only difference here with a genuine PMA session is that we won't immediately start from a 'trigger' moment that negatively activated us during our daily life. Instead, we will first start with an amount of questions to build up trust in your subconscious brain.

Experience the language of your subconscious

This exercise lets you relive events in your life. It is very important that you understand that your conscious memory system hasn't given you all the answers that you need to become more successful. The reason is, that the memories you need for that are hidden from your consciousness. The only way to get to them, is to go where they are hiding, the subconscious! To allow the subconscious to give you the wanted mental pictures, you have to let go! This means you do not direct the subconscious, but allow it to come up with whatever it wants, without asking yourself whether this has anything to do with what you "think" it is related to. The PMA questions will evoke spontaneous images from your subconscious. Once that first image is there, focus on what you feel with that image, even if it's only a very little alteration in your feelings. Focus on where and how you feel this in your body. From this point on, look at the last image and feel… just look and feel and let your subconscious do all the work! Your subconscious mind will never complain or stop, as long as your conscious mind does not block it! You will experience that if you just look and feel, then the next mental picture will automatically pop up. The more you practice this process the faster you will go. Each new picture that pops up after that, will carry more physiological reactions. Just focus on the alterations in your feelings, and follow the response of your subconscious.

Do not combine PMA with other techniques

It is of major importance to understand that the subconscious reacts like a computer. In order to activate the program of your choice, or to activate a specific analysis, you have to hit the correct keys on your keyboard. In other words, if you don't speak the language of your computer, then you don't get the desired answers! Your subconscious acts in the same way. You have to use its language and you have to respect its language rules in order to get the desired answers! PMA is not just another philosophy or "trick". It is totally based on the language of the subconscious. Therefore you cannot expect to receive correct information from you subconscious if you mix the PMA 5-step program with other methods. All other methods that are effective have some aspects in them involving the subconscious language. That is usually enough to make impressive changes at a Cluster level. Please keep in mind that none of the other methods, when they were developed, was aware of the existence of Bad Clusters! They had no real insight in the neurophysiological connection between factual data and their ever present physiological load, and no knowledge of the power of the Inhibiting Friend Mechanism. Remember, the subconscious is a stimulus/response mechanism. You will only get to the Bad Clusters if you understand and speak the language of the subconscious. Is this difficult? Regarding your computer, it is important that you have and use the right command without adding or changing any figure or letter in its command in order to have the right answers, otherwise, it will be difficult to work with it and to learn. And to learn to work with PMA is easier than learning how to work with a computer. With this in mind, let us now take the next step and practice the following exercise:

Read the first question of the exercise. Close your eyes (it's not necessary, but it usually works better) and go to the first picture that pops up! Assume that the first question is: What was the first home you lived in all by yourself, or together with your partner? Now imagine that the first image you see is yourself sitting on the beach. It would be obvious that you would say to yourself: *"No, no... this is not the answer to the question. Let me just look so I can find another picture."* Don't do that! Your subconscious brain was activated by the question and came up with the answer. But you may think this was not the answer requested! True, that is why you never got the answers you needed in the first place! We need the pictures with the highest relative code. In this example, the subconscious caught two main aspects in the question:

1. *Your first home*
2. *Your partner*

In this specific example you made the decision to buy a home when you were sitting together on the beach. This moment of decision together with your partner is obviously of more importance (higher relative code) to you than your first house.

This is why the subconscious came up with the picture of you and your partner at the beach. Never doubt your subconscious! It works like a machine based on the stimulus/response rule and does not make any mistakes. Learn to trust it! Please read one question at the time. Close your eyes and go to the first mental image your subconscious offers you, regardless if this is the answer to the question or not. Once that first image is there, focus on what you feel with that image, even if it's only a very little alteration in your feelings. Focus on where and how you feel this in your body. From this point on, look at the last image and feel, just look and feel, and let your subconscious do all the work! Remember: *Your subconscious mind will never complain or stop, as long as your conscious mind does not block it!* If you just look and feel, you will experience that the next mental picture will automatically pop up. This process will go faster and faster the more you practice. Each new picture that pops up after that will carry more intense physiological reactions. Just focus on the alterations of your feelings. And follow the response of your subconscious.

The tools that allow you to communicate with the subconscious

As we discussed before, you have to follow the rules of the language of the subconscious. Taking all these rules into consideration leads you to the following basic technique:

1. Always start with an *event.*
2. Find the most powerful *moment* in that event.
3. Find the most powerful *detail* in that moment.
4. Now just focus on the detail and *feel* the response of your body
5. Wait until a *new event* (picture) *spontaneously* pops up.

After a mental picture- the next event- pops up spontaneously, you will again follow the same procedure:

Event – Moment – Detail

followed by

LOOKING and FEELING

Keep repeating this process until you reach the content of the Bad Cluster. How do you know when to stop? Your body will tell you. Just seconds before you reach the Bad Cluster, your physiology will intensify significantly. Then the Bad Cluster content will reveal itself to the conscious brain. In the following seconds, the negative physiology will disappear completely! The content of that eliminated Bad Cluster will never bother your physiology again. It is gone forever! Instead of that, you feel a tremendous relief, and after some hours, you'll feel a large increase of energy. It is all about feelings and reliving the moment. As soon as you activate a Bad Cluster, you will feel its negative physiology. Keep in mind, it is never the PMA session that activated the Bad Cluster. It was activated before the session. That was the reason that its contents revealed itself during the session. In almost all cases the Bad Cluster was activated numerous times before and created a negative feeling. If you add up all those occasions that the physiology of the Bad Cluster was activated, you now have the symptoms of its negative physiology stored in a large amount of Clusters. The moment you reach the content of the Bad Cluster, you will start to understand a lot of moments in your life that you felt activated but did not understand why. You will also understand all the inhibiting belief systems you created based on those inexplicable feelings. Realize:

- Whatever it is that created a Bad Cluster in your past, it did not kill you!

- The second thing you have to be aware of is the fact that reliving does not mean that you have to experience the entire magnitude of the pain of the original event. It will be there for only a very brief moment and then it'll be gone forever to make place for positive energy.

- Keep in mind that your Inhibiting Friend will do whatever it takes to protect you. It will therefore come up with a lot of 'nightmare' type of unrealistic pictures. Just look at them and don't ignore them! *We do not look for the objective truth in a session.* The only thing *we are looking for are mental pictures that* you could not remember consciously and that *are loaded with negative physiology.*

Our next exercise contains questions of all kinds of events in your life. Just read the question and go to the very first event that pops up. As soon as the event pops up, continue by using the fundamental technique as explained above. You might already reveal some Bad Clusters here, although many of the questions will evoke pleasant events in your life. The principle is the same. Go to the most dominant moment, followed by the detail. Just focus on the detail and become aware of your feelings (where in your body and what it is that you feel), until a new picture *spontaneously* pops up. Have fun and enjoy the ride!

Signals to train your brain

Experience with all your senses the mental pictures that spontaneously pop up when you read the following questions:

1. A recent happy moment?
2. The colors of the clothes you wore yesterday?
3. A situation in which you felt relaxed?
4. Someone was angry at you?
5. You saw children playing?
6. You had the feeling you could “take on the whole world”?
7. You finished a job you started?
8. You were appreciated by someone?
9. What occurred this morning at ten o’clock?
10. You started a project?
11. You felt really comfortable?
12. Someone loved you?
13. Someone betrayed you?
14. You saw someone you hadn’t seen in a while?
15. You had more strength in you than you possible?
16. You finished something that someone e finish?
17. You explained something clearly tha understood?
18. You gave someone a compliment?
19. You were very nervous?
20. You met someone that you didn’t l
21. You felt secure?
22. Someone interrupted you?
23. You gave an apology?
24. You prepared a meal?
25. You did something you didn’t ex
26. You had to stay somewhere you
27. You broke the authority of som
28. You saw something that impres

29. Someone misunderstood your intentions?
30. You listened to music?
31. You finished an assignment?
32. You interrupted someone?
33. You had a very relaxing feeling?
34. You compared yourself to someone else?
35. You had pain and it made you afraid?
36. You made a difficult decision?
37. You had an experience that you hope you will never go through again?
38. You felt alone and abandoned?
39. Someone pushed you away?
40. You did something that was forbidden but you liked it?
41. You wanted everyone to leave you alone?
42. You were floating in the water?
43. You were very content with your life?
44. You stood firm to your opinion?
45. Someone told you they appreciated you?
46. You were making a big mistake?
47. You were totally exhausted?
48. An animal you loved died?
49. You had the feeling that nothing could go wrong that day?
50. You were enjoying a meal with friends?
51. Someone kissed you?
2. You pushed yourself to the limit?
. You were enthusiastic?
You were looking at someone in a different way?
You were intensely happy?
'ou changed clothes?
ou experienced something exciting?
u had a feeling of power?
neone trusted you?

60. You couldn't say goodbye to something?
61. You had a good conversation?
62. You refused something?
63. You had a relationship with someone that others warned you about?
64. You made plans for a vacation?
65. Someone you loved ignored you?
66. Someone lied to you?
67. You couldn't get enough of something?
68. You didn't have the guts to talk to someone?
69. Your father taught you something?
70. You watched a movie that increased a lot of emotions?
71. Someone told you something and you knew it was a lie?
72. Someone's presence gave you an unsafe feeling?
73. You began a relationship that you later regretted?
74. You didn't want to talk about something?
75. You were afraid for your life?
76. You didn't give your opinion and were sorry afterwards?
77. You had the feeling that you were used?
78. You entrusted someone with a secret?
79. You refused to accept something?
80. You had a sense of fear but didn't know why?
81. You were afraid of dying?
82. You were enthusiastic about something?
83. You were impressed by nature?
84. You suddenly knew something for sure?
85. You had to persuade yourself to do something you did not like?
86. You couldn't approach someone that you really loved?
87. Someone you loved very much died?
88. You panicked?
89. Your earliest experience of pain?
90. You were amused?

You can repeat this exercise as often as you want. And you will see that every time you do this, new pictures will pop up. Do you feel confident enough to practice a real PMA session now? Before we do this, we want to discuss some final aspects of the subconscious language.

The importance of language in your session

A newborn baby cannot speak. It has to learn to speak a language. Scientific experiments have demonstrated that we all have preprogrammed modules for language when we are born. We have to develop these modules over the years and fill their Database with words and phrases. Language is a very important module. For instance, try to reason and argue, or even think or make plans for the future, or evaluate your past, all without the use of words and phrases! The capacity of reasoning, arguing, thinking, making plans for the future, and evaluating our past, distinguishes mankind from other species! There is no doubt that language is important! How important is it in your session? As we see in this diagram, we put language in the center and all the senses around it. Why? All the senses can exist and be experienced on their own, but it is language that works as a catalyst that lifts our consciousness to a higher level.

LANGUAGE AND MODULES

CLUSTERS

SPREAD OUT ALL OVER THE BRAIN
STORED IN DIFFRENT MODULES

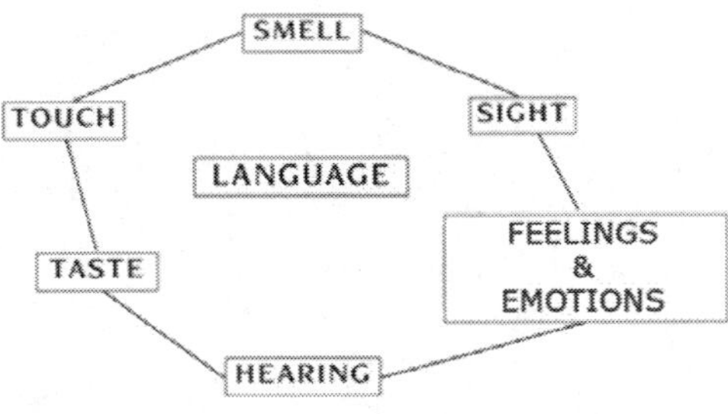

Language in itself has very little meaning without the Database and processes of our senses. Let's examine the proof.

Examples:

What do you see if you hear the word *paard*? If you do not speak Dutch, you won't know what the word *paard* means. Yet, if you understand Dutch, you will immediately see an image of a horse in your mind. There are hundreds of different languages and hundreds of different words to describe a horse. What does this tell us? It tells us that words are just sound constructions that only get their meaning when you attach it to some kind of mental picture (smell, sound, picture, feeling, taste or touch). What do you see when I say "Supercalifragalisticexpialadocious"? Mary Poppins… although the word in itself means nothing, it received its meaning because Mary Poppins put a meaning to it! Words and languages help us during our sessions to make connections and address certain issues.

Exercise:

What do you see if I say "dog"? What kind of dog do you see? What do you feel if you think of that dog? Now imagine that this dog just walked outside into the heavy rain and is all wet. Go near the dog. Smell its wet fur! Now pet the dog! Does your feeling change? Watch out! It's going to shake off the water…!

Now let's analyze this simple little experiment. It was the questions, the words that you heard, that brought up the change in pictures and feelings. How does this work?

- The word *dog* activated a picture. Usually this will only activate some Fragments or Sub-clusters.
- The moment I asked you to imagine that dog all wet from walking in the rain, and then to smell it, I activated a whole new sense: the smell.
- When I asked you to pet it, your sense of touch also got involved.
- At the warning that he was about to shake off the water, complete Clusters were activated and you were ready to react!

Now what does this example show us? Language activates Clusters or parts of Clusters! It works the same with Bad Clusters. The benefit of language in your sessions is that it leads you to the content of the Bad Cluster a lot faster. By activating more Sub-clusters through language, you intensify the physiology (feelings). This will speed up the whole process. If we do a session and we use language to describe what we feel, our subconscious will make lots of connections. Keep in mind that the more connections the brain makes, the more comparison material becomes active. So it helps to bring all our sensory experiences into action. This is important because we need a large amount of activated Clusters to analyze the content of the Bad Cluster. The Bad Cluster was never analyzed in the past! In order to analyze it now, you need material to compare and connect it to. These connections cause the elimination of the negative physiology once the Bad Cluster has been brought to our conscious by reliving it. Make good use of language during your own session! Describe in words what you see and feel. Activate all senses if possible! You can say things out loud, but you don't have to. If you don't want to say out loud what you see and experience in your session, say it in your head but do describe in words what you see and feel! By using words you will speed up the process of making the proper connections and it will give you so much more enjoyment and insight of yourself and the human behavior in general.

You will be surprised

What will surprise you most is discovering how many of your belief systems, preferences, habits and decisions are based upon Bad Clusters. The same goes for unexplainable fears and emotional blockages. The more you clean up or eliminate these things, the more mental energy will be released. Your learning capabilities and memory will also improve, and your psychological and psychosomatic complaints will disappear.

The PMA session based on activation

After successfully going through all the previous exercises, you will get to the point that you are ready to practice the PMA self-improvement. This won't be just an exercise anymore; this is the real power of PMA, which is what enables you to control your mind and belief systems. PMA helps you to instantly feel better and will serve you for the rest of your life! Always stay alert in order to cooperate with your Friend Mechanism, for it is your protection mechanism! You will benefit most from PMA if you are able to apply it instantly when you need it most. This is what the real sessions are all about! If the situation allows you to, you can apply PMA immediately after you feel that you are activated by something. If the circumstances do not allow it, you should do it as soon as possible afterwards. In that case, you might want to write down some 'keywords' to remember the exact moment and detail so you can use it later on in your session. As soon as you know the exact *WHEN* you became activated, you can start your session. Now, continue until you feel the physiological tension rise to a level that you spontaneously see the images of the Bad Cluster. Immediately, you will experience relaxation in your body. The inhibiting and negative physiology of the Bad Cluster will never bother you again after that one reliving! It's gone forever!

Once again keep in mind:

- During a PMA session you *relive*
- This means: There is *no* reasoning, just move one from one mental picture to the next.
- *Do not* think, reason, or rationalize about the mental pictures that pop up.
- Just experience whatever your subconscious offers you spontaneously.
- Hear, smell, see, feel (touch) and taste.
- Allow all *spontaneous* emotions and mental pictures, and do not suppress them!

This may look hard at first, but in fact, it is the easiest thing to do, it all happens automatically if you don't block it! You'll only have to learn to do nothing and let your subconscious do its job! Before you start your session read the following steps carefully.

The basis of the PMA method

Step 1

Try to find a place where you can sit, or lay down comfortably without being interrupted by music, phones or other people. Ask yourself: Is there anything that bothered or activated me recently? This could be an irritation at my work place with clients or co-workers, something at home, driving my car, etc., or something that recently created a sudden mood change?

Step 2

Now, try to be there and relive that situation in your mind. What is the moment in that event that affects you the most? Try to focus only on that moment. Relive that moment over and over again. What is it that you feel in your body? Where do you feel it? Head, chest, stomach, arms, legs, back, etc. How do you feel it? Is there an itch, tension, pressure, pain, heat, cold, etc.? Focus on the feeling and try to intensify that feeling. Don't fight it, but allow it totally, welcome it. It's trying to tell you something.

Step 3

Now focus on the mental picture of the moment again. In that moment there is a detail that affects you the most! It is usually a detail that captures your attention automatically, or just the opposite! In that case, you don't want to see that detail and you're trying to avoid it. Relive that moment until you feel what the detail is. Don't think about what the detail could be! *You will feel it!* Your body will tell you! Just pay attention. Just look and feel, don't think! Once again, let your subconscious do what it does automatically, without conscious interfering! As soon as you know what the detail is, focus on that detail. What do you feel if you focus on that specific detail?

Step 4

Focus on the feeling and become fully aware of what you feel! Where do you feel that? Head, chest, stomach,

> arms, legs, back, etc. How do you feel it? Itch, tension, pressure, pain, heat, cold, etc. Focus on it and allow it; intensify it! Focus on the detail! Now combine both. Just look and feel! Don't do any other thing than look and feel. Let your brain do what it automatically does! Stay in the picture! The detail that intensifies your physiology is in that picture and nowhere else! Keep looking and feeling until another picture pops up spontaneously!

This is not a long process; it can take place in a matter of seconds, due to the tremendous speed of the subconscious processing! After the image of another event pops up, you start again with step 2, followed by step 3 and 4. Tension will build up in your body. The feelings will become stronger. But don't fight it! Don't think about it what ever pops up. Just continue until you experience an event you could not remember before. This can be whole events or details of an event that you could remember but you had no conscious memory of these details. As soon as the whole content of such an event pops up, you will feel the relaxation. Keep doing this until you experience a state of total relaxation. Whatever comes up next, go there, don't dismiss it as irrelevant or unrelated. It is always related through the logical language of the subconscious, and that is the one we must follow here. If this new picture is less painful, or even pleasant, you have been directed away from the Bad Cluster by the Friend Mechanism. You can again go back to the previous picture and look for the most painful detail. Allow yourself to intensify the pain and fear and look for the next picture in that direction. You will know when you get to the Bad Cluster. It is something in your life that you recognize immediately, but yet it comes to your consciousness for the first time ever. Ultimately, it will be processed as a normal Cluster and the harmful physiology will leave your body instantly, and never to return. You will experience a great relief that will positively affect you in all the ways we have discussed before.

Find the moment

To achieve the most effective PMA sessions, we use those moments in our life where we are signaled or activated. Some people find it difficult to pinpoint those moments. The pressures of life may have conditioned us to not pay attention to ourselves anymore. Then we realize we don't feel so good or are not able to perform the way we want to, but we don't remember instantly when that feeling started. However, if we want to do an effective PMA session, we must remember *WHEN* that feeling occurred. We already know that asking *WHY* won't give us the answer. Of course we have to learn to pay more attention to ourselves, but, what if we can't find the trigger-signals that activated the feelings? This exercise shows us how to do that.

The procedure

What can you do if you didn't pay attention to the exact moment that you experienced the changes? You'll have to find the moment afterwards. How do you do that? Just go back in time, inside your head. Don't think, but relive those moments! So you should not see yourself doing things again, but be there, doing it again in your mind. Go back to where you remember that you became aware of the changes in your feelings or behavior. From that point, start to ask yourself:

- *Did I experience these changes when I woke up this morning?*

- *What about breakfast, lunch, or the discussion with that customer, etc.? Were the changes already there?*

In this way, you will find the last moment you remember that the change occurred. When you have already found the moment that you became aware of the changes for the first time, all you have to do next is to think about the time in between these two moments.

- Now you try to focus on the change. Try to relive that changed feeling or behavior.

- After you recall the changed feeling, ask yourself: What was it that irritated me in the period between those two moments?

- Don't think about it! Just look and listen to your body and wait for the spontaneous picture your subconscious comes up with! Your subconscious will not make mistakes. Every picture that pops up is connected to the activation! Don't deceive yourself by reasoning that this next picture has nothing to do with it. Remember, it is the subconscious that makes the decisions, not the conscious mind.

Based on the subconscious language rule that selection is always based on the highest relative value, the first moment that will pop up is always the moment the feeling started! Just learn to trust your own brain! You will enter a whole new stage of possibilities in your life. What's more, you have that *desirable power* inside to become what you always knew you had in you!

Chapter 11 - Build happy relationships with PMA

We all long for the most pleasurable kind of relationships. Whether you're a couple in a long-term partnership, single, but on the verge of marriage, a parent, child, neighbor, friend or even part of a business relationship, this revolutionary program can help you to avoid becoming part of the large number of relationships that suffer from monotony or frequent misunderstandings in communication. PMA will show you the secret of how to attain optimal levels in relationships. Most relationships would be a lot stronger if there was a better understanding of each other's feelings. Why is it so difficult to relate to other people and let them know how you feel?

A relationship is based on the effect two people have on each other. These effects are primarily based on how you the messages and behaviors of the other person are received. The way you receive their signals depends entirely on how you interpret those signals. Your interpretation always depends on your previous experiences; or, in other words, the comparison material that you have already stored during your life. If you are consciously aware of all your previously stored comparison material, then everything is okay. By practicing PMA you will be surprised to find out that the majority of all our irritated reactions and conflicts are based on hidden comparison material that you cannot consciously recall. Applying PMA will teach you how to find this hidden comparison material (memories) in your brain.

After finding these hidden comparison materials, you will immediately experience the unwanted feelings flow away. In return, you will receive a tremendous feeling of relief combined with motivating energy. It empowers you and allows you to think more clearly and lively, regardless of how long these negative feelings have existed. At this point you will start to realize how the unknown contents of Bad Clusters have inhibited your true potential and capacity in your relationships towards others.

You cannot understand a Bad Cluster

Although the workings of our brain are very logical, it appears that the content of a Bad Cluster is completely illogical. Don't think that you will get anywhere in trying to understand the contents of Bad Clusters. You sometimes hear people say that they "understand" where their symptoms come from. This may be true for a physical damage that you have as a result of an accident, but definitely not for the large group of symptoms that we call psychosomatic symptoms. You cannot understand a Bad Cluster. You also cannot recall it until it is exposed through the PMA technique. A Bad Cluster can be activated by various words, locations, objects, as well as by certain individuals or their behaviors, as soon as they contain a certain amount of memory moments. As you read the following example, it will be good to realize that whenever we communicate or associate with other people, we establish a relationship of some kind. This means that activation and negative responses occur in all those relationships from time to time.

> ***Example*:**
> A woman was already married to the same man for twenty years. During the fifth year, the marriage suffered a crisis. Her husband committed adultery. She decided to forgive him and wanted to continue the marriage. Bad Clusters were created the very moment she learned of

the adultery, as well as the moment when she confronted him with the truth. She learned of the adultery through a friend who called her on the telephone to tell her. The friend had seen her husband at the beach in Atlantic City in a passionate embrace with another woman. Her world caved in! It can't be true; she must be mistaken! But her friend affirmed, *"No, I'm not wrong about this. Does your husband have green and yellow striped swimming trunks?"* The wife replied, heart broken, *"Yes, indeed he does."* Her friend described what the other woman looked like: *"She had long blond hair, was slim and was wearing a white bikini."* Slowly the woman regains her balance and, as if she were in a trance, hangs up the phone.

The result

What is the content of this Bad Cluster? The telephone call took place in the kitchen. None of the following data in the Bad Cluster is analyzed. They all have the same value.

- ◊ The smells in the kitchen
- ◊ The interior of the kitchen
- ◊ The telephone
- ◊ The words *beach*, *other woman*, *passionate*, *embrace*, *slim*, *white bikini*, etc.
- ◊ Striped swimming trunks

All these details are coupled with the Physio-cluster, where all the physiology of how she felt at that moment is stored. Her heart was beating wildly, she felt nauseous, and she felt her throat close up. She paled and felt as if all the blood drained out of her head and it felt as if she were going to faint. Every one of these tidbits of data is now empowered to activate the Bad Cluster. If current data is ever similar enough to that in the Bad Cluster, it will be activated; even if the overall event is completely different from the event causing the Bad Cluster.

> ***Result*:**
> That evening she confronts her husband with the story her friend told her. They are sitting together in the bedroom. At first he denies it in every way, *"Darling, you know that you are the only one that I love. I would never even dream of doing such a thing."* She then confronts him with the fact that one of their friends saw him there. His resistance breaks down and he admits that it is true. Once again her world caves in! So it really is true! *"But darling, I didn't want to. I was tricked into it! She means nothing to me; I don't feel anything for that woman."* As he is saying this, he rubs his chin nervously and makes a grimace. He is wearing a blue shirt and a red tie, which he loosens anxiously.

He doesn't understand her violent reaction

So what are the contents of this second Bad Cluster?

- ◊ The interior of the room
- ◊ "*I didn't want to*"
- ◊ "*tricked into it*"
- ◊ Rubbing the chin
- ◊ Grimace
- ◊ Blue shirt
- ◊ Red tie
- ◊ Loosening of the tie

Although the first and the second Bad Clusters are completely different in content, the reason they were created is the same for both, namely her husband's adultery. Don't assume that these two Bad Clusters can from now on only be activated in exactly the same situations. They could very easily be activated in situations that to you, appear to have absolutely nothing to do with the circumstances where the Bad Cluster was originally created. Let's take a look to see how it went with this couple: After a few months she caught him in the arms of that same blond woman. Because she was so hurt by his second betrayal, she divorced him. Fortunately, three years later, she met a great guy and married him. They were very happy until…

> ***Activated*:**
> She is sitting outside on a sunny summer evening, in the back yard. Her beloved husband has arrived home from work. He has already taken off his jacket, and he is wearing a blue shirt and a red tie. Because of the heat, he loosens his tie and opens the top button of his shirt. He tells her that he has to go see his boss this evening. She gets angry because she had already made plans for this evening. Her husband tells her that it won't last long, insisting, *"It's not a big deal. We just have to pop in and make an appearance. We'll be home early."* He is a little upset by her violent reaction and he makes a grimace and rubs his chin.

A Bad Cluster is activated

Suddenly she has a very uneasy feeling. Everything starts to turn, her heart races, and she feels as if her throat is pinched closed. She has no idea what is happening. Just two minutes ago she felt fine. Will she remember now? Does the overall situation resemble the one that the Bad Cluster was created in? Her relationship with her new husband has been excellent. Nonetheless, the Bad Cluster has been activated. She can make absolutely no connection with the adulterous situation of her first husband and the present, because there is simply no way that the subconscious can read the Bad Cluster, so it is not passed onto the conscious brain, although the symptoms of the activated physiology are clearly felt. The incoming sensory data activated an abundance of comparison material. What sort of data did it get to work with?

> Loosening of the tie from a blue shirt, red tie, loosening of the top button, *"it was nothing"*, a grimace, and rubbing of the chin.

The incoming data activates several Clusters that have some or all of these pieces of data, but it also activates the Bad Cluster. The subconscious cannot ignore it because the data is so similar to the Bad Cluster data and the Bad Cluster data has such a high relative code. As soon as it is activated, the Physio-cluster attached to it is also executed. All the sorrow in it is felt by the woman. There was, of course, nothing threatening about the present situation. Nothing in her surroundings is hazardous or dangerous, therefore she will not create another Bad Cluster, but what she is now feeling will be stored in a Cluster. Also, the data of a blue shirt, red tie, loosening of the tie, a grimace, and the chin rubbing are all stored in this Cluster. This Cluster can then be used in the future as comparison material because the data is analyzed. As soon as that happens, that Cluster will activate the Bad Cluster again. Why? Because this Cluster is loaded with similarities that are also in the Bad Cluster.

Will you go to Atlantic City with me?

In our example of the adultery, a Bad Cluster was created during the telephone conversation with her friend that had seen her husband with the woman at the beach in Atlantic City.

> ***The next conflict***
>
> It is another warm day. She is standing in her underclothing in front of the mirror. The frilly white bra and white panties are in stark contrast to her tanned skin. She thinks: "*... just like a "'white bikini'"*. She is quite pleased with what she sees. Then the telephone rings and she excitedly runs to the kitchen to answer it. It is a friend of her seventeen year old daughter. She's a lovely thin girl with long blond hair. She can picture her daughter's friend in her mind as she hears her voice. The girl asks if she wants to go to the beach with her and her parents: the beach in Atlantic City.

Both Bad Clusters are activated

Suddenly a very irritating feeling overcomes her. Her heart starts beating rapidly and she feels like her throat is closing up. A feeling of panic takes control over her. What activated the Bad Cluster this time? The fact that there were sufficient memory moments available. What were they?

- ◊ The white bikini she thought of when she looked at herself in the mirror
- ◊ The kitchen's interior
- ◊ The fact that she imagined seeing the figure and long blond hair of her daughter's friend
- ◊ The telephone conversation
- ◊ The invitation to the beach

◊ The words *Atlantic City*

This entire image contained enough similarities for the subconscious to activate the Bad Cluster and its connected negative physiology. Now she really starts to experience strong feelings of insecurity and she has no idea why. As soon as her husband comes home, she will tell him about the uneasy feeling that came up a few days ago. They discuss the incident and how she felt about it, but also how she felt the same negative feelings this afternoon after the phone call. The two Clusters that she made are now connected to each other. So now one Cluster is made from the data of the two preceding Clusters, and furthermore, they are attached to the other two as comparison material. Now her husband starts to get really worried about her health. He loosens his tie and rubs his chin nervously while making a grimace. Hey, now what? She starts to feel bad again. All the same symptoms arise. Why? The two incidents that she just talked about had a number of memory moments that were in a Bad Cluster. It got even more complicated when her husband loosened his tie, rubbed his chin, and quivered at the mouth. The subconscious receives the similarity and activates the Bad Cluster that was created when she was told about the adultery. Now both of the Bad Clusters are activated.

Now just imagine what this could mean to their relationship. She is feeling terrible! It is the feeling of insecurity and fear, but also the feeling of betrayal that was activated. What do you think will be the effect in her actions and behavior towards him? He tries to comfort her and tries to hug her. She is pushing him away and leaves the room telling herself: *"He does not understand me!"* (belief system). From this point on she will, whenever she is activated, look for confirmation of her belief system that he does not understand her. This is just one example of the many possibilities how a relationship can be disrupted. Keep in mind that her second husband did nothing wrong at all. Yet he is the one who has to now deal with her feelings and negative behavior towards him. More than likely, her behavior will activate some of his Bad Clusters, which of course are not caused by her, but probably originate from a period before he even knew her.

It is not the other, it is your comparison material

Successful relationships are not based on rational arguments but on feelings. As we understand by now, these feelings originate from our activated comparison material. If we have a violent or abusive partner, then it is correct to say that our negative emotions are caused by behavior of our partner. But if we can assume that our present relationship is based on mutual love, respect and appreciation, then PMA can do miracles for your relationship. Many relationships suffer from misunderstandings that could totally be avoided if they would only understand the subconscious processes. Feelings are not mainly activated by what your partner does, but are the result of the emotional load of the comparison material that it activates in your subconscious. As you will find out, the majority of that comparison material has nothing to do with your partner. In most cases it goes way back to a time you did not even know each other, as the following example shows.

The suitcase clicks shut

If we understand the power and effects of a Bad Cluster, then the reactions we mentioned in the examples seem completely logical and explicable. If one compares two situations, one where a Bad Cluster is created and another that activated it, we can see that there is no logical connection between the two events. There is no similarity in the situation or intentions of the two incidents. In that regard, the motive of the Bad Cluster's activation is, therefore, completely illogical! We also want to take a look at some other examples:

***Example*:**
A young married couple has a considerable amount of tension in their marriage. They really love each other but they continue to have arguments. He has a job that takes him away from home several nights a week. Every time this happens, he leaves the house with an argument. As soon as he closes the door behind him, he feels sorry. Neither of them really wishes to fight and argue at these times. She claims that it really doesn't bother her to be alone at night. Nor does she have anything against his job or the fact that he has to be away so frequently. So there appears to be no logical connection between his departure and the arguments they have. And yet, each time that he walks out the door, she feels miserable. Her heart beats frantically, she is frightened to death, and feels intensely sad and angry, all at the same time. This has been going on for months. What is the cause of her symptoms and her behavior?

***Session*:**
She is asked to relive the last argument they had. She describes what happened. Now she is asked to determine at exactly what moment the symptoms and emotions arose in her. After going over the entire incident several times, she suddenly realizes the exact instant her bad feelings came up. It was the moment that her husband headed for the bedroom to pack his suitcase. He opened it up and put his clothing in it. He shuts the suitcase. The clicking of the lock seems to be the exact detail when she starts to feel bad. Instantly, she makes a leap in her

> memory back to her youth: She is ten years old. Her mother and father are fighting constantly. This particular evening it is so bad that her father yells he is leaving and never coming back. He walks to the bedroom and packs his suitcase. Her world collapses. Her father, her friend, her everything, is going away, … going away forever! It can't be so, it mustn't be so! As if she were nailed to the ground, frozen, she stands and watches how he packs his suitcase. She sees him throw everything into the suitcase and close it. *Click*, *click*, the suitcase is closed and locked up. Her father slams the door behind him. She is left standing there. She is in a state of panic. Her heart is beating in her throat and she is controlled by panic and anger. She suddenly understands that this is the same feeling that she has when her husband leaves. Needless to say that both developed several belief systems to explain the "unreasonable" behavior of the other.

What were the memory moments that activated the Bad Cluster? Departure, bedroom, packing a suitcase, the clicking of the lock, and the slamming of the door. All this data was in the Bad Cluster and was sufficiently similar for the subconscious to activate the Bad Cluster. After the session, several of her physical symptoms instantly disappeared. The tension between her and her spouse also disappeared when she told him that it was not his behavior that caused her anger but that he was unwillingly activating subconscious comparison material from her past. By seeing her change and understanding the power of these subconscious processes, he started to do sessions as well. Their relationship reached a new level of communication and understanding.

Did you learn anything from it?

How is our behavior affected by Bad Clusters? How can we explain repeated patterns of fighting, arguing, overreacting, fearful behavior, and a certain level of predictability in reactions in terms of Bad Clusters? All of us can perhaps recall many such moments when we reacted in such an irrational way. We don't even understand ourselves and why we behaved in such a manner. It could be a one-time incident. However, there are also patterns of reacting that keep recurring. In certain situations you react in the same irrational way. For those who know you well, they find it easy to predict how you will react. There are scads of examples for this. We will look at one which is easily recognized by most of us.

> ***Example:***
>
> A couple has been married for several years. The wife is a good cook and she takes good care of her loved ones. The husband gets home late for dinner on a regular basis; it happened again today. She has carefully heated and reheated the meal several times, and is rather irritated by this. On the other hand, the husband has a less than pleasant day at the office behind him. He was so caught up, he didn't notice how late it was getting. He only looks forward to going home and having a pleasant evening, letting his troubles fade away. When he walks cheerfully into the kitchen, he notices that the look on his wife's face is enough to kill a dead man. She angrily speaks out, *"Where on earth have you been? I've been waiting forever with this food! Everything is spoiled now! You never think about me! I slave away here all day and this is the reward I get?!"* Now, his mood swings way below sea level and he dishes it right back to her, *"You think I sit around the office all day*

> *doing nothing? I work myself to death for you. Or do you think my job is so great? Do you have any idea what I do all day? I had a lousy day at work and then I have to come home, and what happens? I get the same hassles at home!"* Dinner is eaten in silence. He may as well forget about that nice pleasant evening at home. Rationally, we can expect this to happen in a relationship maybe once or twice. After one or two repetitions of this, it should become quite clear to both that such exchanges accomplish nothing. Against all logic, we see that patterns develop nonetheless and are repeated year after year. We repeatedly behave in a manner that is irrational, incomprehensible and senseless. In this case, what is active are the Bad Clusters, and many other Clusters with the content of that behavioral pattern. We have to realize that the above behavior can lead to destructive belief systems like: *"He has no respect for what I do for him,"* or, *"She is not supporting my efforts in taking my job seriously."* These are just two examples of the many negative and inhibiting belief systems that can be created in the attempt of explaining the inexplicable negative symptoms of Bad Cluster physiology.

Is there a common cause for this well known behavioral pattern? The only common cause this has, is the activation of Bad Clusters. We can hardly assume that it would be proof of intelligence and of rational behavior to continue fighting about the same topic, like the one mentioned above, year after year. Therefore, it must originate from comparison material that is not approachable for logic and reasoning. It is purely emotionally loaded material. During PMA sessions it will become very clear that the activation moments, also called trigger moments, differ from person to person, as well as the content of the Bad Clusters that cause the behavior.

The secret of successful relationships

It is often said that the secret of successful relationships is communication. There are many counselors that advise couples on how to behave and to respond to each other. The counselor is usually very good and true, and although the couples are determined to apply the advice, they fall into the same old behavioral patterns over and over again. The reason is, the advice was understood by the conscious brain which does all the logical reasoning, but it did not change any of the negatively loaded Bad Clusters that caused their behavior in the first place. A scientific research team studied the behavioral patterns of many couples. This finally led to the discovery of four basic attributes that determines the success or failure of a relationship. With astonishing accuracy they could predict if the marriage would last or end in divorce, purely based on these four attributes:

- *Defensive behavior*
- *Obstructive behavior*
- *Criticism*
- *Contempt*

If these four behavioral patterns were regularly present in a relationship, it would be more than 87% certain that this relationship would end in a divorce within four to six years. And of all four attributes, contempt is the worst. If there is no mutual respect, then the first three of the attributes would almost automatically come into the picture. Keep in mind that all four are not rational attributes but are totally based on feelings! Will any of these attributes help you to establish a healthy and happy relationship? Of course not! We also have to realize that this does not only apply in the case of marriages, but in all kinds of relationships. Whenever you deal with people on a regular basis you create some kind of relationship. If you want it to last, or even better, if you want to create successful relationships, PMA will give you the most powerful tool to discover your subconscious comparison material that creates your decisions and behavioral patterns. By using the PMA technique, as explained in this book, you can eliminate every existing barrier between you and others.

To get to the root-cause, just start with a moment that the behavior of the other person gave you a negative feeling. Follow the basic PMA procedure: *Event – Moment – Detail – Feel*, until spontaneously, a new picture pops up. This picture is your next 'Event'. Keep repeating this process until you find the Bad Cluster. It will not only help you to understand your own reactions and behavior, but also that of the other person. If you can convince the other person to also apply the PMA tools, then a completely new era of your relationship will start with totally new levels of communication and understanding.

PMA means freedom!

You will come to know yourself and learn why you do things the way you do them and why you see things the way you see them. You will feel comfortable and function better, and understand why people in your surroundings (at home or work) act and react the way they do. A better understanding about others will surely lead to better relationships and a higher level of success in performance. PMA is a matter of choice! Do you feel the need and desire to face your subconscious comparison material that controls you? Do you dare to make the journey through your brain, looking for pictures that on a daily basis have a negative effect on you, and then change them into positive energy? If you can answer *yes* to these questions and clean up your Bad Clusters, you will feel relieved, confident, more aware, better equipped to handle the challenges of life, and capable of seizing the opportunities life offers you. You will know the truth about yourself, and that truth will set you free. Dare to live! You deserve happy and successful relationships.

Chapter 12 – Take control of your life

Learn to understand yourself and others

No one in the twentieth century has free time. So we need to buy the time and simply say no to other things that aren't necessary. You will discover that not all relationships are 'healthy'! If you find it important to please people, you will gather 'parasites' around you that take advantage of you and consume an important part of your energy. Learn to say: "*No.*" Ask yourself if everything that you are presently doing is absolutely necessary. If not, then don't do it! Some people may think, *"Yes, but then people will get angry at me."* Think about that: Someone who actually gets angry at you because you have the desire to improve your welfare, is quite obviously more concerned about his own advantage and not yours. Realize that such people are parasites that will slowly suck you dry. Learn to say "no" to these people. If they get angry and drop you as friends, then be happy! Now you will have some time for yourself and for others who are worth your time.

The tragic fact in these situations is that these parasites are always hanging around people who are willing to do something for them and who are unable to say no. Usually the victims of the parasites are sensitive people longing for close friendships, but are often disappointed by their friends. Parasites can invariably sense that you are incapable of saying no. These parasites suck up your time and then you have none left over for the people who are worth spending time with, people that could become real valuable friends. Free yourself of these parasites! By doing something for your own welfare, after a while you will function better, and therefore, you will be more helpful to the world around you. You will have insight as to why others behave the way they do and why they react they way they do. You will understand that there is nothing more fascinating on the face of this Earth than the human mind, *your* own mind. You will embark on a journey of discovery in your own brain and you will increasingly enjoy it.

Pay attention to the solution

Many people are under a lot of stress because they don't understand that focusing on a problem is never the answer. They come up with all kinds of worrying scenarios, but do not reach a state of positive decision and action! They keep the problem alive. They take tranquilizers, anti-anxiety or anti-depressant medications in order to keep the root-cause of their problems alive, instead of finding a solution. The medication will suppress the symptoms but will not change anything about the cause of the problem. The stress, anxiety or burn-out symptoms are like a red warning light on the dashboard of your car. Of course you can take a hammer and smash the red light, but will that solve the problem?

Stop worrying about the problem.

Pay attention to the solution!

Usually it doesn't take much time to understand a problem. Train yourself to not pay attention to the problem anymore after you have understood all the aspects of the problem. From that point on it is a waste of time to focus on the problem! Worrying hasn't solved one single problem so far, it only makes it worse! Remember, pay attention to the solution. If you have a problem, find as many solutions as you can come up with! Use your energy to solve the problem and do not stick to the problem reflecting on it from a million perspectives.

Don't ask why, but ask when

If Thomas Edison would have continued focusing on the problem, we might still be in the dark at night! However, he thought up hundreds of solutions to his problem until he discovered how to make a light bulb! Successful people never focus on a problem. As soon as they see the problem, they develop solutions and start to work on those solutions. They also believe in their solutions! If you want to become successful you have to focus on the solutions of how to get what you want. The majority of the people don't understand what the real problem is. They think the solution is a matter of "positive thinking" or conditioning or motivating themselves. By now you understand what the real problem is. Therefore, start to focus on the solutions. Train yourself to pay attention to the signals your body is giving you. Pay attention to how you respond, feel and behave. Realize that the way you respond, feel and behave is always a reaction caused by your comparison material that is activated by the combination of incoming sensory data.

Pay attention to *WHEN* you are activated and stop worrying about the question *WHY*. If you find out *when* you are activated and find the connected comparison material, you will automatically know *why* you where activated! The solution will definitely not be found by continuing to ask yourself *why* you don't have the success you want or deserve. The solution is to focus on your own reaction, feelings and behavior in order to find your Bad Clusters and eliminate them.

Good advice, no help

Does the solution lie within seeking good advice? In practice, we have learned that it is not a good long-term solution. Oh, it's not that you don't agree with the good advice that everyone gives you. Usually you agree with them right away! But once you analyze your life a few weeks or months later, then you realize that you used only a very small amount, or none, of the good advice after all. *"I thought we had agreed the last time we spoke that we were going to do things differently?" "Yes, you're absolutely right, but I just can't seem to be able to do it, and sometimes there simply is no other way. I really try to do it differently, but, there's always some reason why it doesn't work."* Do these arguments and belief systems sound familiar? Often, in spite of knowing better, we continue to behave foolishly and undermine our own health.

The origin of your goals

Here you have a start in skyrocketing your success! Let's start to change your goals and belief systems that inhibit you from being more successful, happy and healthy. This would mean that you can set your goals in true freedom and can achieve them without any unnecessary obstacles getting in your way. If you are a person who says *"I always reach my goals"*, then ask yourself: Am I truly happy inside, or am I only pursuing the goals I know I can achieve in my present status? Are these the real goals you would set if you had total freedom and enough energy? Do you realize that your goals are strongly connected to your belief systems? Your belief systems and your goals are both coming from your comparison material. So, what gives the comparison material power and creates the drive? It is the attached physiology.

> ***Exercise*:**
> In how many areas of your life do you have goals? Start to write them down. Be specific and don't be shy. If your goals are too easy then they are not a goal that truly drives you. Set your goals for next week, month and year. Don't be unrealistic. If your goals are unrealistic you will be discouraged in trying to achieve them. As soon as you have set your goals, then ask yourself, for each one, why you want to achieve it.

Through your belief systems you will end up at the true source of your goal: your comparison material. If it consists of normal Clusters you will easily be able to come up with reasons why you want to achieve that goal. If you can't do that, there's a good chance that you're dealing with a driving force that is rooted in a Bad Cluster. You know what to do then. You have found another clue that will lead you to your true potential.

How to achieve your goals

Goal setting is almost a standard ingredient of every seminar on personal effectiveness. In PMA we also address this subject, but for a different reason. Having goals is essential in our life. In PMA we go a step further and investigate what the source of your goals are. A goal derives its power from its source. By getting to the source, and changing it (in the case of a Bad Cluster), you will be able to give so much power to your goals that you are actually going to achieve them. Let's have a look at your present goals and create some new ones where needed. Goal setting is not only valid for the long term, we can set daily goals every day.

> ***Exercise*:**
> What are your goals for the end of next week? Is that really what you want and are you satisfied with that? Or can this goal become more powerful? If you want to change that goal, what do you have to do?

Most people don't think about goals. They just "live" their life, and every day of the week is the same. Don't be like that, there is so much to achieve and enjoy in life. Just take the opportunity and dare to live!

> Can you set a goal for yourself right now and decide that you will achieve that goal before the end of next week? Please write it down and note what you can do to achieve this; really believe that you are going to make this work! You will be surprised how inventive you will become. If you really want to achieve something, use the PMA tools and you will definitely get there!

Setting goals does not create commitments but it gives you the drive and direction to achieve them! Without goals, you do not have any drive or direction, you'd wake up in the morning and wouldn't have a reason to get out of bed! Even on a day off from work, you always need goals to get you going! It can be simple things like taking a shower, putting on your clothes or having breakfast. Maybe you think these are all normal behaviors and have nothing to do with goals because of the fact that you're not tired anymore (so you get out of bed) and now you are hungry (so you make breakfast), but these feelings are caused by physiological changes and they drive you to do these everyday things, they are part of your daily goals

You have to believe in your goals

Drives always originate from physiological changes! Whether this is hunger, thirst, desire, love, anger, responsibility, etc., it is always the feeling that drives you towards your goals. We have many goals we do not even consider as goals. We see those as normal behavioral patterns. Were you born with them? No, somebody taught us these patterns. Did we always like them? Most of us didn't like them if it involved cleaning our room, getting up in time to get to school, and a lot of other patterns that our parents tried to teach us. Why did we obey? If we didn't, our parents or teachers would be angry at us. That was emotional pain. For some of us, staying in bed or not going to school was pleasure. So it all comes down to the choice between pain and pleasure. Or in other words, feelings! It is easy to set goals. You just sit down with a pen and a piece of paper and start to write! You want to become a billionaire, live 150 years, want to be famous, etc… No, this is not how it works! We already discussed that goals originate from feelings. If there are no feelings involved, your goal will have no power; it will give you no drive! Let us examine this diagram to see where your real goals come from.

What really shapes your world and abilities?

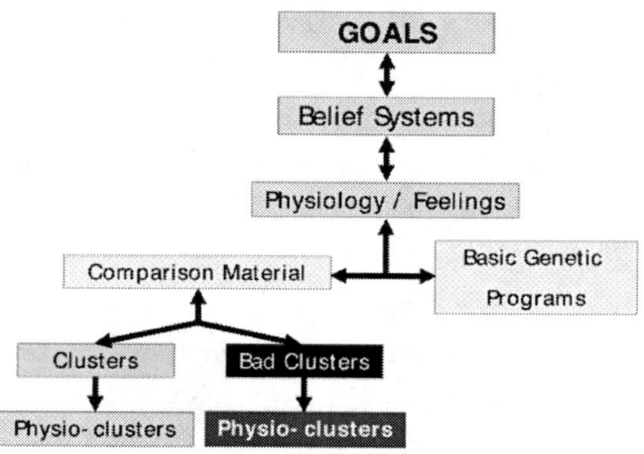

We cannot set an effective goal if we do not believe that this goal is something that we really want. This means that our goals have to come from our belief systems. If that is not the case we do not really want them, and do not really believe in them! A goal you don't believe in, is of no value! If you try to pursue it, it will give you a constant negative feeling and you will condition yourself negatively regarding it. And by doing that, you will strengthen the belief systems that you can't reach your goals!

Widen the circle of your possibilities

You probably bought and read this book in order to learn and experience the benefits of the PMA technique. A lot of other programs are being studied but, usually, only a few people will benefit from these. How come? This is because people hate to put too much time and effort in a program which they are not sure will really benefit them. It's like a workout, like physical exercises. You have to work hard and sweat a lot before you see just minor improvements in your muscles, figure, or most importantly, your health. Wouldn't it be wonderful to just sit in a lazy chair, enjoying well deserved rest, and grow muscles and become healthier after a while? We all know this won't happen. If we want to have a wonderful figure and good health, we have to exercise and sweat! Here is the good news: You don't have to do heavy workouts or sweat with PMA to become more healthy, happy and successful. You can sit down in your lazy chair while you are doing your exercises. In the meantime, you can develop courage, good health and energy!

Courage is the only thing you need!

You need the courage to give yourself permission to look in the mirror and discover who you really are and why you feel, act and behave like you do! To become more successful in all aspects of life, you need to grow. Everything that grows needs space to do so. A lot of people restrict themselves to such a narrow space that they will never see their full potential. Most people live in a very small circle. Why don't they widen that circle? It is because of their comparison material. What other people enjoy, can give others so much fear that they don't want to do those same things. In their comparison material this is no fun! They feel that doing this will activate pain. That is why this illustration shows a man trapped in a circle.

If he widens it in the direction of pleasure, it will also automatically widen in the direction of pain. That's why he won't allow himself to widen the circle towards pleasure and, consequently, remains in a smaller circle. Unfortunately, this restricts his possibilities to extend his success and happiness! He will not widen the circle if he has no possibility of avoiding the pain.

Do the pleasurable things you never did

Using the easy tools of PMA, lets make the proper connections and definitely feel the freedom and joy you deserve, without being bothered by pain. Without knowing the tools of PMA you wouldn't be able to eliminate the negative physiology of a Bad Cluster because you did not know the existence of that type of material. Now you know how to approach that material and how to eliminate its unhealthy and inhibiting physiology forever. This means that it isn't scary anymore to face the 'real you' in the mirror. With this knowledge we can widen our circle and even provoke the pain.

Why would I do something like that? Because I want to grow, expand, and become the maximum of what I can become! I need to stop sabotaging and lying to myself! Now I know that I can feel total freedom (Freedom = the absence of inhibiting fear), after I've eliminated whatever negative physiology becomes active, I will allow myself, yes, if necessary, force myself to become more successful in life and expand my possibilities. How do you do that? You expand towards the pleasure. You're telling me here that I should focus on practicing pleasurable things? That's right! But before you start drawing the wrong conclusion, I do not mean the things you already like to do! What you should focus on are the pleasurable things that you desire to do but you never had the courage to do them! Things that other people do and enjoy very much, but you feel reluctant to do. These resistances are based on the fears that created our belief systems. This fear could be installed by the behavior and opinion of our parents, spouse, company, community, family, religion, culture or many other sources. This fear will inhibit you from doing the things you like, or would like, if you tried them. And many of these things would lead you in the direction of a much more successful and pleasurable life. Our belief systems and our goals are based on our comparison material, Clusters and Bad Clusters. After we find our Bad Clusters and eliminate their physiology, we will lose the fear that inhibits and blocks us. We all want to achieve that as fast as possible. To speed up the process you have to provoke the Bad Clusters. How do you do that? By doing the things you always wanted, but you did not have the courage to do! So make these things your goals! You can do this both in your personal life and in your work.

Application in your daily life

If you want to become more successful in your work and personal life, then try to find those things that stop you from being more effective and start doing them. Overcome your fears by facing them! Do you for instance have difficulties with:

- *Communicating with employees or customers*
- *Organizing*
- *Motivating people*
- *Cold calls*
- *Solving problems between two or more employees*
- *Setting your priorities*
- *Finishing what you started*
- *Expressing yourself effectively*
- *Controlling your finances*
- *Share your deepest feelings with the ones you love*
- *Confronting others with their responsibilities and mistakes*

These, and many other issues that are related to Bad Cluster material, could be solved with PMA. Would this influence your behavior and your success? Make mastering these things your new goal. Condition yourself to enjoy this exploration process and love what you are doing. Is that difficult to do? Not at all, you just have to decide, and do it! What will happen if you just do it? You are widening your circle towards pleasure, and a circle will widen equally to all sides. So now the material that blocks you from going towards the pleasure will become visible. Great! Now you can eliminate the attached physiology forever because now you know how to do that! Don't allow "jamming stations" from the past to ruin your future any longer! Do your PMA session with the already activated material and you will gain much more space.

The opportunity to grow

This diagram shows you how it works. Every time you overcome a problem that inhibits you from being successful, or every time you reach a goal you could not reach before, you are widening your circle.

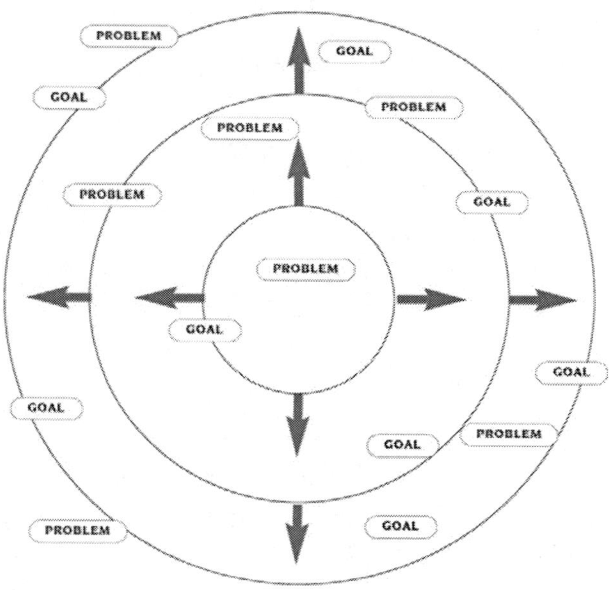

Look what happens! By achieving your goal, or conquering a problem, your circle widens in all directions and will place your Bad Clusters in the spotlights. Now you can easily trace and eliminate them. After you eliminated the Bad Clusters that narrowed your circle, your circle will widen in all directions. Now, due to your personal growth, you are capable to solve all the problems inside this larger circle and able to reach all the goals you could not reach before. This is the route to your success! Keep in mind that whatever material you clean up with PMA will be cleaned up forever! No repetition, no conditioning, the problems are just gone!

How far and how deep can you go with PMA?

Once you learned and practiced PMA, you will never forget it. It is like skating, riding a bike, or swimming, once you know how to do it, you'll never forget it! PMA is not just another method. It is the blueprint of our neurophysiology, of our total being! Once you understand PMA to its full extent, you understand yourself, and others, in a way you never did before.

For how long and to what depth can you apply PMA? To any depth and at any length of time that you decide! You learn about yourself and those around you during your entire life! Is it dangerous if you go too deep? You can never go too deep with PMA! Actually, the deeper you go, the less dangerous it becomes. The real danger lies in not eliminating your Bad Clusters! If you do nothing, and leave them as they are, they will not only inhibit and block you, they will also harm your emotional and physical well being! Keep in mind that here we have the tremendous difference between PMA and other methods! Most of the other methods are based on conditioning, but they do not clean up the real root-cause of the problem because they are not based on the awareness of the existence of

Bad Clusters. Even if you feel relief with common conditioning programs, they only work on the level of Clusters and not the root-cause of your problems, the Bad Clusters! You do not clean up the real source; therefore, the Bad Clusters will become active again whenever there are enough memory moments around you! By performing PMA, you eliminate the real cause once and for all. Even if you decide not to go very deep, you clean up anyway. Remember it is a reliving of what you endured in the past! Therefore, it can never be dangerous to do that. On the contrary! The deeper you go, the more "space", freedom and energy you will have! The issue here is not so much how deep you can go, but mainly how deep you want to go! Your subconscious brain will never complain or stop delivering mental pictures, as long as your conscious mind does not block it! Remember you are in control all of the time! How deep you want to go depends on what your goals are. If you want answers, want to overcome specific fears, and/or want to become more successful in life, you do not need to go that deep. PMA is the ultimate tool for reaching your goals. With this tool, you will find more answers than you could ever imagine about yourself, human behavior, emotions and the hidden processes of your mind.

Do something with what you've learned!

Many people are convinced procrastinators. Don't fall into that trap! Make a plan today regarding when and how you will apply what you learned from this book. Write down at this very moment what days in the week and what moment of the day you will practice PMA, starting today! Make a schedule and stick to it! Don't fall into the trap of denial, either! There are always some people who tell themselves that they can control their Bad Clusters. They can't! Nobody can! You cannot close down all of your senses from the input, so you will in fact get activated! The activation of Bad Clusters happens in the subconscious. It's all based on the rule of stimulus/response. Compare it to a computer key. Pushing the same key in a program will always get the same response. This is the same with the signals that enter the brain. ***Your will has no control over it!***

Fear versus freedom and pleasure

We all have Bad Clusters. The most important physiology attached to a Bad Cluster is fear! Fear is an inhibiting force as well as a driving force in human behavior. How can it be both?

> ***Example*:**
> The fear of becoming poor can drive you to earning a lot of money and can change you into a workaholic. The fear that the community, family, or group that you are a part of will not accept and appreciate you, can drive you to all kinds of behavior that you basically don't want, but you do it to be accepted and appreciated by others.

This is a 'fear inspired' behavior that makes you vulnerable to all kinds of 'parasites' that will try to control your life! A lot of people have difficulties saying "*NO*" to others. They often end up doing things they don't want to, simply because they are afraid others won't like them anymore when they say "no" to them. The parasites are usually real 'masters' in creating guilt trips in your mind. Bad Cluster fear can also inhibit and block your future. Many people would like to have their own business, or move on to another company, approach others in a different manner, and build new relationships, but the fear blocks them from doing so. They just vegetate in an everyday routine. They are not happy, and fear withholds them. They are too frightened to change. Every community, group, club, religious organization, culture, family and company has its own rules and regulations.

There is nothing wrong with that, as long as you agree with them. Apart from the written rules and regulations, these groups create their own "code", their own unwritten rules and regulations. Those rules tell you that you can't do this or you can't behave or dress like that. None of these rules are written down. The group makes them up. This is one of the effects of what is called "group thinking". It is usually the unwritten rules and regulations of group thinking that block us if we become free and open-minded. This simple drawing of freedom shows you how the majority of people live.

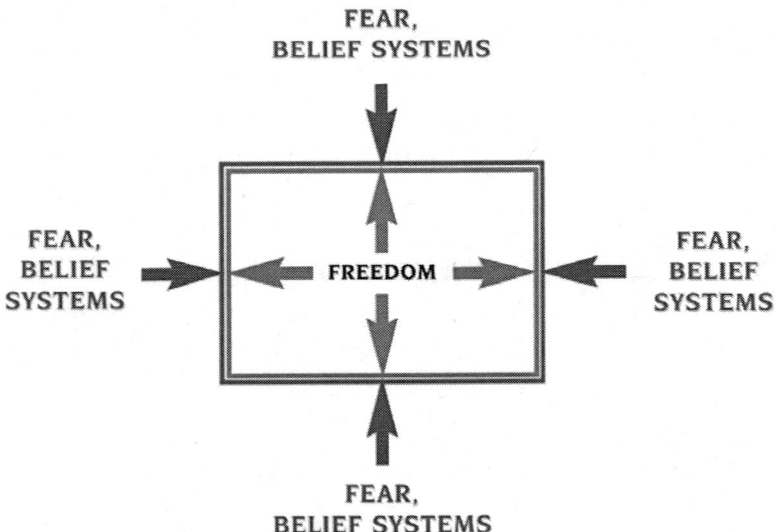

It is all those unwritten rules and expectations of the social group that will limit your freedom. *"You have to do this,"* and, *"I expect you to do that,"* and, *"You can't do that,... just think of what others would think!"*

Freedom is the absence of inhibiting fear

What is freedom? There are many theories and opinions regarding it. Unfortunately, there are people who cannot distinguish between freedom and selfishness. They think that they have the right to be free no matter how many other people have to pay the price or suffer the inconvenience of their so-called freedom. This has nothing to do with freedom! Real freedom is based on mutual respect that creates an environment that makes it possible for all people to live without the demands of others and without infringing the freedom of others. In a free environment you can think, say and do whatever you want as long as you do not harm others or infringe their personal freedom and rights. The next drawing shows what real freedom is about.

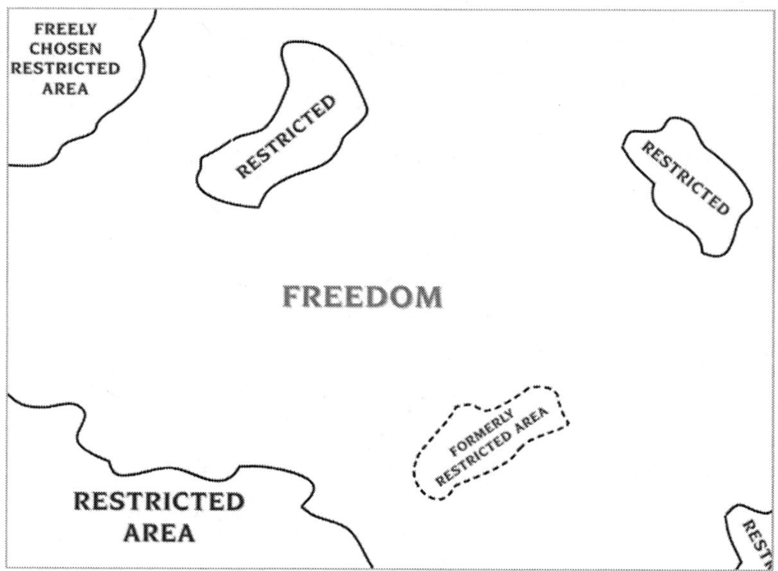

Based on our respect for others, and based on our conscience, we determine the restricted areas with our own free will! We have the right to change those areas throughout our life. Real freedom means that we have the right to change the opinion that we may have at this very moment. There is a simple rule that was expressed by Dr. Friday in his book, *Friday's laws*: *"I am responsible for everything I do and say, I am not responsible for your response."* Does this sound reasonable to you? Are you also familiar with the strong desire to change things in your life but yet, you are not doing it? How come? What are your belief systems that stop you? Are you afraid of the response you may get from your environment?

Use PMA to overcome those roadblocks. How? By imagining that you are approaching that other person and telling him/her that you made a decision that things will change, followed by your explanation of how and why it will change. Just imagine that, and imagine how they would respond to you. It is usually your own idea of how they respond that holds you back! Let it all happen in your imagination! Accept the feelings this will cause. Allow those feelings and give your subconscious the freedom to spontaneously come up with any picture it wants. From there, follow the standard procedure: *Event – Moment – Detail - Feel.* Now, allow the next picture to pop up spontaneously.

Practical tools to apply your new knowledge

Consider a Bad Cluster as a fire below the surface. You never know when it will pop up to the surface. It will pop up unexpectedly and it can burn everything down! So what we want to do is use the tools we acquired here before something like that occurs! Other Bad Clusters are almost constantly active and we have completely adapted to their limiting effects to such an extent that we have forgotten who we would be without these constant influences. These also can be traced and eliminated to give you a quick entrance into a new world of feeling healthy and regaining the energy to take on the whole world. To do that in the most effective way, we need awareness! You need awareness of where you are standing at this point in your life. How do you get this awareness? As a human being, we can argue, plan, reason and feel. The combination and interaction of these aspects make us unique and deliver us to a higher level of awareness. Use these aspects to know yourself and the status you are in. We all have awareness, but there are different levels of awareness we can reach. We can have awareness of our environment, other people, the ones we love, our job, etc. The level of awareness we speak about here, is the awareness of yourself, your body, your own behavioral patterns and feelings! We all have Bad Clusters and we all have an Inhibiting Friend Mechanism that pushes us away from pain. Total awareness would mean that we understand and are aware of all our behaviors, habits, thoughts, decisions, feelings, likes and dislikes. Some do better than others in this respect. How come?

The more Bad Clusters we have, the more power our Inhibiting Friend Mechanism will develop and push us away from the awareness that we have these Bad Clusters. If that were not the case, we would automatically discover all our Bad Clusters. And due to the fact that Bad Clusters contain pain and fear, our Inhibiting Friend Mechanism will push us into all kinds of habits and behavioral patterns that distract our awareness from where we should go to reveal and eliminate the Bad Clusters. The more active Bad Clusters you have, the lower your level of self-awareness will be! You will end up focusing more and more on unimportant things around you, making yourself believe that these things are truly important to you. These behavioral patterns and habits will definitely not help you to get rid of your Bad Clusters!

Changing your belief systems

You are not born with fear, life teaches you that! Fear is meant to be a warning signal to avoid pain. If it causes lasting fear or emotional and/or psychosomatic problems, than you can be sure that it is Bad Cluster related. A very clear example of that is 9/11. Many people suffered tremendously from the attack of the Twin Towers at September 11, 2001 and those who survived the disaster, we can be absolutely sure that they created Bad Clusters there. However, thousands of people all over the United States, who were <u>not present</u> in New York at that time, suffer since that day from all kinds of psychosomatic complaints and inhibiting fears. Their negative physiology is <u>not</u> caused by this horrible event, but only <u>triggered by it</u>. The way these people perceived the information activated already existing Bad Clusters in their subconscious. Just imagine how often they were confronted with this information through the media. This kept the activated Bad Clusters active.

We are born with a lot of possibilities and a certain amount of energy. Don't waste that energy by focusing on all kinds of unimportant things. Use your energy to become totally aware of yourself, your possibilities, your feelings! The use of energy is similar to the use of money: You can only spend it once! Therefore, spend it well! Now you have learned how to truly change things permanently. There is no method that goes as deep as PMA. We don't change the book, we don't change the paper, we restore the damaged alphabet! It all comes down to your own decision! We sometimes feel resistance in making decisions, even if they benefit us. Keep in mind: resistance is a feeling! Feelings originate from your comparison material. Ask yourself: Is it logical to sabotage yourself? No, it's not! If it is not logical, then it can only come from Bad Clusters! Their content is illogical and unanalyzed. Being successful and happy is within reach of everybody, but it doesn't instantly come to you. You have to do something about it and make it happen! Always remember, your Inhibiting Friend Mechanism will come into action with all kinds of arguments as to why you don't have the time or the need to do this. Keep in mind, you installed those arguments and belief systems yourself, and you are the only one that can make the decision to change them! It is all a matter of priority. How much do you appreciate and respect yourself? Do you really want to find out about yourself and become increasingly successful in your personal life and business? You think your problem is that you have no time to do this or that other people don't give you that time because they keep leaning on you? Stop sabotaging yourself! Don't focus on the "problem", but on the solution. It is that mental imprisonment that we are going to do away with. It's all within your reach and you *can* do it! We are going to challenge our own internal fears and pain. Let it come, and deal with it once and for all!

No matter what is in your path, there is always a solution! You just have to be able to focus on it, and PMA gives you the tools to do just that. PMA is an all-encompassing system. Your issues are not exempt from it. There is a quote from Agatha Christie that says: *"Curious things, habits. People themselves never knew they had them."* But now we know that we have them and realize how their web-like construction can entangle us! You will increasingly experience how strong your Inhibiting Friend Mechanism can be and in how many ways it influences and even controls your life! Nevertheless, realizing all this also makes you aware of the fact that you now have the power and possibilities to free yourself from all inhibiting factors and release that *desirable power* within you. You will discover how powerful PMA is. It will change your way of thinking and processing incoming sensory data, even if you decide not to practice PMA!

You will recognize your own behavioral patterns and those of the other persons that you never recognized before. How come? Because PMA shows you how your brain works. Subconsciously, you already knew all this! Now you have become aware of it. This makes quite a difference! Have you ever experienced that someone pointed out one of your specific behavioral patterns, or a certain phrase or word you repeatedly use? What they told you is not really new to you, but you were never aware of it. What happens after they told you? Are you just going to forget it, or do you start to pay attention to it, whether you like it or not? PMA is just like that, only this time it is not about a specific word, phrase, or behavioral pattern; much more is at stake now. PMA is about the core of all things, your health, what you think, say and do! It is about who you are! PMA makes it possible to change your belief systems! Remember, your inhibiting belief systems won't change if you don't get to your Bad Clusters. After you have eliminated the physiology of your Bad Clusters, then the driving force behind your belief systems will be changed forever.

No taboo during a PMA session

You will never get to your deepest hidden energy sources if you start a session with reservations. There should be no taboos, no topics that should not be brought up when you use the PMA technique! No one can put a puzzle together if some of the pieces are missing or if some pieces of another puzzle are thrown in. Someone who does the exercises without any taboos or restraints, while making use of the subconscious language, will experience sensational progress. Assuming that you fully cooperate with your subconscious and faithfully do the exercises, even if at first not all goes smoothly, you can continue to expect that you will notice significant results after just a few sessions. Many have noticed amazing results from just one session.

However, by applying the PMA technique you learn more than just a self-help method. You learn to master a lifetime tool and you will never forget it. It will be useful in many situations in your life!

Get the leverage you need to become more successful

Now we are all familiar with the phrase: *"Love your neighbor like yourself."* Do you love and respect yourself enough to take the time to practice PMA? Or are your duties and responsibilities towards others always more important to you than your own health and happiness? This is a question many people need to ask themselves. You might be one of them. It is inherent to human nature to procrastinate (literally shift things to tomorrow; to habitually put things off). Don't fall into that trap. If you understand PMA and feel that this is how the mind/body relationship really works, then <u>do something about it</u> and don't procrastinate!

Tools that help you practice PMA to your benefit

Be aware that practicing PMA doesn't cost you time, instead, it *gives* you time. To avoid procrastination you have to plan a specific day and time to do your session. Do not allow anything to interfere with that! If you take this seriously, you will experience its positive results. This is an important basic principle that people sometimes have difficulty with! If you want to succeed, just do it! PMA isn't something you just know about, it's something you practice! After a while of practicing, you do not need to plan a specific time anymore. You will take that time whenever you feel it's necessary to do a session. By then you will have experienced such strong benefits, that nobody will have to remind you of doing sessions. You do not need long practicing hours before you know how to do PMA. As soon as you understand the concept, and you do by now, you can do it!

The only thing that you have to learn is to give yourself permission to look and feel, even when the *movie* gets scary! Now, you know everything you need in order to immediately apply PMA! If you will actually do it, then it's all up to you! By now, you have identified your internal inhibiting mechanisms, so they will not be in control any longer as long as you don't want them to! So this has nothing to do with practicing or getting used to it; this is purely a decision you make. You know what's at stake. The choice is between the exciting road to your freedom and *desirable power*, or the familiar road of your Inhibiting Friend Mechanism and your "trusted" belief systems. You've been down that road before; you know where it leads...

Continue on

After mastering the PMA method, it will empower you for the rest of your life. It will help you to better understand your own behavior, as well as the behaviors of others. Endeavor to discover how ingenious and wonderfully your brain has been created and what a great capacity for happiness, health, and success has been lying dormant in your brain for years, just waiting to be awakened. Think, search, experience, and surprise yourself. Much success and pleasure is in the discoveries you make of your true self and all your hidden talents and potential!

I wish you lots of success and fun in everything you choose to do in your life!

Acknowledgement

I want to thank my wonderful team – Ingrid Schabbing, Marleen Korthuis-van der Sleen, and Thomas M.J. Korthuis - for the great support and help they always give me and all the efforts they put into the creation and realization of this book. Without their help and support this would not have been possible. I also want to thank Becky Diaz for all her efforts to read and correct the text.

References

PMA is developed from a combination of experimental practice and connecting the dots of experiments and discoveries in the fields of psychology, neuroscience, physiology, biology and quantum physics. The reproducible facts and outcomes of these experiments and findings form the foundation of the PMA approach. To study and compare these facts, you have to combine the facts that are shown in the following books and you will discover that they all support the PMA approach. However, to come to the same conclusion, you will have to be very thorough in eliminating every existing interpretation of those facts. Keep in mind that the majority of the contents of textbooks are not formed entirely by the scientific facts, but mainly by the interpretation of those facts. Facts never lie! However, those same facts have led to many opponent explanations and interpretations. To discover the harmony between these facts in PMA and how they support the PMA explanation, always ask yourself: Is this a reproducible fact, or outcome, or is it just an interpretation?

References and Literature Progressive Mental Alignment

Adamec, R.E. (1989), 'Kindling, Anxiety and Personality.' In: Bowlig T.G. and Trimble (red.), *The clinical relevance of Kindling.* Wiley, Chichester, pp. 117-135.

Alley, T.R. and Hildebrandt, K.A. (1988), in: Alley, T.R. (red.), *Social and Applied Aspects of Perceiving Faces.* Lawrence Erlbaum, Hillsdale, N.J.

Arnsten, A. F.T., *The Biology of Being Frazzled. Science,* June 12, 1998; 280: 1711-1712 [DOI: 10.1126/science.280.5370.1711] (in Research).

Bach-y-Rita, P. (1995), Non-synaptic Diffusion Neurotransmission and Late Brain Reorganization. Demos, New York.

Barlow, H.B. (1987), 'The Biological Role of Consciousness.' In: *Mindwaves*, pp. 361-381. Basil Blackwell, Oxford.

Basbaum, A.I. (1996), 'Memories of Pain.' In: *Sci Am Med*, pp. 22-31.

Benson, F. (1997), in: Feinberg, T. and Farah, M. (red.), *Behavioral Neurology and Neuropsychology*. McGraw Hill, NY.

Birnbaum, S.G., et al. Protein Kinase C Overactivity Impairs Prefrontal Cortical Regulation of Working Memory, *Science,* October 29, 2004; 306: 882-884 [DOI: 0.1126/science.1100021].

Blakemore, C. (1977), *Mechanics of the Mind.* Cambridge University Press, Cambridge.

Bower, G. (1992), How Might Emotions Affect Learning? In *Handbook of Emotion and Memory: Research and Theory*, S.-A. Christianson, ed. Hillsdale, NJ, Erlbaum.

Carter, R., and Frith, C. (1998), *Mapping the Mind.* Weidenfeld and Nicolson.

Churchland, P.M. (1993), *Matter and Consciousness.* MIT Press, Cambridge, Mass.

Cohen, and Servan-Schreiber, D. (1993), A Theory of Dopamine Function and Its Role in Cognitive Deficits in Schizophrenia. *Schizophrenia, Bulletin, 19,* 85-104.

Cohen, M.S., Kosslyn, S.M., Breiter, H.C. (1996), 'Changes in Cortical Activity During Mental Rotation: A Mapping Study Using Functional MRI,' in: *Brian*, 119, pp. 89-100.

Cohen, N.J., and Eichenbaum, H. (1993), *Memory, Amnesia, and the Hippocampal System.* MIT Press, Cambridge.

Cooper, R.K., and Sawaf, A. (1997), *Executive EQ: Emotional Intelligence in Leadership and Organizations*. Perigee Trade.

Covey, S.R. (1989, 2004), *The 7 Habits of Highly Effective People: Powerful Lessons in Personal Change*. Free Press, New York.

Crick, F., and Mitchison, G. (1983), "The Function of Dream Sleep." *Nature 304*, pp. 11-114.

Csikszentmihalyi, M. (1990), *Flow: The Psychology of Optimal Experience*. HarperCollinsPublishers.

Czerner, T. (2001), *What Makes You Tick? The Brain in Plain English.* John Wiley & Sons.

Daimond, M.C., Scheibel, A.B., Elson, L.M. (1986), *The Human Brain.* Collins.

Damasio, A.R. (1999), *The Feeling of What Happens.* Harcourt, Brace.

Damasio, A.R. (1994), *Descartes' Error: Emotion, Reason, and the Human Brain.* Grosset/Putnam, New York.

Deci, E.L., and Flaste, R. (1995), *Why We Do What We Do: The Dynamics of Personal Autonomy, Understanding Self-Motivation.* G.P. Putnam's Sons.

Deutschman, A., *Change or Die*, Fast Company, May 2005 edition, issue 94, www.fastcompany.com/magazine/94/open_change-or-die.html

Domhoff, G.W. (2003) *The Scientific Study of Dreams: Neural Networks, Cognitive Development and Content Analysis.* American Psychological Association.

Emmelkamp, P.M.G. et al., *Fysiologische disfunctie en gezondheid,* Facultiteit der maatschappij en gedragswetenschappen van de universiteit van Amsterdam, http://www2.fmg.uva.nl/psychologieincludes/psyresearch/1_2004KP.pdf

Fransen, H. (2003), *Bondgenoot, autobiografie van een immuncel.* Uitgeverij De Zaak, Groningen.

Freud, S. (1996), *The Standard Edition of the Complete Works of Sigmund Freud.* Vol. 1-23. Hogarth Press, London. (Originally published in 1923).

Frijda, N.H. (1986, 1999) *The Emotions: Studies in Emotion and Social Interaction.* Cambridge University Press, Cambridge.

Frith, C.D. and Dolan, R.I. (1997), 'Abnormal Beliefs: Delusions and Memory,' paper presented at the May 1997 Harvard Conference on Memory and Belief.

Fuster, J.M. (1980), *The Prefrontal Cortex: Anatomy, Physiology and Neurophysiology of the Frontal Lobe.* Raven Press, New York.

Gazzaniga, M.S. (2000), *The Mind's Past.* University of California Press.

Gazzaniga, M.S. (1992), *Nature's Mind.* Basic Books, New York.

Goleman, D. (1998) *Working with Emotional Intelligence.* Bantam Books, New York.

Goleman, D. (1996), *Vital Lies Simple Truths: The Psychology of Self Deception*. Simon & Schuster.

Goleman, D. (1995), *Emotional Intelligence.* Bantam Books, New York.

Gregory, R.L. (1997), *Mirrors in Mind.* Oxford University Press, New York.

Hartmann, E. (1998), "Nightmare after Trauma as Paradigm for All Dreams." *Psychiatry* 61, pp. 223-238.

Hirst, W. (1994), Cognitive Aspects of Consciousness. In The *Cognitive Neurosciences,* M.S. Gazzaniga, ed. MIT Press, Cambridge.

Hobson, J.A. (2002), *Dreaming: An lntroduction to the Science of Sleep*. University Press, Oxford.

Hoogendijk, W.J.G., et al. (1996), *Circadian Rhythm-Related Behavioral Disturbances and Structural Hypothalamic Changes in Alzheimer's Disease.* International Psychogeriatrics, 8, 245-252.

Humphrey, N. (1992), *A History of the Mind.* Simon & Schuster, New York.

Joseph, R. (1993), *The Naked Neuron*. Plenum, New York.

Kinsbourne, M. (1995), 'The Intralaminar Thalamic Nuclei,' in: *Consciousness Cognition*, 4, pp. 167-171.

Kosslyn, S. (1996), *Image and Brain*. MIT Press, Cambridge, Mass.

Leavitt, F., and Labott, S. (1996), Suppressed memories. *Journal of Traumatic Stress, Vol. 9, pp. 483-496.*

LeDoux, J.E. (2002), *Synaptic Self: How Our Brains Become Who We Are*. Viking.

LeDoux, J.E. (1996), *The Emotional Brain: The Mysterious Underpinnings of Emotional Life*. Simon and Schuster, New York.

LeDoux, J.E. (1992), Emotions and the Amygdala in J.P. Aggleton, ed., *The Amygdala: Neurobiological Aspects of Emotions, Mystery, and Mental Dysfunction*, pp 339-51.Wiley-Liss, New York.

Lipton, B.H. (2005), *The Biology of Belief: Unleashing the Power of Consciousness, Matter, and Miracles.* Mountain of Love/Elite Books, Santa Rosa, CA.

Lipton, B.H. (2002), *Nature, Nurture and the Power of Love: The Biology of Conscious Parenting,* DVD.

Lipton, B.H. (2001), *The New Biology: Where Mind & Matter Meet,* DVD.

Lipton, B.H. (2001), *The Biology of Perception: The Psychology of Change*, DVD.

Lipton, B.H., *The Science of Innate Intelligence: Biological Consciousness and the New Medicine*, Part 1 and 2, VHS.

Mandler, G. (1992), Memory, Arousal, and Mood. In *Handbook of Emotion and Memory: Research and Theory*, S.-A. Christianson, ed. Hillsdale, NJ, Erlbaum.

Mann, S. (1999), *Hiding What We Feel, Faking What We Don't: Understanding the Role of Your Emotions at Work.* Element Books Limited, Dorset.

Marshall, J.C., et al. (1997), *The Functional Anatomy of Hysterical Paralysis*. Cognition, Vol.64.

McGaugh, J.L., Introini-Collison, I.B., Cahill, L.F., Castellano, C., Dalmaz, C., Parent, M.B., and Williams, C.L. (1993), Neuromodulatory Systems and Memory Storage: Role of the Amygdale. *Behavioural Brain Research* 58, 81-90.

McTaggart, L. (2003), *The Field: The Quest for the Secret Force of the Universe*, Harpercollins Pub Ltd.

Nathanielsz, P.W. (1999), *Life in the Womb: The Origin of Health and Disease.* Promethean Press, Ithaca, NY.

Nature 441, 398-401 (25 May 2006) | doi:10.1038/441398a; Published online 24 May 2006

Nørretranders, T. (1993), *The User Illusion: Cutting Consciousness Down to Size*. New York, Penguin Books.

Oschman, J.L. (2000), *Energy Medicine: The Scientific Basis of Bioenergy Therapies,* foreword by Candace B. Pert. Churchill Livingstone.

Panksepp, J. (1998), *Affective Neuroscience: The Foundations of Human and Animal Emotions,* Oxford University Press.

Pert, C.B. (2000, 2004), *Your Body is Your Subconscious Mind*, Audio Cassette, Audio CD.

Pert, Candace (1997), *Molecules of Emotion: The Science behind Mind-Body Medicine*. Scribner, New York.

Piët, S. (1998), *Emotie management: Werken met emoties van jezelf en anderen.* Uitgeverij Contact, Amsterdam /Antwerpen.

Pinker, S. (1994), *The Language Instinct: How the Mind Creates Language.* Morrow, New York.

Pinker, S. (1979), *How the Mind Works.* W.W. Norton, New York.

Pray, L.A. (2004), "Epigenetics: Genome, Meet Your Environment." *The Scientist* 14-20.

Ramachandran, V.S., and Blakeslee, S. (1998), *Phantoms in the Brain: Probing the Mysteries of the Human Mind.* Harper Perennial.

Ramachandran, V.S. (1996), 'What Neurological Syndromes Can Tell Us about Human Nature: Some Lessons from Phantom Limbs, Capgras Syndrome, and Anosognosia,' in: *Cold Springs Harbour Symposia*, Vol. LXI, pp. 115-134.

Rock, A. (2004), *The Mind at Night: The New Science of How and Why We Dream.* Basic Books.

Rolls, E.T. (1995), 'A Theory of Emotion and Consciousness, and Its Application to Understanding the Neural Basis of Emotion,' in: *The Cognitive Neurosciences* (red. Gazzinga M.S.). MIT Press, Cambridge, Mass.

Ruis, M.A.W., et al., *Housing Familiar Male Wild Type Rats Together Reduces the Long-Term Adverse Behavioural and Psychological Effects of Social Defeat.* Psychologie February 1999, pp. 50, 59.

Ryan, K.D., and Oestreich, D.K. (1998), *Driving fear out of the workplace: Creating the High-Trust, High-Performance Organization.* Jossey-Bass Inc., San Francisco.

Schacter, D.L. (1996), *Searching for Memory: The Brain, the Mind and the Past.* Basic Books.

Searle, J. (1992), *The Rediscovery of the Mind.* MIT Press, Cambridge.

Shimamura, A. (1995), Memory and Frontal Lobe Function. In *The Cognitive Neurosciences*, M.S. Gazzaniga, ed. MIT Press, Cambridge.

Siegel, D.J. (1999), *The Developing Mind: How Relationships and the Brain Interact to Shape Who We Are.* Guilford, New York.

Silverman P.H. (2004), "Rethinking Genetic Determinism: With Only 30,000 Genes, What Is It That makes Humans Human?" *The Scientist* 32-33.

Smith, D. (1998), *British Psychological Society*, Annual Conference, Brighton.

Solomon, R.C. (1993), The Philosophy of Emotions. In *Handbook of* Emotions, M. Lewis and J. Haviland, eds. Guilford, New York.

Strand, F.L. (1999), *Neuropeptides, Regulators of Physiological Processes (Cellular and Molecular Neuroscience).* MIT Press, Cambridge, Mass.

Tsong, T.Y. (1989), "Deciphering the Language of Cells." *Trends in Biochemical Sciences* 14: 89-92.

Wu, X., Feng, J., et al. (2003), "Immunoglobulin Somatic Hypermutation: Double-Strand DNA Breaks, AIDs and Error-Prone DNA Repair." *Journal of Clinical Immunology* 23(4).

Zeki, S.M. (1993), *A Vision of the Brain.* Oxford University Press, Oxford.

Zijderveld, *G.A. van (1995), The Role of Adrenaline in Anxiety Disorders: A Psychophysiological Study.* Vrije Universiteit, Amsterdam.

Notes

Notes

Notes